Law and Creativity in the Age of the Entertainment Franchise

Much of the real value in the entertainment industry today lies in franchises – fictional universes, entertainment concepts, reinventions of cultural traditions and celebrity – that create an ongoing presence in the marketplace. The entertainment franchise now shapes the global cultural landscape. However, scholars have devoted little attention to how intellectual property law has changed or is being stretched in practice to accommodate this type of creativity and form of enterprise.

Covering law and practice in jurisdictions such as the United Kingdom, the EU, the USA, Australia, Spain and the Caribbean, this collection explores the 'fit' of intellectual property laws with specific franchises and tracks the way creators and entrepreneurs work around law's limitations. Case studies include mega-film franchises, fan activity, hip-hop, the management of celebrity reputation, flamenco, 'Disneyfied' theatre, film and television funding, arts festivals and 'Carnival in a box'.

KATHY BOWREY is a professor at the Faculty of Law, University of New South Wales, Sydney.

MICHAEL HANDLER is an associate professor at the Faculty of Law, University of New South Wales, Sydney.

Cambridge Intellectual Property and Information Law

As its economic potential has rapidly expanded, intellectual property has become a subject of front-rank legal importance. Cambridge Intellectual Property and Information Law is a series of monograph studies of major current issues in intellectual property. Each volume contains a mix of international, European, comparative and national law, making this a highly significant series for practitioners, judges and academic researchers in many countries.

A list of books in the series can be found at the end of this volume.

Law and Creativity in the Age of the Entertainment Franchise

Edited by

Kathy Bowrey and Michael Handler

CAMBRIDGE
UNIVERSITY PRESS

CAMBRIDGE
UNIVERSITY PRESS

University Printing House, Cambridge CB2 8BS, United Kingdom

Cambridge University Press is part of the University of Cambridge.

It furthers the University's mission by disseminating knowledge in the pursuit of education, learning and research at the highest international levels of excellence.

www.cambridge.org
Information on this title: www.cambridge.org/9781107039896

First published 2014

Printed in the United Kingdom by Clays, St Ives plc

A catalogue record for this publication is available from the British Library

Library of Congress Cataloguing in Publication data
Law and creativity in the age of the entertainment franchise / edited by Kathy Bowrey, Michael Handler.
pages cm – (Cambridge intellectual property and information law)
Includes bibliographical references and index.
ISBN 978-1-107-03989-6 (hardback)
1. Authorship. 2. Intellectual property. 3. Copyright. 4. Franchises (Retail trade) – Law and legislation. 5. Entertainers – Legal status, laws, etc. I. Bowrey, Kathy, editor. II. Handler, Michael, editor.
K1440.L39 2014
346.04′8 – dc23 2014032211

ISBN 978-1-107-03989-6 Hardback

Contents

Figures

Contributors

JOSÉ BELLIDO is a senior lecturer, Kent Law School, University of Kent

LIONEL BENTLY is Herchel Smith Professor of Intellectual Property and Director, Centre for Intellectual Property and Information Law (CIPIL), Faculty of Law, University of Cambridge

LAURA BIRON is a lecturer in philosophy, University of Kent

KATHY BOWREY is a professor at the Faculty of Law, University of New South Wales, Sydney

MICHAEL HANDLER is an associate professor at the Faculty of Law, University of New South Wales, Sydney

SHARON LE GALL is a lecturer at the Faculty of Law, University of the West Indies

DAVID LINDSAY is an associate professor at the Faculty of Law, Monash University

FIONA MACMILLAN is a professor of law, Birkbeck, University of London and Visiting Professor of Law, University of Roma Tre

JOHNSON OKPALUBA is a visiting lecturer, Dickson Poon School of Law, King's College London

DAVID ROLPH is an associate professor, Sydney Law School, University of Sydney

BRENT SALTER is a visiting fellow at the Faculty of Law, University of New South Wales, Sydney and PhD student, Yale Law School

Acknowledgements

This book is the product of an Australian Research Council (ARC) Discovery Project Grant entitled 'Entertainment Rights in the Age of the Franchise' (DP0985948). We thank the ARC for its financial support and Leanne Palmer at UNSW for her administration of the grant over a number of years.

The collection of essays in this book is largely based on a series of papers delivered at a workshop entitled 'Culture Industries and the Franchise', held in Sydney in July 2011. We thank the participants at the workshop for all their work – for embracing the themes of our project, for their generosity in commenting on each other's papers at the workshop and for their efforts in turning their workshop papers into the chapters in this collection. We are also grateful to Angela Sutton for her assistance in organizing the workshop.

Thanks go to the participants at the International Society for the History and Theory of Intellectual Property (ISHTIP) workshops at Università Bocconi, Milan in June 2009 and Université Panthéon Assas (Paris 2) in June 2013 for their helpful feedback on the papers we presented at those workshops, which helped influence our own chapters in this collection. Thanks also to the numerous colleagues with whom we have discussed our ideas over the course of this project, including Catherine Bond, Jason Bosland, Robert Burrell, Lesley Hitchens, Jill McKeough, Albert Moran, Joellen Riley, Brad Sherman, Kim Weatherall, and the Australian lawyers, entertainment industry professionals and agents we spoke to in 2011 and 2012.

Sincere thanks go to our team of UNSW research assistants who have worked on our franchise project since 2009 – Louise Buckingham, Sophia Christou, Lizzie Fuller, Marie Hadley and Bailee Walker – for their diligence and for helping shape the contours of the project. We also express our gratitude to Jennifer Kwong from UNSW, and Kim Hughes, Richard Woodham and Jo Breeze from Cambridge University Press, for their excellent editorial work on this collection.

Finally, we would like to thank our families for their love, support and willingness to engage with our franchise project and our ideas over the last few years. Without them this book would not have been possible.

Part I

Introduction

1 Franchise dynamics, creativity and the law

*Kathy Bowrey and Michael Handler**

1 The importance of studying franchises

The invention of an entertainment concept rich enough to sustain a franchise has become an accepted indicator of original creative genius in the twenty-first century. However, the relationship between creativity, economic opportunity and intellectual property law in the context of entertainment franchises is not well understood. One of the reasons for this relates to the complexity of factors involved, as well as the role of serendipity. A short consideration of the origins of a world-famous franchise, now entering its fiftieth year, provides a case in point.

1.1 'Hold tight and pretend it's a plan!':[1] *The* Doctor Who *franchise*

Given its origins, it is a wonder that *Doctor Who* even lasted beyond its first four episodes in 1963. The show had been conceived of by the BBC's Head of Drama, Sydney Newman, in early 1963, as little more than an educational, science fiction drama that would appeal to children, in order to plug a gap in Saturday evening programming.[2] The idea of a science fiction programme was frowned upon by some within the BBC, who disliked the genre's associations with comic books and American pulp fiction, something that helps explain the initial lack of institutional support for the development of the show.[3]

Copyright doctrine places the author of the script – a literary and a dramatic work – at the pinnacle of relevant legal and creative relationships. The production of the script is presumed to provide the necessary

* Our thanks go to José Bellido and Catherine Bond for their comments on this chapter.

[1] Doctor Who, in 'The Doctor, the Widow and the Wardrobe', *Doctor Who* (BBC television, 2011).

[2] See further B. J. Robb, *Timeless Adventures: How Doctor Who Conquered TV*, rev. edn (Harpenden: Kamera Books, 2013), pp. 18–22.

[3] J. Leach, *Doctor Who* (Detroit, MI: Wayne State University Press, 2009), p. 5.

impetus that makes possible the initiation of the making of a film and the eventual television broadcast. However, in commercial film and television production this is not necessarily the real sequence of events, as can be seen in the development of *Doctor Who*. In the first half of 1963, Newman worked on the concept of the show with the Head of Serials, Donald Wilson, and BBC screenwriter, C. E. Webber. Webber started developing the idea of an episodic 'loyalty programme' consisting of science fiction stories revolving around a number of constant, or 'loyalty', characters.[4] The interest here was not the creation of a stand-alone copyright work, but the production of a successful television series, recognizable in terms of its genre, key characters, appealing cast members and recurring dramatic elements that would draw audiences to return to see more. Newman is credited with coming up with the idea of a time-travelling doctor and, in some accounts, the name of the show,[5] while Wilson is said to have come up with the idea of a time machine able to dematerialize and rematerialize.[6] Scripts for various episode arcs (known as serials) were developed, but by June 1963 it was decided that Webber's script, which had been intended for the first four episodes, was not up to scratch. Instead, it was replaced with a caveman-themed script, based on a draft by Webber, with the writing credit going to Anthony Coburn,[7] who is thought to have come up with the idea of the outside of the Doctor's time-travelling machine, called the TARDIS, to be a blue police box.[8] Shortly afterwards, the BBC allocated an untested producer, Verity Lambert, and an untested director, Waris Hussein, to the show.[9] They were unimpressed by the quality of Coburn's script and asked for rewrites.[10] The creative contribution of the authors of the scripts was therefore structured by the briefs provided by the relevant 'non-authors'

[4] This is the language used in a memorandum from C. E. Webber to D. Wilson, 'Science Fiction', 29 March 1963, at http://bbc.co.uk/archive/doctorwho/6402.shtml.

[5] D. Howe, M. Stammers and S. Walker, *Doctor Who – The Handbook: The First Doctor – The William Hartnell Years, 1963–1966* (London: Virgin Publishing, 1994), p. 173; cf. Robb, *Timeless Adventures*, pp. 24–7 (outlining the collaboration between Webber and Newman in developing the Doctor's character, and suggesting that either Newman or caretaker producer Rex Tucker came up with the title).

[6] Robb, *Timeless Adventures*, p. 22; 'Who Created Who?', *BBC Two* (online), at http://bbc.co.uk/programmes/p01kqt9x/features/who-created-who.

[7] Robb, *Timeless Adventures*, p. 34.

[8] A. Cartmel, *Through Time: An Unauthorised and Unofficial History of Doctor Who* (New York: Continuum, 2005), p. 4. See also J. Legge, 'Who Owns the Tardis?', *Independent on Sunday*, 10 November 2013, p. 4.

[9] Lambert was primarily responsible for the casting of William Hartnell as the First Doctor.

[10] Robb, *Timeless Adventures*, p. 35. A pilot episode was filmed in September 1963, but featured so many production errors that Newman and Lambert decided that it needed to be reshot (see *ibid.*, pp. 39–40).

(i.e., department heads, directors and producers), in full knowledge that different writers might have been needed to be contracted to keep producing scripts on schedule if the series took off.

The first episode, 'An Unearthly Child', was broadcast the day after the assassination of President John F. Kennedy to modest ratings and a BBC-commissioned report indicating ambivalence amongst the audience.[11] The second episode received lukewarm reviews.[12] In light of this muted response and high production costs, the BBC came close to cancelling the programme within its first four episodes.[13] Factoring in the capriciousness of the audience is an ongoing challenge in popular television production. Whereas copyright law constructs the audience as largely passive recipients of cultural products and without significant power, a failure to engage key demographics as indicated by audience surveys and ratings data is often decisive in relation to the future of the programme. In the case of *Doctor Who*, it was only after the broadcast of the next serial, written on commission for the BBC by Terry Nation and entitled *The Daleks*, which introduced the eponymous cyborgs, that the show started to achieve genuine ratings success and, more importantly, enter the British public consciousness.

From these uncertain beginnings, featuring numerous creative contributions from a mix of BBC employees and independent contractors pulling in different directions, *Doctor Who* has become one of the longest-lasting and most productive franchises in history. The first three years after the show's debut saw the production of *Doctor Who* board games, craft sets, projector slides, comic strips, three novelizations of various serials and the first *Doctor Who Annual*, alongside three new seasons of the show. It was also a period of 'Dalekmania', giving rise to Dalek costumes, Dalek toy models made by at least four different companies,[14] two licensed Dalek films[15] and a Dalek stage play.[16] The BBC and Terry Nation exercised varying degrees of control over this spin-off activity,[17]

11 Leach, *Doctor Who*, p. 11.

12 M. Crozier, 'Television', *Guardian*, 2 December 1963, p. 7 (describing it as 'a depressing sequel' and that the 'Wigs and furry pelts and clubs and laborious dialogue were all ludicrous').

13 M. Bould, 'Science Fiction Television in the United Kingdom', in J. P. Telotte, *The Essential Science Fiction Television Reader* (Lexington, KY: The University Press of Kentucky, 2008), p. 215.

14 See 'Doctor Who Toy History', at http://doctorwhotoys.net/doctorwhotoyhistory.htm.

15 *Dr. Who and the Daleks* (Amicus Productions, 1965) and *Daleks – Invasion Earth: 2150 AD* (Amicus Productions, 1966), both featuring Peter Cushing as the Doctor.

16 *Curse of the Daleks* (1965).

17 N. Perryman, '*Doctor Who* and the Convergence of Media: A Case Study in Transmedia Storytelling' (2008) 14 *Convergence: The International Journal of Research into New Media Technologies* 21, 23.

but it was still embraced by fans.[18] At the end of this period, the producers of the programme came up with the idea of allowing the character of the Doctor to 'regenerate', meaning that he could take a new physical form; a narrative device allowing them to replace the actor playing the Doctor with another. This allowed for continuity and renewal within the series (with seven different actors taking on the role up to the show's cancellation in 1989 after twenty-six seasons), without overly compromising the identity of and viewer loyalty towards the character or the extended universe. In the 1970s, the BBC registered a number of 'Doctor Who' logo trade marks for goods ranging from games, toys, clothing, to cosmetics and toothpaste.[19]

In an apparent paradox, the cancellation of the show in 1989 only helped expand the *Doctor Who* universe. Between 1991 and 1997, Virgin Publishing, a BBC licensee, produced around 100 books containing new stories about the First to Seventh Doctors, aimed at the adult audience that had grown up with the show, with fans being able to submit new story proposals.[20] The *Doctor Who Magazine*, which had started publishing in 1979, continued through this period, with fans and former *Doctor Who* scriptwriters taking a leading role in editing and shaping the content of the publication.[21] Following a 1996 made-for-television movie entitled *Doctor Who*, featuring the only screen appearance of the Eighth Doctor, the BBC started producing its own book ranges, including *The Eighth Doctor Adventures* and another series based on earlier Doctors, relying on many of the authors who had written for Virgin Publishing. Audioplays aimed squarely at fans were released in the late 1990s by Big Finish, another BBC licensee, featuring actors from *Doctor Who* reprising their roles.[22] Unlicensed activity also flourished during this time, including the production of audiobooks and a television series by the company BBV, featuring actors from *Doctor Who* drawing on their celebrity by taking on roles that alluded to their *Doctor Who* characters.[23]

18 A. McKee, 'How to Tell the Difference between Production and Consumption: A Case Study in Doctor Who Fandom', in S. Gwenllian-Jones and R. E. Pearson (eds), *Cult Television* (Minneapolis, MN: University of Minnesota Press, 2004), pp. 175–81 (criticizing arguments that such activity can be dismissed as being 'non-canonical').

19 See trade mark registrations UK1068701, UK1068702 and UK1068703, all dating from 1976.

20 Perryman, '*Doctor Who* and the Convergence of Media', pp. 23–4.

21 McKee, 'How to Tell the Difference between Production and Consumption', p. 172.

22 A. O'Day, 'Event TV: Fan Consumption of Televised *Doctor Who* in Britain (1963–Present)', in G. Leitch (ed.), *Doctor Who in Time and Space: Essays on Themes, Characters, History and Fandom, 1963–2012* (Jefferson, NC: McFarland and Co., 2013), pp. 15–16.

23 McKee, 'How to Tell the Difference between Production and Consumption', pp. 174–5.

Such was the level of goodwill that the *Doctor Who* franchise had maintained over this time that the television series was able to be relaunched by the BBC in 2005. This came with an even stronger focus on franchise-related activity, accompanied by more extensive 'Doctor Who' trade mark registrations.[24] Most notably, the new series has given rise to two spin-off television series, aimed at different audiences: *Torchwood* (based on Jack Harkness, a character in the new series and designed to explore more adult themes than *Doctor Who*) and *The Sarah Jane Adventures* (based on a popular companion of the Doctor from the 1970s and designed for teenagers). Both of these spin-offs have themselves been spun-off into novels, audiobooks and online content.[25] In addition, since 2005, the BBC has produced behind-the-scenes documentaries,[26] a children's television series[27] (itself featuring an animated serial based on *Doctor Who*)[28] and other television content, including a lavish docudrama about the show's early 1960s origins.[29] The BBC has also produced over fifty *New Series Adventures* books, featuring stories and audiobooks about the Ninth to Eleventh Doctors; launched its own magazine, *Doctor Who Adventures*, aimed at six to thirteen year olds; produced a huge range of licensed merchandise; and built a significant online presence for fans, featuring video clips, episode commentaries, interactive games, mobisodes and 'metasites' featuring enhanced details of fictional elements contained in the television show.[30] Separate from the BBC's activity, fan clubs around the world have continued to thrive, with major festivals and conventions attracting stars of the show and generating continued buzz.[31] Most recently, a permanent exhibition called 'The Doctor Who Experience' has opened in Cardiff, near the BBC's Roath Lock 'centre for excellence'

24 New 'Doctor Who' logo marks were registered (EU4406229; UK2376000) in numerous classes covering goods and services including electronic and video games, books and magazines, clothing and footwear, games and toys, broadcasting, concerts and shows. A number of updated logo marks, for similar goods and services, were registered in 2009 (UK2527703; UK2527895; UK2527896; UK2527901).

25 Supported by trade mark registrations for the word marks TORCHWOOD (UK2394209) and THE SARAH JANE ADVENTURES (EU6301808), covering similar goods and services to the 'Doctor Who' registrations. *The Sarah Jane Adventures* also featured the character K-9, a robotic dog that had been part of *Doctor Who* since 1977. A further spin-off television series called *K-9*, consisting of live action and animation, premiered in 2010. *K-9* is not a BBC production, but uses the original model of K-9, and contains allusions to the *Doctor Who* universe.

26 *Doctor Who Confidential* (2005–11).

27 *Totally Doctor Who* (2006–7).

28 *The Infinite Quest* (2006–7).

29 *An Adventure in Space and Time* (2013).

30 Perryman, '*Doctor Who* and the Convergence of Media', pp. 26, 28–33.

31 For an American perspective on the franchise, see L. Porter, *The Doctor Who Franchise: American Influence, Fan Culture and the Spinoffs* (Jefferson, NC: McFarland and Co., 2012).

for drama where *Doctor Who* is filmed, as part of attempts by Cardiff Council and the Welsh government to revitalize a downtrodden part of Cardiff Bay by turning it into a creative industries hub.[32]

Intellectual property rights clearly underpin ongoing investment in the *Doctor Who* franchise. It is axiomatic that these laws have a significant role to play in supporting this form of creative enterprise. However, as this brief history suggests, intellectual property law is more of a background presence than the central driver of this creative activity. In this regard, the voluminous literature on the centrality of copyright in providing an incentive to produce[33] warrants unpacking in relation to the creative industries and, in particular, in relation to the success of entertainment franchises.

1.2 The aim of this collection

By starting with *Doctor Who*, we do not mean to suggest that it is the world's oldest entertainment franchise. Such activity can be traced back at least as far as the beginning of the twentieth century. For example, Beatrix Potter's book *The Tale of Peter Rabbit*, first published commercially in 1902, soon branched into dolls, board games, wallpaper and porcelain.[34] Pat Sullivan's 'Felix the Cat' began as a New York newspaper strip in 1917, was turned into globally distributed animations in 1921, and soon came to support a myriad of character merchandising.[35] Also following suit from the early days of the film era is a certain mouse from Walt Disney's animated short *Steamboat Willie*, first screened in 1928. Mickey Mouse soon supported a huge range of merchandise marketed across the globe that remains of interest to fans, consumers and to copyright law today.[36] But it is in the last fifty years, since *Doctor Who* first screened, that the entertainment franchise has become typical of a mode of production that has shaped the global cultural landscape. Inescapable franchises from our time, such as *Star Trek*, James Bond, *Star Wars*, *Batman*,

[32] 'Work Starts on BBC Wales Drama Village in Cardiff Bay', *BBC News Wales* (online), 24 June 2010, at http://bbc.co.uk/news/10402789.

[33] For discussion in a law reform context, see I. Hargreaves, *Digital Opportunity: A Review of Intellectual Property and Growth* (May 2011), at http://ipo.gov.uk/ipreview.htm; Australian Law Reform Commission, *Copyright and the Digital Economy*, Report 122 (November 2013), at http://alrc.gov.au/publications/copyright-report-122.

[34] L. Lear, *Beatrix Potter: The Extraordinary Life of a Victorian Genius* (London: Penguin, 2008).

[35] J. Canemaker, *Felix: The Twisted Tale of the World's Most Famous Cat* (New York: Pantheon, 1991).

[36] T. Susanin, *Walt Before Mickey: Disney's Early Years, 1919–1928* (Jackson, MS: University Press of Mississippi, 2011); L. Lessig, 'Free Mickey Mouse', *The Economist* (New York), 12 October 2002, p. 67.

Superman, *X-Men* and *Harry Potter*, might immediately spring to mind, although, as we will see, the cultural phenomenon in which audiences participate in extended relationships with fictional universes and cultural content extends well beyond such entertainment blockbusters.

Franchises involving films and television series have been well documented and interrogated in cultural studies scholarship, in particular in the work of Henry Jenkins on 'transmedia storytelling'[37] and Derek Johnson on media franchises and industrial institutions.[38] Cultural studies writers have also begun tracing the changes in content necessary for franchises to circulate globally and still connect with local audiences.[39] There is also considerable business law scholarship on franchising, which mainly focuses on 'how-to' aspects, such as the licensing of trade marks, 'know-how' and reputation to create income streams across time and space.[40] However, there is scant consideration of how value or custom is generated and sustained in the reputation associated with the franchise. In both disciplines, there has been very little scholarly work addressed to how the law, and intellectual property law in particular, has changed or is being stretched in practice to accommodate this type of cultural activity, creativity and form of enterprise.

Staying with *Doctor Who* as an example, it is clear that there are likely to be interesting, formal legal issues in trying to identify who owns and has the ability to exploit various individual aspects of the franchise, such as the characters played by actors, the Daleks or the TARDIS, the associated books, recordings, toys and other merchandise, and events and exhibitions. These are likely to give rise to complex, multi-jurisdictional licensing issues. However, there seems to be a much more fundamental issue at stake. Looking at the franchise *as a whole*, the question might be asked as to what sustains the economic and cultural value of this sort

[37] See especially H. Jenkins, *Convergence Culture: Where Old and New Media Collide* (New York University Press, 2006), ch. 3; H. Jenkins, S. Ford and J. Green, *Spreadable Media: Creating Value and Meaning in a Networked Culture* (New York University Press, 2013).

[38] See especially D. Johnson, *Media Franchising: Creative License and Collaboration in the Culture Industries* (New York University Press, 2013). See also D. Johnson, 'Franchise Histories: Marvel, *X-Men* and the Negotiated Process of Expansion', in J. Staiger and S. Hake (eds), *Convergence Media History* (New York: Routledge, 2009); D. Johnson, 'Participation is Magic: Collaboration, Authorial Legitimacy, and the Author Function', in J. Gray and D. Johnson (eds), *A Companion to Media Authorship* (Chichester: Wiley-Blackwell, 2013).

[39] See, e.g., A. Moran (ed.), *TV Formats Worldwide: Localizing Global Programs* (University of Chicago Press, 2009). See also the collection of articles in (2013) 8(2) *Critical Studies in Television: The International Journal of Television Studies*.

[40] See, e.g., M. Hero (ed.), *International Franchising: A Practitioner's Guide* (London: Global Law and Business, 2010); S. Giles, M. Redfern and A. Terry, *Franchising Law and Practice* (Sydney: LexisNexis, looseleaf).

of phenomenon? Along with cultural studies scholars, we are doubtful that this can simply be located in the traditional, disaggregated objects of legal protection – the 'films', 'television broadcasts', 'sound recordings' and other 'works' that are generated. So is the real value tied up with something more nebulous and unfamiliar to the formal law – things that can be described at a higher level of abstraction, such as concepts, creative identities, personalities and other distinctive cultural identifiers, all of which are designed to generate continued consumer engagement and create an ongoing presence in the marketplace? If so, then how exactly are artists, owners and entrepreneurs (many of whom are not necessarily going to be connected to the original broadcaster) commercializing these more diffuse forms of 'creativity'? And how are they using the law and existing legal categories and concepts to do so?

This collection of essays aims to address these broader questions in exploring the relationship between law and creativity in the context of entertainment franchises. In the remainder of the first part of this chapter, we set the scene for the collection by engaging with the breadth of the concept of the 'entertainment franchise'. We show that it is a more complex, fluid concept than is sometimes appreciated, and that similar cultural and economic dynamics extend well beyond film- and television-related production to encompass a much wider range of creative output. We then show that the assumptions that what is of value to the entertainment industry, reflected in legal categories of protection that underpin legal scholarship, are problematic, meaning that the role that law plays in supporting creativity in this sector tends to be mischaracterized. Instead, we aim to show that while formal legal categories and legal narratives can and do limit our view of the relationships that are in play, it is a mistake to assume that law is merely a 'passive' follower of culture and economy in this context (that is, that law only steps in to manage transgression of established expectation). We explain that attention needs to be focused on how existing legal concepts, such as 'authorship' and 'property', are being actively extended to create new cultural meaning and value, and how more attention needs to be paid to existing managerial and professional practices that allow for authorship to function more effectively in the context of entertainment franchises.

In the second part of this chapter, we provide an overview of each essay in the collection, both in terms of how each constructs and engages with the extended notion of the entertainment franchise, and how each addresses one or more of the key themes of the collection. Collectively, the aim of the chapters is to help recharacterize law as far more active and foundational in constructing the very idea of culture and of economy.

1.3 *Defining the entertainment franchise*

As should be obvious from some of the examples already given in this chapter, the entertainment franchise is a familiar concept in contemporary culture. However, it is a concept that is rarely articulated with much precision. One difficulty, especially for those approaching the subject from a legal disciplinary background, is that, as noted above, the entertainment franchise is only tangentially related to the business law construct of a 'franchise' or 'franchising'. The legal concept essentially involves a business owner giving a number of independent parties the right to carry on that business under a system or plan determined by the owner.[41] This legal definition is useful in setting up the general idea that can be applied to the entertainment franchise: that, at its core, there is an entity exercising overarching control over distributed activity, and that, in turn, goods or services produced by any given franchisee will have a consistent, familiar quality, thereby allowing for the management of consumer expectation through the maintenance of brand reputation. However, while the legal notion of the business franchise might have analogues with some forms of cultural activity (such as the replication of television formats around the world),[42] it does not come close to capturing the complexity of the entertainment franchise. A further issue for legal scholars is that the language of the 'entertainment franchise' is not commonly used by lawyers, at least outside the USA. In interviews we conducted with representatives from Australian broadcasters and film and television funding bodies for this project, we were struck by the fact that a number of interviewees said that they did not associate what they did as relating to 'entertainment franchises', dismissing this as an American concept and instead referring to their management of more traditionally understood 'broadcast rights' or 'format rights'.[43]

A second difficulty is that when describing cultural production, the term 'franchise' is often used in a limited and pejorative sense, especially in the popular media. It is most commonly used to describe a major Hollywood blockbuster, consisting of multiple films and associated merchandising, that has been based on commercially proven and culturally ingrained source material, whether a well-known series of books, comic

41 For an illustrative legal definition, see Trade Practices (Industry Codes – Franchising) Regulations 1998 (Cth), Schedule: Franchising Code of Conduct, cl. 4.

42 See generally Moran, *TV Formats Worldwide*.

43 For our interview methodology, see K. Bowrey and M. Handler, 'Instituting copyright: reconciling copyright law and industry practice in the Australian film and television sector', in this collection.

book characters, computer games, toys or even theme park rides. In addition, the term is often used to signify the 'creative bankruptcy and foregone economic determination of contemporary media industries'.[44] Franchises are often seen as formulaic, risk-averse exercises by major studios, with the 'pre-awareness' of the brand not only designed to maximize global box office returns and the chances of cost recovery, but also to save on the costs of marketing an 'unknown' entity that may well be more creative, but is untested in its capacity to generate large audiences.[45] Franchises are set up as posing a 'challenge to choice, diversity and creativity . . . by their mechanistic, almost viral drive toward self-replication'.[46]

Whatever one thought of the merits of the fifth *Resident Evil* film, or the decision to split J. R. R. Tolkien's 'The Hobbit' across three movies released over three Christmases, it is clear that a notion of the entertainment franchise that focuses on Hollywood film blockbusters and is used to signify a dearth of creativity is too limited. A more useful and neutral articulation of the entertainment franchise, drawing on the work of scholars such as Johnson, is that it describes a network of property or property-like rights in connected cultural content, often distributed across multiple media, together with associated marketing and merchandising, all of which is sought to be 'owned' or managed by a controlling entity.[47] To this should be added the idea that the goal is to ensure continuing consumer engagement with the cultural phenomenon not only across multiple media but also across time – a depth of experience that sustains consumer loyalty and motivates more consumption.[48]

Seen in these broad terms, it is possible to see entertainment franchises as going well beyond film and television productions and their related merchandise and commercial tie-ins. Further, we suggest that similar dynamics can be seen beyond the realm of the sort of 'storytelling' that

[44] Johnson, *Media Franchising*, p. 1.

[45] For discussion, see E. Aarseth, 'The Culture and Business of Cross-Media Productions' (2006) 4 *Popular Communication: The International Journal of Media and Culture* 203. See also C. Clarke, 'The Art of Leaving 'Em Wanting More', *Guardian*, 10 December 2010, p. 3; P. Hoad, 'The New Abnormal', *Guardian*, 1 November 2013, p. 12.

[46] Johnson, *Media Franchising*, p. 2.

[47] Cf. Johnson, 'Franchise Histories', p. 14 ('a perennially extensible network of content in the service of several wide-reaching culture industries').

[48] Jenkins, *Convergence Culture*, p. 96. This may involve 'additive comprehension', where a piece of information introduced in one element of the franchise is designed to shape a consumer's understanding of the franchise as a whole (*ibid.*, pp. 123–30). This can, of course, come at the risk of alienating fans who feel that the franchising activity (whether it be a proliferation of spin-offs or an increased focus on merchandising) will lead to a dilution in quality of what they perceive to be the core product: see, e.g., M. Campbell, *Doctor Who: The Complete Guide* (London: Constable & Robinson, 2011), p. xii.

characterizes narrative-based mass media franchises. For example, franchise dynamics can be seen in musical theatre and drama productions, in particular in large-scale blockbuster musicals (often based on successful films, but increasingly on successful pop artists' back catalogues) that play throughout the world, and which in turn have an impact on the geography of drama and theatre precincts in cities. The same dynamics can be seen in attempts by celebrities in the entertainment industry to extend, exploit and manage their reputations across multiple media – for example, a chef starring in television shows and engaging in book deals, product endorsements, speaking engagements and public appearances. Although franchise-like activity is not commonly associated with the music industry, similar dynamics can be seen here in the way the industry, at various times, has sought to commodify and extract commercial value from traditional musical styles or modes of performance, or extend the life of back catalogues by exploiting the reputation of old artists and works in new products. And it can be seen in attempts to commodify cultural events or spectacles, such as carnivals or festivals, by replicating them throughout the world.

While the collection does engage with franchises in their more immediately recognizable forms (for example, the exploitation of fantasy worlds across hit films, comic books and related merchandise), the authors of the essays in this collection are interested in exploring franchise dynamics in the broader sense outlined above. What unites the chapters is an interest in entertainment products where the cultural and economic value can be said to sit somewhere outside the originating 'work' generated and the role that the law plays in enabling the production and management of such phenomena.

1.4 *Looking beyond existing legal categories and interrogating law's relationship with creativity*

We mentioned before that while much has been written about entertainment franchises from a cultural studies perspective, this is an area that has received relatively little attention in legal scholarship. This is most likely because of a series of assumptions that are made about the relationship between law and industry practice. To explain, it is uncontroversial to note that the entertainment industry is comprised of different sectors (music, film, television, literary, art, performance, etc.) and that this industry structure is, to a large extent, reflected in the various categories and sub-categories of copyright that are intended to reward and promote the commercialization of 'creativity' within these sectors. Much legal scholarship therefore accepts that those legal categories, in turn, reflect the products that are likely to be of value within the entertainment industry. On this basis, such scholarship focuses on the operation of those categories, emphasizing disputes and court decisions that give rise to difficult doctrinal issues and, in particular, determining the merits of competing authorial claims.[49] This legal approach involves disaggregating the franchise, identifying its constituent elements, and asking questions familiar to intellectual property lawyers such as whether each discrete element is a copyright work, who is its author or are its authors, who owns copyright in the work, and what sort of conduct infringes the owner's rights.[50]

This is not to dismiss the importance or complexity of this sort of scholarship. Our issue is more that such an approach overlooks that what is of value in the entertainment industry is not simply a set of discrete works, but instead sits somewhere above and outside the domain of the existing legal constructs. As Kathy Bowrey has argued previously:

> Commodification is no longer thought of as beginning with a 'core' or primary work such as a film, show or book that, having proven its value in terms of consumer attractiveness, then crosses over to subsidiary markets, products and channels. The market aspiration is to protect the entire process of creating future value, where calculating that value exceeds expectations of selling the product in its original form to a 'primary market'... The property at stake in the entertainment industry is not the material form or cultural artefact, with a customary 'primary' channel of distribution. It has become a far more abstract future expectation of audience pull or fan appeal associated with an idea or concept that can be distributed in numerous commodity forms and via many outlets.[51]

However, recognizing that such a shift has taken place does not mean that the law has become irrelevant, or that the law must be reformed to accommodate these changes in culture by aligning more closely with this new form of property. Rather, it means that we need to rethink and reinvent the methodologies we use to discuss intellectual property law and its manifestations in shifting media landscapes. It also requires a

[49] A notable recent example, discussed in Chapter 2, is *Lucasfilm Ltd* v. *Ainsworth* [2009] FSR 2; aff'd on appeal [2012] 1 AC 208.

[50] Further, while some legal scholarship recognizes the broader form of value that might lie in 'image', 'persona' or 'celebrity', above and beyond any creative works that are produced, such scholarship often focuses on the various, limited ways that such concepts are protected through existing legal categories (such as defamation, passing off, or publicity rights). See, e.g., S. Smith, *Image, Persona and the Law*, 2nd edn (London: Sweet & Maxwell, 2008); P. Loughlan, B. Macdonald and R. Van Krieken, *Celebrity and the Law* (Sydney: Federation Press, 2010); G. Black, *Publicity Rights and Image: Exploitation and Legal Control* (Oxford: Hart Publishing, 2011).

[51] K. Bowrey, 'The New Intellectual Property: Celebrity, Fans and the Properties of the Entertainment Franchise' (2011) 20 *Griffith Law Review* 188, 195.

consideration of a wider range of claims that have been made to create and own culture, creative concepts, fictional and real identities and niche markets. If the entertainment franchise entails a different kind of 'genius' to that privileged in copyright through its traditional celebration of the author and the original work, with a blending of creative vision with sustained economic enterprise, understanding this phenomenon requires a different approach in legal scholarship. It requires, in turn, a re-interrogation of the construct of authorship, a better understanding of the role of management in generating ongoing consumer interest and a discussion of the limits to owning culture. This volume is consequently divided into three Parts, with each Part devoted to an exploration of one of these three key themes.

Part II, entitled 'The productivity of the author model: authors, collaborators and non-authors', critically assesses the postmodern notion that 'authorship' is a way of limiting meaning that confers too much control on authors/producers. It is accepted that intellectual property law is essentially a dynamic of allocating properties. However, the writers in this Part explore how extended ideas of authorship are being deployed to create and expand the cultural meaning and value of franchises. They reflect on subtle shifts in the way ownership claims have been rearticulated by originating authors and creators in the face of enduring fan loyalty and unanticipated interest in their works by later generations. They also note the extent to which mega-successful creators necessarily accommodate some creative play by audiences, fans and other artists, in order to revitalize interest in their productions. A mix of philosophical and practical considerations are considered as explanations for these new authorship claims.

Part III, entitled 'Managing authorship', looks to a much-neglected area in intellectual property law scholarship – the managerial and institutional support required for 'authorship' to function profitably. Doctrinal preoccupation with private rights and formal demarcations of ownership tends to oversimplify how the law works in practice. Creator motivation is often reduced to a transactional view of relationships that underestimates the importance of co-operation between parties, generosity, goodwill and other broader cultural concerns. These chapters consider how artists talk back to the law through interventions in the marketplace of ideas, as well as how the social relations involved with large-scale cultural production are formally and informally regulated with a view to mobilizing support for particular enterprises and to minimize conflict. The writers in this Part share an interest in how creators position themselves to work around the limits of the law, without necessarily confronting these legal limits directly.

Part IV, entitled 'Group rights and culture', looks at a phenomenon not normally associated with commercial franchises – cultural festivals. These chapters discuss how many of the features and pressures of conventional franchises have impacted on these events, but also show how festivals, as events with embedded historical links to cultural group identities, remain more or less outside of mainstream intellectual property consideration. The writers challenge this construction, showing how festivals do not exist outside law or economy, but nonetheless remain constructed in law as 'fringe' activity. This is discussed as both a strength and a weakness to the vitality and future of these kinds of cultural events.

2 An overview of the collection: exploring authorship, management and the limits to owning culture

In this section we explain in more detail the approach taken by the authors of each chapter, and how each chapter draws out the themes of the collection as a whole.

2.1 Part II: the productivity of the author model: authors, collaborators and non-authors

Part II of the collection reflects on the endurance of the traditional author model in the entertainment industry, notwithstanding that the entertainment franchise requires this concept to be deployed in new and innovative ways.

In Chapter 2, 'The author strikes back: mutating authorship in the expanded universe', Lionel Bently and Laura Biron use the example of George Lucas's *Star Wars* to explore new theories of auteurism devised by film commentators to help explain shifts in the nature of film production associated with the emergence of the entertainment franchise. Extended authorial-like creation claims of film impresarios like George Lucas have been explained in terms of: the 'auteur-director', familiar to romantic theory; the 'commercial-auteur', credited with the commercial strategy for distribution and marketing of the film franchise; the 'franchise-auteur', standing behind the totality of the *Star Wars* universe and, in particular, its character merchandising; and, lastly, the 'brand-auteur', a director 'signature' associated with the entirety of the blockbuster product.

Authorship is considered as a productive starting point for validating new assertions of cultural standing because authorship is an established vehicle for awarding credit to cultural production. But it is not the romantic ideal of originality or creativity traditionally associated with authorship that is activated here. Authorship becomes associated with crediting an economic 'talent'. Thus, it is reverence for an economic triumph that is incorporated into the new cultural logic of authorship.

Bently and Biron then explore the status of these franchise-related authorial claims under copyright and trade mark law, noting a lack of corresponding reinvention of the relevant legal constructions to accommodate the shift in film production. They conclude that there is a tension between the cultural phenomenon of film authorship and its conceptualization within intellectual property law, and are uncertain as to the consequence of this non-alignment.

The chapter throws up important questions about intellectual property law's contribution to new cultural and economic developments, and whether legal constructs of authorship are sufficiently productive, in an economic sense.

David Lindsay's Chapter 3, 'Franchises, imaginary worlds, authorship and fandom', suggests that the contemporary fascination with franchises and imaginary worlds owes its heritage to religion, and Christianity in particular. While not wanting to overplay the connection or offend readers, he relates the territorial ambition of the medieval Church to that of entertainment empires and the personal commitment of religious followers to the devotion of fantasy and comic world fans. However, in the contemporary context, investment in the making of imaginary worlds is also linked to the allure of experiential goods for consumers and fans. It is at this point that Lindsay embarks on a more detailed exploration of the economics of contemporary fantasy and comic franchises.

He argues that collaboration is essential to the longevity of these imaginary worlds and their franchise value. Thus, as with Bently and Biron's analysis, his argument is that to some extent copyright's construction of the key relationship as being between the author and work, or the content owner and audience, is unhelpful. Lindsay argues that creators need to walk a tightrope between maintaining the distinctive qualities of the universe and actively engaging consumers and fans. This requires relaxation of authorial control and management of a tension between openness and closure, given the importance of fan participation to enduring interest in the imaginary world.

Offering a sophisticated account of fan activity, Lindsay notes that the fan community can itself be deconstructed into canonical and non-canonical co-guardians of the fantasy world. He argues that with different fan identities comes an additional layer of complexity to rights management, including canonical fans policing other fans, out of respect for the importance of the author/creator. Most provocatively, and contrary to the idealization of fan participation present in 'transmedia' advocates such as Jenkins and other new media critics, Lindsay argues that uncertainty surrounding copyright infringement is essential to ongoing engagement between the franchise owner and fans. He argues that the threat of copyright infringement is a key tool that needs to be deployed to maintain a hierarchical relationship between creator and fans. Lindsay defends the power imbalance that copyright creates by arguing that the image of the creative individual author is the essential organizing principle for regulating the commercial and semantic relations of the imaginary universe. Without due respect for the persona of the creator, around which the imaginary universe revolves, the imaginary universe will fail to survive as a distinctive kind of cultural experience.

Lindsay suggests the productivity of the author function is its capacity to regulate cultural meaning and build brand value as generated in the franchise. Thus, to Lindsay, an authorial concept of rights ownership is integral to securing meaningful fantasy relationships that sustain commodification. Without this reference point, the imaginary universe loses its distinctiveness, and thereafter its economic value.

Chapter 4, 'Digital sampling and music industry practices, re-spun', like Lindsay's chapter, also provides a counter-narrative to conventional accounts of authorship as a constraint on creativity. Johnson Okpaluba interrogates the commonly repeated claim that a pro-licensing culture took hold in American hip-hop only after the successful copyright infringement action in *Grand Upright Music Ltd* v. *Warner Bros Records, Inc.*,[52] leading to the creative deterioration of hip-hop in the following decade.

The author reflects on sampling practices and hip-hop styles before, at the time of, and after the case. He argues that it is too simplistic to assert that there was ever a golden age of lawless sampling or that after *Grand Upright* hip-hop artists were newly intimidated into clearing samples. He also rebuts the claim that, overall, hip-hop artists ceased making innovative music under threat of litigation at the behest of rent-seeking labels. Rather, he argues that labels did not see hip-hop as a major threat to income streams that needed closing down. The major labels had already appreciated the value of facilitating licensing of samples in hip-hop well before the *Grand Upright* litigation, with licensing practices already in place.

Major labels and authors understood that artistic reputation and the commercial value of works and back catalogues were related to the conditions that regulated access to musical creations. For some artists, a

[52] 780 F Supp 182 (SDNY, 1991).

relaxed attitude to sampling was acceptable. For others, tighter control was desired. However, the licensing practices that emerged in hip-hop had less to do with general industry agreements about how legal rights to sampling should be managed in relation to hip-hop and more to do with finer nuances of the musical market and with the attitude of both sampled and sampling artist personalities as they sought to position themselves in relation to ever changing cultural interests, creative and commercial opportunities.

The chapters in Part II show that rather than original creators and media owners being in combat, the author function can be deployed to mutual advantage to extend the cultural life of a work and unleash the franchise potential that revolves around an extended notion of authorship and creative endeavour.

2.2 *Part III: managing authorship*

Artists, agents, managers, professional associations, artistic communities and investors are actively involved in the creation of cultural products and their dissemination, and we need to look behind the formal legal classification of interests and allocation of rights to understand how the law works in practice. The chapters in this Part look at the legal and social relations that sustain cultural activity over time, beyond those supported by traditional notions of copyright entitlement. One of the main problems of viewing the entertainment industry through the author model is the way a preoccupation with identification of ownership of rights displaces consideration of the creative and innovative ways through which cultural work is supported, economic value is created, culture is turned into product and brand value is sustained through management and professional activities.

While a defamation action is conventionally considered in terms of enforcing a legal right to reputation, David Rolph, in Chapter 5, 'Building and rebuilding reputations: reflections on the role of defamation law in the life of a celebrity', shows how, in relation to celebrity litigants, defamation can assist 'franchise-like' image control or brand management. It can help facilitate the projection of a particular persona or 'public' identity desired by the celebrity through restraining the circulation of conflicting, disruptive or unwelcome messages. However, as Rolph shows in his account of the backlash against the celebrity Jason Donovan flowing from his defamation action against *The Face* magazine in 1991 over imputations of homosexuality, the decision to sue can also have other consequences that damage the celebrity's reputation. Rolph's chapter considers how a defamation action can give impetus for the celebrity to talk back to the law by embarking on more conventional franchise activity in the form of the celebrity memoir. In Donovan's case, this was part of a not altogether successful attempt to restore his damaged reputation. In Rolph's chapter, we see a complex interweaving of legal and non-legal mechanisms utilized to enhance celebrity image or brand control. In placing defamation litigation in the context of a much broader discussion of image-control strategies, Rolph presents a more complex, nuanced view of reputation than is usually presented in legal scholarship. Here, reputation is dynamically constructed through the ongoing intersection of the domains of law and media and commercial enterprise, throughout the public life of the celebrity.

Brent Salter and Kathy Bowrey's Chapter 6, 'Dramatic copyright and the "Disneyfication" of theatre space', reflects on the relevance of US literature about the 'Disneyfication' of theatre space to the Australian theatre scene. US critics have argued that there has been a shift in the experience of theatre, in the use of public space and in the idea of what theatre is, that has followed from urban redevelopment of Times Square in New York. The result has been the homogenization of the theatrical precinct, with the incorporation of merchandising and shopping into theatre attendance. The aim is no longer that of assembling audiences for discrete shows, but to draw global consumers who come to 'experience' the precinct. Along with the changes to the character and use of public space, critics also discern shifts in the labour relations of theatre as a consequence of the size and scale of the investment and the nature of productions attractive to swathes of global tourists. As writers and directors become corporate employees, distributions of power linked to ownership of copyright also have less relevance, and the legal relations of theatre come to mirror that of cinema. While Disneyfication was originally confined to large, prominent commercial theatre precincts, scholars have also suggested that similar dynamics have also affected American not-for-profit theatre.

The Australian commercial theatre scene is also dominated by franchised theatre spectacles. Salter and Bowrey investigate whether there have been corresponding changes to entertainment consumption in 'Australian theatre', which is culturally structured around the not-for-profit sector. They find that Australian theatre production remains a playwright model, with the centrality of the author function maintained through the standard-setting of the Australian Writers' Guild and the absence of corresponding theatre producers' or directors' guilds. However, the financial struggles of the sector lead away from concerns over labour relations and copyright. The larger problem raised by theatre practitioners is over inadequate funding and lack of public policy to support the production of original Australian works, which impacts on the sustainability of the sector and, in turn, on retention of talent within Australia. Salter and Bowrey's research highlights the importance of co-operation within artistic communities to the viability of national cultural production. They also argue that the main danger of Disneyfication comes from the lack of relevant Australian law or public policy to support the aspirations of this small professional community, leading to its slow death. Disneyfied theatre may be all that remains as it is a profitable form of global production.

Kathy Bowrey and Michael Handler's Chapter 7, 'Instituting copyright: reconciling copyright law and industry practice in the Australian film and television sector', raises similar questions about the role of law in supporting Australian production, in the context of film and television. The authors sought to investigate why standard industry agreements in Australia contain 'rights' to television 'formats' and 'derivative' and 'spin-off' rights to literary and dramatic works and films – a franchise trade based on concepts unknown to Australian copyright law. Drawing upon interviews conducted with public broadcasters, film funding bodies, and guilds representing producers, directors and writers, what they found took them by surprise. The legal and cultural relations in play were far more complicated than they, or copyright law's formal categories and demarcation of rights, had entertained, and understanding Australian standard industry labour relation agreements, as agreed to by major players, was far more important a factor than was expected.

Bowrey and Handler argue that copyright ownership is of little productive use in mobilizing capital and labour in this small entertainment market. Accordingly, such work has to be done by public funding bodies, media regulations and industry labour agreements. The management provided by guilds and quasi-public institutions provides an alternative and supplementary mechanism for ordering the copyright trade. The authors argue that there is a need to recognize and value the work of these other institutions better to understand why there is a gap between how copyright jurisprudence constructs private rights ownership and how income streams are generated in practice in the Australian film and television industry. They construct the key relationships in terms of social contract and common enterprise, displacing the traditional focus on ownership of exclusive property rights.

José Bellido's Chapter 8, 'Flamenco music in copyright historiography', is also concerned with the role of institutions in regulating creativity, in particular copyright management agencies. He argues that it was the lowly, lascivious and exuberant reputation of flamenco, associated with its place of performance, that disrupted ready integration of the art form into copyright in Spain in the early to mid-twentieth century. More-conventional legal explanations of the obstacles – flamenco's traditional and folkloric roots; the ephemeral performance elements; the lack of written works – are also addressed. However, Bellido argues that concerns about copyright formalities were readily overcome through management strategies and technologies of mapping and documenting performances. But, while economic self-interest motivated the relevant collecting society, the Spanish Collecting Society of Authors (*Sociedad de Autores Españoles* (SAE)), to take over the task of copyright registration previously conducted by the state, as well as to encompass flamenco music within its purview, the low cultural status of this art form and its practitioners proved to be a significant stumbling block. Attempts at inclusion of flamenco artists profoundly disrupted the organization of the guild again and again, notwithstanding flamenco being one of the more profitable entertainments managed by the SAE. Acceptance of flamenco was eventually advanced through the Spanish music recording and publishing house Hispavox (now EMI). Flamenco long-playing gramophone records were a very profitable form of popular music for Hispavox, and having one's name on the LP was accepted as a form of evidence of an authorial input. Music publishers were permitted to join the SAE from 1963 to contribute to management and co-ordination of the interests of authors, music publishers and producers.

Bellido points to the importance of understanding legal rights in the entertainment industry as also being distinctive cultural claims. He suggests that while money can provide a common language and an incentive to co-operate, as an organizational matter, cultural expectations can be much harder to manage than the legal technicalities. His case study suggests that, as a consequence of the tensions that can emerge, agents and institutions that manage legal rights are also engaged in defining and redefining our cultural experience. As such, management practices of defining the art, the product and the availability of rights, and of controlling the manner of consumption, are not secondary matters in copyright law. Rather, the agency and efficacy of these professionals is fundamental to defining the nature of our shared cultural experience.

Combined, the chapters in Part III point to the importance of other institutions and managerial relationships that are neglected and poorly understood due to a preoccupation with the author model. The focus on individual and private property rights tends to displace recognition of collective cultural and economic aspirations. This theme is taken up more broadly in the next section of the volume.

2.3 *Part IV: group rights and culture*

In the age of the franchise, what is the relationship between law on the one hand and cultural products that the formal law has not historically recognized on the other hand? Does culture really need an owner? These are questions confronted by the last two chapters in this collection, both of which focus on cultural festivals.

Fiona Macmillan's Chapter 9, 'Arts festivals: property, heritage or more?', asks what turns out to be a profoundly provocative question: what kind of entity is a festival? In interrogating this question, Macmillan reflects on the significance of the legal classification tools we draw upon to read cultural phenomena, in particular the priority afforded to copyright and, more generally, the legal sacralization of private property rights through which we come to read culture and its products.

Festivals are often described in terms of copyright subject matter – the 'film' festival, the 'music' festival or 'art' festival – and as merely an alternative forum of distribution for these kinds of copyright works. However, this is shown to be clearly inadequate. Macmillan argues that the expectation of spontaneity, audience participation and fracturing of the everyday that marks out the festival as a special and distinctive kind of cultural event challenges the fit within intellectual property logics and the associated legal recognition afforded to orderly, disciplined labour relations. Contemporary festivals defy easy classification, bridging older agrarian traditions and the present day.

While human rights and cultural property laws provide an alternate legal framing for the festival, Macmillan argues that these too are problematic. The same public/private distinction that privileges private property, and the same undertheorized public domain that runs through intellectual property, are repeated in cultural heritage law. As currently constructed, cultural heritage law also lacks the conceptual foundation to challenge the hegemony of private property. Nonetheless, through cultural heritage law raising the significance of public rights, Macmillan argues this creates the possibility for a more profound theorization of intangible cultural property. The avenue suggested is through developing the idea of *res universitati*, a particular notion of a domain of non-exclusive property under Roman law. She argues that the property concept of *res universitati* defines a bounded creative community that distinguishes 'ours' from 'theirs'. Brought to bear upon our understanding of cultural heritage rights, it may provide an avenue to preserve productive synergies such as those evident in the festival, while maintaining the incentive to produce such synergies through the exercise of rights against outsiders.

Macmillan's chapter reminds us of the endurance of cultural forms that resist contemporary legal classification. The festival engages time, space and sociality in ways that defy the priorities suggested by the sacralization of private property rights. Alternative models of cultural commodification have always remained on the margins of the spatialization imagined by intellectual property law. However, she argues that the endurance of the festival as a vibrant and effective domain of cultural expression is also made vulnerable by the marginalization of its productive energy by the law. Hence, Macmillan suggests the need for a creative rethinking of the law and its priorities in order to prevent the law, as represented by the dominant logic of intellectual property, from destroying that which it cannot comprehend.

The concluding chapter in the collection, Sharon Le Gall's 'Franchising carnival: issues of rights and cultural identity', complements Macmillan's theorization of the legal classification of festivals. She provides a detailed history of a particular festival – the Trinidad and Tobago Carnival. Le Gall shows how the form and function of the event has changed in response to colonial and postcolonial politics, and how in light of these transitions the role of law in regulating carnival has been transformed. Carnival builds the collective, political identity of the people, and in the nineteenth century aspects of Carnival were regulated by criminal laws to suppress noisy, disruptive activity that was seen to challenge the local legal order. But, later, carnival came to be conceived of more broadly as a genuine cultural 'tradition' and as an expression of the independence of the people of Trinidad and Tobago. In the mid-twentieth century a Trinidad and Tobago-style carnival came to be replicated across the Caribbean islands. It also travelled with the Caribbean diaspora and was transplanted in North America, Europe and Africa. There are now regional initiatives to export it further, through concepts such as 'Carnival in a box'. This franchise involves selling accumulated local knowledge and expertise required to run a successful carnival event to other cities, in particular to cities in Africa, where there is an interest in connecting with Caribbean ancestors.

While Macmillan suggests a reimagined scope of property law could better protect the festival, and in so doing help secure its survival as more than a franchised cultural form distributing copyright works to subsidiary markets, Le Gall's history shows there is no neat way of classifying the Trinidad and Tobago-style carnival. The identity of the festival is contingent. It is political, cultural and economic in character and it is impossible to separate these aspects. Intellectual property rights are integrated into the contemporary carnival franchise to support some of the entrepreneurial aspirations behind its franchising. The protection available is fragmentary and tangential. However, Le Gall argues there is not really a need for intellectual property law to do more here. Le Gall argues that the carnival franchise is not necessarily about property rights at all. She says it is about identity politics, but notes that traditional knowledge protection is also not particularly apt to protect cultural identity in this circumstance.

Le Gall's chapter problematizes our expectations of law. She argues that in the case of the Trinidad and Tobago-style carnival it is the vitality of carnival, the appeal of the event in connecting peoples and places across history, time and place that is what is worth protecting. Advancing new rights claims is not necessarily an appropriate avenue to support this activity. The positioning of the franchise at the margins of the law is a strength in invigorating this cultural trade by allowing the cultural and economic aspects to merge and fold back onto each other across different times, peoples and places. Here, the lack of private or communal property rights helps grow cultural identities and cultural trade. Thus, Le Gall's study poses what is for many lawyers a counter-intuitive logic. Here, the relative absence of law enables, rather than undermines, cultural trade in the age of the franchise.

3 Conclusion

As a whole, this collection aims to interrogate commonly repeated complaints about law's relationship with creativity. It is often suggested that intellectual property and related laws act as a restraint on creativity.[53] Laws are said to interfere with the free and authentic flow of cultural exchanges. Copyright, in particular, is criticized as unfairly privileging the author over the claims of other creators, users and fans. In combination with trade mark law, copyright is said unreasonably to protect the reputation of famous brands, with private economic interests trumping other cultural claims.[54] Further, individual rights are seen as undermining group and collective claims to culture.[55]

53 See, e.g., L. Lessig, *Free Culture: The Nature and Future of Creativity* (New York: Penguin Press, 2004); W. Fisher, *Promises to Keep: Technology, Law, and the Future of Entertainment* (Redwood City, CA: Stanford University Press, 2004); K. McLeod, *Freedom of Expression®: Overzealous Copyright Bozos and Other Enemies of Creativity* (New York: Doubleday, 2005).

54 See, e.g., R. Coombe and A. Herman, 'Culture Wars on the Net: Intellectual Property and Corporate Propriety in Digital Environments' (2001) 100 *South Atlantic Quarterly* 919; Jenkins, *Convergence Culture*; S. K. Katyal, 'Performance, Property, and the Slashing of Gender in Fan Fiction' (2006) 14 *Journal of Gender, Social Policy and the Law* 461; A. Chander and M. Sunder, 'Everyone's a Superhero: A Cultural Theory of "Mary Sue" Fan Fiction as Fair Use' (2007) 95 *California Law Review* 597.

55 See, e.g., F. Macmillan, 'Human Rights, Cultural Property and Intellectual Property: Three Concepts in Search of a Relationship', in M. Burri-Nenova and C. B. Graber

The chapters, each in their own way, confront the polarization of law and culture that is common to many contemporary critiques of intellectual property law. Rather than looking for ill-fits and mismatches between law and cultural practice, the authors in this collection more commonly look to how legal and cultural relations are inter-related. They are not necessarily advocating for reform of relevant laws to suit an idealized opinion about how intellectual property laws and culture should be interacting. Rather, they are looking more carefully at existing creative legal, business, managerial and professional practices that allow for legal obstacles and shortcomings to be overcome, side-stepped, ignored and turned back into opportunities. This leads to the emergence of a much more nuanced and contingent positioning of law in relation to culture.

What we hope to achieve in this collection is to reinvigorate debates about the relationship between law and industry through broadening out discussion of cultural products to consider how they circulate, regardless of how they are classified by formal laws. This involves, in part, looking at how cultural activity centred on franchise-like behaviour leads to the stretching of foundational legal tropes such as 'authorship' and 'property', as well as looking to the role of the state and other public and private institutions in generating mega-success. We believe it is important to consider that legal practice, driven by the economic imperatives, is often far more innovative than is given credit for in sustaining cultural enterprise. The possibilities of law are reinvented in this process. However, the significance of a shift may not be readily discerned, especially by a conservative profession, for a considerable time. Our main point is not that intellectual property law is marginal to the entertainment franchise, but that the character of these laws, and copyright in particular, is shifting its shape. Law is less fixed or secure, and starting to mirror some of the ephemeral features of the entertainment franchise. While the author function and reputation still provide a hook to anchor certain rights claims and to vest cultural control, these notions are increasingly deployed in surprising and potentially destablizing ways that warrant much further scholarly consideration and debate.

(eds), *Intellectual Property and Traditional Cultural Expressions in a Digital Environment* (Cheltenham: Edward Elgar, 2008).

Part II

The productivity of the author model: authors, collaborators and non-authors

2 The author strikes back
Mutating authorship in the expanded universe

Lionel Bently and Laura Biron

1 Introduction

In recent years, the difficulty of finding a common legal or cultural answer to the question of how to identify the author of a film has been compounded by the emergence of the entertainment franchise – a phenomenon whereby the cultural industries have been able to exploit the commercial potential of films as networks or franchises of related products, rather than single cultural products. New conceptions of authorship have emerged within film studies to take into account the changing dynamic of the entertainment franchise, moving beyond the 'director-as-author' model associated with *auteurism*, focusing instead on executive production, authorship of the underlying story and 'brand' authorship. The aim of this chapter is to explore these conceptions of film authorship in more depth, highlighting an underlying tension that exists between film or franchise authorship as a cultural phenomenon and the question of how to identify the author from the standpoint of intellectual property law.

2 Authorship and film

The position of the 'author' within the film industry is a matter that has been widely discussed, even when the focus is limited to the film itself. Although it is taken for granted that film-making is a collaborative process,[1] for much of the late twentieth century a theory of the director-as-author, or auteurism, which was first developed in French

[1] Until the 1960s, Hollywood, in particular, had been dominated by the 'studio system', the nature of which highlighted the film as an industrial production controlled by corporate decision-makers, leading some to argue that 'movies made . . . during the heyday of the old-style studio era should be regarded as collective endeavors and analyzed accordingly': V. W. Wexman, 'Introduction', in V. W. Wexman (ed.), *Film and Authorship* (New Brunswick, NJ: Rutgers University Press, 2003), p. 8.

cinema,[2] held sway even amongst commentators dealing with Hollywood movies.[3] Perhaps the most well-known advocate of the theory was Andrew Sarris, first with his famous 1962 essay 'Notes on the Auteur Theory',[4] and later with his 1968 book, *The American Cinema*.[5] The claim, put simply, was that:

> [o]ver a group of films, a director must exhibit certain recurring characteristics of style, which serve as his signature. The way a film looks and moves should have some relationship to the way a director thinks and feels.[6]

Sarris went as far as to claim that such characteristics were more common in US film than elsewhere because 'so much of the American cinema is commissioned'. Importantly, in this conception, the auteur is necessarily the director, and the creativity and expression of the author's personality lies in directing the actors, movement, action, choosing the camera angles and the framing of the image.[7] Moreover, the film was often said to be 'visually distinctive' in some way,[8] enabling the auteur's *mise-en-scène* or personal signature to be apparent in the work.

However, auteurism was also subject to significant critical analysis in film studies, particularly through the influence of structuralism and post-structuralism, which highlighted the inter-textual and fragmented nature of authorship, and challenged the romantic notion of the author as, in Michel Foucault's critique, 'the figure that, at least in appearance, is outside [the work] and antecedes it'.[9] In French cinema, this process arose within auteurism itself, through the movement known as auteur-structuralism.[10] Although this theory still focused on the director as auteur, its method was to highlight the director's authorial voice as an unconscious process to be uncovered by viewers and, following Roland Barthes, to view the meaning of the text (or film) as constructed by its

[2] In particular by François Truffaut's essay, 'A Certain Tendency of the French Cinema', in the journal *Cahiers du Cinéma*. The essay is reproduced in B. K. Grant, *Auteurs and Authorship: A Film Reader* (Oxford: Blackwell Publishing, 2008).

[3] Grant, *Auteurs and Authorship*.

[4] A. Sarris, 'Notes on the Auteur Theory in 1962' (1962–3) 27 *Film Culture* 1 (reprinted in Grant, *Auteurs and Authorship*).

[5] A. Sarris, *The American Cinema: Directors and Directions, 1929–1968* (New York: Dutton, 1968).

[6] Sarris, 'Notes on the Auteur Theory in 1962', p. 7. See also Grant, *Auteurs and Authorship*, p. 1 ('some directors may express an individual vision, a worldview, over a series of films with stylistic and thematic consistency').

[7] J. Caughie (ed.), *Theories of Authorship* (London: Routledge & Kegan Paul, 1981), p. 13.

[8] Wexman, 'Introduction', pp. 2–3.

[9] M. Foucault, 'What is an Author?', in P. Rabinow (ed.), *The Foucault Reader* (New York: Pantheon Books, 1984), p. 101.

[10] Wexman, 'Introduction', p. 4.

spectators, rather than something antecedently planted in it by a self-conscious author.[11] Auteur-structuralism soon became just one of many forms of *ciné*-structuralism, the general effect of which movement led one commentator to claim that film scholars had stopped discussing authorship at all by the 1990s.[12] Despite the neglect of authorship, however, film theorists still continued to speak of the important role of directors in the analysis of film, even if they were simply the 'source of an unconscious process of textual writing'[13] rather than explicitly recognized as auteurs.

If questions about film authorship have been controversial amongst film commentators, the question of who is the author of a film for legal purposes, in particular for copyright law, seems to have been even more hotly contested. One general difficulty is the fact that there is no universal system of copyright law, but merely a collection of national copyright systems that, through international agreements (the most significant of which is the Berne Convention for the Protection of Literary and Artistic Works),[14] operate many similar standards. Moreover, in the context of authorship of films, variations between copyright systems are still quite pronounced. Even though films ('motion pictures' or 'cinematographic works') are recognized as a distinct category of work within the Berne Convention,[15] rather than being indirectly protected as a combination of screenplay (dramatic work), choreographed movement (dramatic work) and photographs, different jurisdictions have reached different answers to the question of who should be viewed as the author. The writer of the screenplay, the writer of the dialogue, the director, the composer of music, the editor and the producer are amongst the many different authors or co-authors recognized in different legal systems. Indeed, at the 1948 Brussels Congress that revised the Berne Convention, the Chair of the Sub-Committee spoke of 'the impossibility of defining the author of a cinematographic work'.[16]

[11] R. Barthes, 'The Death of the Author', in S. Heath (ed.), *Image, Music, Text* (New York: Hill and Wang, 1977).

[12] D. Andrew, 'The Unauthorised Auteur Today', in J. Collins, H. Radner and A. P. Collins (eds), *Film Theory Goes to the Movies* (New York: Routledge, 1993), p. 77.

[13] Wexman, 'Introduction', p. 1.

[14] Opened for signature 24 July 1971, 1161 UNTS 31 (entered into force 15 December 1972).

[15] See art. 1(2) ('cinematographic works to which are assimilated works expressed by a process analogous to cinematography').

[16] Reproduced in S. Ricketson and J. Ginsburg, *International Copyright and Neighbouring Rights: The Berne Convention and Beyond*, 2nd edn (Oxford University Press, 2008), Appendix 28, p. 272; http://global.oup.com/booksites/content/9780198259466/15550028.

The challenge of reaching an agreed upon view about film authorship in both law and film studies reflects at bottom the intrinsically collaborative nature of film-making and the attendant difficulty of identifying one person, or a manageably small number of people, whose input into the making of a film can be analogized to the input of a writer or painter into the construction of a poem, novel or portrait. The huge expense involved in making films, and the ease with which they might be copied, seems readily to justify their protection by copyright, but offers no clear solution to the task of identifying the author. At the same time, it might be argued that the need to resolve the question of authorship in film has been made less pressing through the development of legal rules and practices (particularly contract) that offer relatively clear answers to the distinct question of the ownership of copyright.[17] As long as it has been clear who the copyright owner is, and thus who can enforce copyright, a locus exists around which a nexus of 'authorial' transactions – financing, distribution, remuneration, credit and so on – has been able to operate through private and collective bargaining. In Hollywood film-making, for example, the work-for-hire doctrine might notionally designate the production company as the 'author' (and copyright owner), but complex union codes ensure and closely regulate the ways in which many of the participants are recognized and control minimum terms for remuneration. When it comes to films as singular cultural products, then, it is possible that a broad consensus exists about the designation of 'authors' and 'owners', and that legal rules that enable these different aspects of the 'author function' to operate have to some extent assuaged the difficulty of identifying a single author of a film.

3 The entertainment franchise

Even if the difficulty of finding a common legal – let alone cultural–legal – answer to the question of who is the author of a film has been mitigated by certain legal rules, it has also been further complicated by developments in the last decades of the twentieth century, which raise new and pressing questions about authorship for both film scholars and legal theorists. The mid-1970s witnessed the beginning of significant shifts in the nature of film with the emergence of the entertainment franchise, a phenomenon whereby income made from exploitation of a film through its playing before audiences in cinemas, or through television and cable broadcasts, was shown not to be of primary significance when compared to the money

[17] For example, the US 'work for hire' doctrine and the presumption of transfer in French copyright law.

that could be made through other means, including merchandising and, more recently, the making of video games.[18] And for many commentators the release of *Star Wars* in 1977 stands out as a key moment in the development of this process.[19] Film-makers, novelists, cartoonists and so on may have been able to exploit certain secondary markets long before *Star Wars*,[20] but it was with *Star Wars* that the nature of the 'entertainment franchise' became clear: no longer were the eyes of (those financing) the cultural industries focused on the potential of single cultural products, but instead on networks or franchises of exploitation arrangements.[21] What came to matter, commercially at least, was less the cultural 'thing' or 'text' but rather the rights to control derivative and associated forms

[18] For a discussion of this phenomenon in relation to *Star Wars*, see D. Pollock, *Skywalking: The Life and Films of George Lucas* (New York: Harmony, 1983), pp. 254–5; J. S. Lawrence, 'Introduction: Spectacle, Merchandise, and Influence', in M. W. Kapell and J. S. Lawrence (eds), *Finding the Force of the Star Wars Franchise: Fans, Merchandise and Critics* (New York: Peter Lang, 2006), p. 1 ('The Star Wars franchise stands as film history's greatest commercial and cultural success').

[19] T. Schatz, 'The Studio System and Conglomerate Hollywood', in P. McDonald and J. Wasko, *The Contemporary Hollywood Film Industries* (Oxford: Blackwell Publishing, 2008), p. 20 ('*Star Wars* quickly evolved into the model New Hollywood "franchise", i.e., the blockbuster-spawning entertainment machine that exploited and expanded the original but in an ever-widening range of entertainment products'); T. Balio, *Hollywood in the New Millennium* (London: Palgrave Macmillan, 2013), p. 80 ('The current vogue of film-licensing began with George Lucas's *Star Wars*... After *Star Wars*, it became standard practice to support franchises and tentpole with massive merchandising campaigns which generated revenues that often rivalled their box office take'). See also T. Schatz, *Old Hollywood/New Hollywood: Ritual, Art, and Industry* (Ann Arbor, MI: UMI Research Press, 1983), p. 194; J. Surowieki (1997), quoted in J. Baxter, *George Lucas: A Biography* (London: HarperCollins, 1999), p. 174 ('It's safe to say that *Star Wars* single-handedly created the film-merchandising business'); J. Lewis, 'Following the Money in America's Sunniest Town: Some Notes on the Political Economy of the Hollywood Blockbuster', in J. Stringer (ed.), *Movie Blockbusters* (London: Routledge, 2003), p. 63 ('It changed not only the way films were made, but how they were promoted, distributed and exhibited to American and international audiences'); P. Grainge, *Brand Hollywood: Selling Entertainment in a Global Media Age* (London: Routledge, 2008), p. 3 (*Star Wars* 'inaugurated the effects-laden era of the merchandised blockbuster').

[20] In the 1940s, Disney made $100 million per annum from 'trinkets': Balio, *Hollywood in the New Millennium*. p. 79, citing 'America's Sorcerer', *The Economist* (London), 10 January 1998, p. 71. David Thomson refers to the earlier merchandise associated with the television show *The Adventures of Davy Crockett* (1954): D. Thomson, *The Big Screen: The Story of the Movies and What They Did to Us* (London: Penguin, 2012), p. 452.

[21] T. Corrigan, *A Cinema Without Walls: Movies and Culture after Vietnam* (New Brunswick, NJ: Rutgers University Press, 1991), p. 20 ('Every conglomerate would pursue the *Star Wars* figures: $27 million invested in 1977 ... returning well over $500 million by 1980, for a 1855 per cent profit in three years'); R. Allen, 'Home Alone Together: Hollywood and the "Family Film"', in M. Stokes and R. Maltby (eds), *Identifying Hollywood's Audiences: Cultural Identity and the Movies* (London: BFI, 1999), p. 118 ('Star Wars demonstrated the extraordinary profitability of licensing the use of a film's title, logo, character likeness, storyline, props and other features').

and activities.[22] The 'thing' had thereafter to 'be strategically available to multiple reiteration across a range of commercial settings from lunch boxes to video games'.[23] The emergence of the 'entertainment franchise' was so widely recognized that even films started to refer to their own franchise potential, as the 1993 film *Jurassic Park* famously did when the camera alighted on the fictional *Jurassic Park* merchandising store, stocked with real life *Jurassic Park* themed merchandise.[24] According to Thomas Elsaesser, the scene 'anticipates that we will like the film so much that we will want to buy the merchandise, and to make it easy for us, it displays it in the film itself'.[25]

There are no doubt a number of important,[26] and many disturbing,[27] characteristics and effects of the 'entertainment franchise'.[28] The entertainment franchise has changed the commercial dynamics of film-making because takings at the box office are no longer necessarily the most important revenue streams. In turn, the capacity to achieve returns from merchandising has become a critical consideration in decisions as to what films are made. The entertainment franchise has also changed the nature

[22] Grainge, *Brand Hollywood*, pp. 52–3.

[23] R. Armstrong, Review of *New Hollywood Cinema: An Introduction* (2003–4) 57 *Film Quarterly* 59.

[24] And also where sceptical scientist Dr Malcolm berates the park owner for being too interested in merchandising, telling him 'before you even knew what you had, you patented it, and packaged it, and slapped it on a plastic lunchbox'.

[25] T. Elsaesser, 'The Blockbuster as Time Machine', in T. Elsaesser, *The Persistence of Hollywood* (Abingdon: Routledge, 2012), p. 271.

[26] 'It is said that the "blockbuster" saved Hollywood and thus . . . the cinema as a popular entertainment medium': Elsaesser, 'The Blockbuster as Time Machine', p. 279. See also Allen, 'Home Alone Together', p. 119 (observing that the shift altered what a film 'is', not just economically but ontologically).

[27] S. Sontag, 'The Decay of Cinema', *New York Times Magazine*, 25 February 1996, pp. 60–1 ('While the point of a great film is now, more than ever, to be a one-of-a-kind achievement, the commercial cinema has settled for a policy of bloated, derivative film-making, a brazen combinatory or recombinatory art, in the hope of reproducing past successes . . . In this country, the lowering of expectations for quality and the inflation of expectations for profit have made it virtually impossible for artistically ambitious American directors, like Francis Ford Coppola and Paul Schrader, to work at their best level. Abroad, the result can be seen in the melancholy fate of some of the greatest directors of the last decades'); D. Thomson, 'Who Killed the Movies?', *Esquire* (New York), December 1996, p. 56 ('Movies are in a very bad state . . . sunk beyond anything we dreamed of . . . I blame Spielberg and Lucas'); D. Denby, 'Has Hollywood Murdered the Movies?', *New Republic* (online), 14 September 2012, at http://newrepublic.com/article/books-and-arts/magazine/107212/has-hollywood-murdered-the-movies ('It has come to this: a movie studio can no longer risk making good movies. Their business model depends on the assured audience and the blockbuster. It has done so for years and will continue to do so for years more . . . The big revenues from such pictures rarely get siphoned into more adventurous projects; they get poured into the next sequel or a new franchise').

[28] Much of the literature focuses on the relationship with the audience, in particular, surrounding fandom. See further D. Lindsay, 'Franchises, imaginary worlds, authorship and fandom', in this collection.

of film, the film itself being just 'one instance in a wider commercial system of objects'.[29] This has transformed film as a cultural experience, as no longer 'merely' a series of images on celluloid consumed by the public in temporarily defined periods at the cinema, but more a diffuse cultural experience in which a film's characters and concepts become reference points for people who may never have seen the initial film. Finally, and most importantly for this chapter, the entertainment franchise has prompted new questions about authorship. It seems to be a common feature of many of the contemporary entertainment 'franchises' that they purport to derive from the creative act of 'an author'. At the same time, the most prevalent idea amongst film commentators – that of the director as author – appears ill-suited to the new environment where the *mise-en-scène* plays so small a role in the so-called 'expanded universe' of computer animation, theme parks and 'potential goodwill' of audiences.[30]

In the remainder of this chapter, we consider some ways in which the entertainment franchise has led to debate over, and re-conceptualization of, the notion of authorship amongst commentators on Hollywood, focusing on *Star Wars* in particular.[31] More specifically, we show how George Lucas has been attributed not only in the romantic-author role of 'auteur-director', but also as fitting new models of authorship: the 'commercial auteur' who is analogous to the executive producer of a film; the 'franchise-auteur' who is responsible for the underlying concept behind the expanded universe; and the 'brand-auteur', who is said to stand as an important indicator of the quality of the products in the franchise, and their marketability. In contrast to the fluid evolution of notions of authorship of film (and ideas of film itself), we outline the legal parameters by which film authorship is determined, and how authorship of merchandise might be conceived. Our aim is to highlight the discontinuities between legal characterization and evolving ideas of authorship in film commentary, with a view to raising some questions about the relationship between authorship in film studies and authorship in law.

29 S. Lash and C. Lury, *Global Culture Industry: The Mediation of Things* (Cambridge: Polity Press, 2007), p. 186.

30 K. Bowrey, 'The New Intellectual Property: Celebrity, Fans and the Properties of the Entertainment Franchise' (2011) 20 *Griffith Law Review* 188, 193.

31 The link of the 'franchise' back to an 'act of authorship' is by no means unique to *Star Wars*, or indeed to cases where the supposed 'author' was fortunate (or prescient enough) to have negotiated an interest in further modes of exploitation. The *Teenage Mutant Ninja Turtles* franchise, for example, which encompasses films, cartoon serials, books and a wide range of merchandise is said to have started life in the authoring of a comic book by Kevin Eastman and Peter Laird in the 1980s. More obviously, the *Harry Potter* franchise traces itself to the act of authorship of J. K. Rowling, writing in Edinburgh in the 1990s.

4 The authorship question: film and franchise

4.1 Lucas as auteur-director?

Although the director-as-auteur model has been questioned and challenged amongst film scholars, this has not stopped some from applying it to *Star Wars*. Most obviously, Lucas is credited as the director and writer of the first *Star Wars* movie.[32] Moreover, he has frequently been described as an example of a film auteur, either specifically in relation to the first *Star Wars* movie, the initial trilogy, or more generally. For example, writing in the respected journal *Film Quarterly*, Denis Wood has said:

> If any contemporary film can be said to be the work of one man, *Star Wars* is such a film. Lucas wrote the story and the screenplay, directed, helped edit and produce the film, and actively involved himself in every phase of the production. However you felt about this film, you felt the strong voice of a single individual speaking through it.[33]

Production manager Robert Watts opined that 'it was a film that was entirely George's'.[34] Another commentator has referred to the first three films in the *Star Wars* series as having been 'the work of a single guiding intelligence'.[35] Douglas Gomery adds that 'filmmakers such as George Lucas . . . have become the cultural idols of a generation in the same way novelists had only two decades earlier'.[36] Lucas has been referred to as a 'genius',[37] 'a great American artist',[38] and commentators have even made the classic associations between Lucas and the obsessive commitment of the romantic author to their work to the point of neglect of worldly concerns, starvation and illness.[39]

However, if we look more closely at the details of the making of *Star Wars* and subsequent films, the positioning of Lucas as a romantic

[32] Released in 1977 under the title *Star Wars*, it is now known as *Star Wars Episode IV: A New Hope*. The film credits indicated it was 'a Lucasfilm production', 'produced by Gary Kurtz', with music by John Williams, and 'presented by' Twentieth Century Fox.

[33] D. Wood, 'The Empire's New Clothes' (1981) 34 *Film Quarterly* 10, 16.

[34] Pollock, *Skywalking*, p. 170.

[35] A. Collins, 'The "Star Wars" Trilogy' (1983) 4 *San Francisco Jung Institute Library Journal* 48.

[36] D. Gomery, 'The Hollywood Blockbuster: Industrial Analysis and Practice', in Stringer, *Movie Blockbusters*, p. 81.

[37] Pollock, *Skywalking*, p. 66. [38] *Ibid.*, p. 272.

[39] See A. Harmetz, 'Today's Hottest Movie Stars – C3PO and R2-D2', *New York Times*, 5 June 1977, p. D1 (referring to Lucas's 'insistence on putting on the screen the precise vision inside his head'). See also Pollock, *Skywalking*, p. 125 (referring to Lucas positioning himself as 'starving').

auteur-director seems strange for a number of reasons. First, after directing *Star Wars*, Lucas handed over direction of subsequent films in the series to others. According to Tom Schatz, Lucas preferred to produce rather than to write or direct films.[40] Indeed, Lucas has often complained about the task of directing.[41] Mark Hamill, who played Luke Skywalker, stated 'if there were a way to make movies without actors, George would do it'.[42] Lucas even admitted he had not done 'anything to make the actors wonderful'.[43] In the two immediate sequels, the 'story' was created by Lucas,[44] but direction was passed on. The screenplay for *The Empire Strikes Back* (1980) is attributed to Leigh Brackett and Lawrence Kasdan, and the film was directed by Irvin Kershner and produced by Gary Kurtz. Similarly, the screenplay of *Return of the Jedi* (1983) is attributed to both Lawrence Kasdan and George Lucas, and it was directed by Richard Marquand and produced by Howard Kazanjian. Although the credits refer to Lucas as director of the next three movies in the *Star Wars* series, these were characterized by 'increasingly sophisticated effects and diminishing narrative energy'.[45] Indeed, Lucas himself has said he is 'much more of a filmmaker than a film director'.[46]

4.2 *Lucas as commercial-auteur*

Recognizing that Lucas does not fit the model of a romantic auteur-director, but driven by the assumption that it would be 'silly to argue' that he is not an auteur,[47] some commentators have sought to redefine film authorship itself. Highlighting the commercial dimensions of authorship, Timothy Corrigan and Warren Buckland have offered alternative conceptions of film authorship that focus less on the act of creation or internal dynamic of the film, and rather on particular designations of 'authorship' as tied up with a function of commerce. According to Corrigan, the 'auteur' is 'a commercial strategy for organising audience

[40] Schatz, *Old Hollywood, New Hollywood*, p. 209. In an interview, Lucas stated: 'Once I started directing, I realised I didn't enjoy it – because of the fact that it isn't hands on': M. Tuchman and A. Thompson, 'I'm the Boss' (1981) 17 *Film Comment* 49, 53.

[41] Pollock, *Skywalking*, p. 93. [42] *Ibid.*, p. 163. [43] *Ibid.*

[44] According to the credit manual of the Screen Writers Guild, 'The term "story" means all writing covered by the provisions of the Minimum Basic Agreement representing a contribution "distinct from screenplay and consisting of basic narrative, idea, theme or outline indicating character development and action"': Writers Guild of America, *Screen Credits Manual* (2010), p. 17, at http://wga.org/uploadedFiles/writers_resources/credits/screenscredits_manual10.pdf.

[45] Thomson, *The Big Screen*, p. 452.

[46] Quoted in D. Goddard, 'From "American Graffiti" to Outer Space', *New York Times*, 12 September 1976, p. 89.

[47] Lewis, 'Following the Money in America's Sunniest Town', p. 75.

reception . . . a critical concept bound to distribution and marketing aims that identify and address the potential cult status of an auteur'.[48] For Corrigan, George Lucas is an example of just such a 'commercial auteur', the celebrity of his agency producing and promoting texts that invariably exceed the movie itself.[49] Similarly, Buckland redefines an author as 'a director who gains control over all the stages of film-making: not just film production, but also distribution and exhibition'.[50] In contrast to the traditional criteria of authorship that focus on the internal aspects of film production, 'mastery of the filmmaking process is no longer a sufficient criterion for authorship status: the director also needs to control external factors such as production, money and the deal-making process'.[51]

In a similar vein, Jon Lewis notes that 'although Lucas did not direct a single film in the 1980s, he is one of the decade's two most successful, important, significant, and valued auteurs'.[52] He describes Lucas and Spielberg as 'blockbuster auteurs' who produce 'high-concept entertainment' (famously identified by Spielberg as movie ideas that are describable in twenty-five, or fewer, words).[53] In relation to *Star Wars*, Lewis notes:

> *Star Wars* was a model new Hollywood product. It was easily cross-promoted and it exploited markets in several parallel entertainment and consumer industries. Given the scale of its financial success, questions regarding its artistic merit seemed altogether beside the point.

Auteurship in this sense is not about directing scenes or positioning the camera, but instead about making deals that enable movies to be made and controlling the post-production process.[54] If directing is less important than generating the concept, securing finance, or post-production addition of sound, special effects and so forth, these should be recognized as places where individual actors or agents make a difference. The

48 Corrigan, *A Cinema Without Walls*, p. 103. See also T. Corrigan, 'The Commerce of Auteurism: A Voice Without Authority' (1990) 49 *New German Critique* 43; T. Corrigan, 'Auteurs and the New Hollywood', in J. Lewis (ed.), *The New American Cinema* (Durham, NC: Duke University Press, 1998).

49 Corrigan, *A Cinema Without Walls*, p. 107.

50 W. Buckland, 'The Role of the Auteur in the Age of the Blockbuster: Steven Spielberg and DreamWorks', in Stringer, *Movie Blockbusters*, p. 84.

51 *Ibid.*, p. 86.

52 J. Lewis, 'The Perfect Money Machine(s): George Lucas, Steven Spielberg, and Auteurism in the New Hollywood', in J. Lewis and E. Smoodin (eds), *Looking Past the Screen* (Durham, NC: Duke University Press, 2007), pp. 65–6.

53 During the filming of *American Graffiti*, Lucas explained that 'scripts should be more like blueprints than novels': L. Sweeney (1970), quoted in Lewis, 'The Perfect Money Machine(s)', p. 81.

54 Lewis, 'The Perfect Money Machine(s)', p. 70.

outcome is that producers or executive producers of films would be considered authors.

4.3 *Lucas as franchise-auteur*

A third way in which Lucas has been seen as the auteur of *Star Wars* is through his association with the 'totality' of the franchise, rather than just the films.[55] On this approach, Lucas is auteur of the franchise because he developed the initial concept or story that initiated the so-called 'expanded universe' of *Star Wars* merchandise. He may even have done so consciously and intentionally. According to Mark Pepvers, Lucas 'created *Star Wars* with the toy by-products in mind. He was making much more than a movie'.[56] According to one biographer, 'Lucas fantasized about R2-D2 cookie jars, Wookiee mugs, and wind-up robots'.[57] Another recounts conversations Lucas had with Charles Lippincott, a publicity supervisor at Lucasfilm, about the merchandising potential of the film,[58] and concludes:

> Lucas never saw Star Wars toys as a lucrative spin-off: to him, they were his best chance of making a profit from a film that would probably not do all that well at the box office. In June 1977, when Star Wars was barely released, he said, 'In a way, this film was designed around toys. I actually make toys. If I make money, it will be from the toys'.[59]

Apparently, the material contained in the expanded universe of *Star Wars* merchandise 'has been carefully vetted for continuity and intent, often by Lucas himself'.[60] Even Tom Schatz, whose comments on Lucas hardly suggest he is a fan, asserts that Lucas is closely involved in the design

[55] It is widely recognized that following the success of his first film, *American Graffiti* (which cost over US$750,000 to make but earned well over $21 million), Lucas negotiated to 'retain' these merchandising rights in his deal with Twentieth Century Fox, in part so that he could better control the promotion of the film. As Lucas himself recalled in an interview, the deal was made at a time where film production companies did not regard them as of any real value: 'How George Lucas Got the Rights to the STAR WARS Sequels', AFI (2009), at http://youtube.com/watch?v=dPJ2gQdKXqk.

[56] M. Pepvers, 'ET and Friends are Flying High', *Business Week* (New York), 10 January 1993, p. 77, quoted in Lewis, 'The Perfect Money Machine(s)', p. 68.

[57] Pollock, *Skywalking*, p. 194.

[58] J. Baxter, *George Lucas: A Biography* (London: HarperCollins, 1999), p. 173.

[59] As it turned out, the franchise was not limited to toys, or even to merchandise. There was a novel, a sound-track album, as well as figures and posters. In a 1985 case in which Lucasfilm Ltd relied on ownership of the STAR WARS trade mark, the court explained it had been used 'to merchandise dolls, toys, comic books, cookies, paper cups, watches, candles and even bubble bath': *Lucasfilm Ltd* v. *High Frontier*, 622 F Supp 931, 932 (DDC, 1985) (Gesell J).

[60] Kapell and Lawrence, *Finding the Force of the Star Wars Franchise*, p. xvii.

of the 'toys'.[61] Likewise, Lawrence referred to the franchise as 'guided by a single creator, George W. Lucas'.[62] According to Derek Johnson, Lucasfilm Ltd is 'the production company of *franchise creator* and overseer George Lucas'.[63] These comments suggest that recognition of Lucas as auteur of the franchise is both an acknowledgement that authorship of the initial concept or story behind the film initiated the development of its franchise, but also that Lucas himself was closely involved in this process, both by way of general oversight and close input into the design of some of the products.

4.4 *Lucas as brand-auteur*

A fourth response amongst film commentators has been to talk of film authorship in terms of brands and marketing. Picking up on the analysis of Lucas as a 'commercial' auteur (discussed in 4.2), it has become common to recognize that the position of the 'author', whether director or producer, in relation to a film, is primarily about marketing. As such, the film industry both promotes and seeks to capitalize on the perception of a particular name as an 'auteur'. Andrew deWaard, for example, has explored how '[t]he industry has come to see auteurs as another distinctive (and marketable) element that can be added to blockbuster appeal . . . the director's name has become part of the marketing equation as an assurance of quality'.[64] Following on from his description of George Lucas and Steven Spielberg as 'blockbuster auteurs', Jon Lewis argues that they also brought a shift in film authorship from signature style to 'signature product':

> [Lucas and Spielberg's] significance isn't really a matter of specific moments or sequences or scenes or films, but rather a matter of participation in a larger industry drama, one revealed not on screen but in the media coverage and idle gossip attending the motion picture today.[65]

61 Schatz, *Old Hollywood/New Hollywood*, p. 194 ('many of [the *Star Wars* toys] he designed himself').
62 Lawrence, 'Introduction: Spectacle, Merchandise and Influence', p. 1.
63 D. Johnson and W. Brooker, 'Star Wars Fans, DVD, and Cultural Ownership: An Interview with Will Brooker' (2005) 56 *The Velvet Light Trap* 36.
64 A. deWaard, 'Joints and Jams: Spike Lee as Sellebrity Auteur', in J. D. Hamlet and R. R. Means Coleman (eds), *Fight the Power!: The Spike Lee Reader* (New York: Peter Lang, 2008). He offers the example of Spike Lee objecting to the establishing of a cable channel 'Spike TV'. Lee complained: 'People don't realize that I'm a brand . . . and all the goodwill that I have invested in it can be contaminated by "Spike TV"': S. Lee and C. Fuchs, *Spike Lee: Interviews* (Jackson, MS: University Press of Mississippi, 2002), p. 288.
65 Lewis, 'The Perfect Money Machine(s)', pp. 67–8.

Interestingly, on this conception of film authorship, the auteurist focus on the 'signature' of the director (see 4.1) is still relevant, but it becomes more about their signature as attached to the wide variety of products that result from the franchise. Perhaps brand auteurship, in this sense, is a combination of the director-auterist's search for an individual director's signature, the commercial-auteurist's focus on marketability and the franchise-auteurist's commitment to a continuing relationship between an individual auteur and all the related products of the franchise.

5 The authorship question: intellectual property law

5.1 Authorship and copyright law

The flexibility with which film commentators have deployed the notion of 'authorship' stands in contrast to the manner in which authorship is usually attributed by the legal system (and by copyright laws more specifically). Copyright law assumes that authorship is a relatively stable category, and much of copyright law seems to be premised on the ability of the system to identify authors with reasonable certainty. At first sight, much of the debate over the status of Lucas as auteur, and the fluid realignment of the notion of authorship to correspond with the way that Lucas and others have operated, seems a long way from copyright law's practice. Indeed, the definition of authorship that is most prevalent across different copyright systems is one that tends to focus on contributions of natural persons to the expressive form of a work, allocating authorship status only to those who contribute substantially and originally to such expression.[66] If this legal conception of authorship fits any of the above conceptions of film authorship, it seems to support the auteur-director model – focused as it is on contribution to expression contained in the work – which is precisely the model that seems inapplicable to the entertainment franchise.

Indeed, just as film scholars were starting to replace auteurism (or at least director-focused auteurism) with a more fluid notion of film authorship, copyright law increasingly recognized directors as authors. In the British recodification in 1988, moral rights of attribution and integrity were conferred on the 'directors' of films, while EU harmonizing directives in the early 1990s required member states to recognize directors as

[66] J. Ginsburg, 'The Concept of Authorship in Comparative Copyright Law' (2003) 52 *DePaul Law Review* 1063.

at least one of the authors of cinematographic or audiovisual works.[67] No attention seems to have been paid to the shift in the nature of film production that we have referred to as the emergence of the entertainment franchise, and the corresponding attempts to recognize commercial and other dimensions of film production as authorial. Furthermore, it is questionable whether contributions associated with commercial auteurism, such as deal-making, financing or post-production control could really be considered contributions to be 'of the right kind' for *authorship* in copyright law, because most copyright laws exclude from consideration initiation, organization and management as potential contributions of authorship.[68]

One way in which many copyright systems differ from romantic auteurism, however, is through their potential to recognize multiple authors of a film, alongside the director. Taking the first *Star Wars* film, for example, where romantic auteurism seems at its strongest, it is questionable whether, in UK law, the screenplay – as distinct from any film in which the performance of such a play is embodied – would be considered a work of sole authorship in Lucas's name. Rather, it might be recognized as a work jointly authored with Bill Huyck and Gloria Katz, who were not named as authors of the *Star Wars* screenplay despite the fact that their contributions to the screenplay led them to be given 2 per cent of the net shares,[69] and could well be considered contributions 'of the right kind' to count as contributions of co-authorship in law.[70] In consideration of the film itself as a cinematographic work, French copyright law would recognize *Star Wars* as a work of joint, rather than individual, authorship. Lucas would be the director, the author of 'the scenario', and probably also the author of the dialogue.[71] However, Lucas would almost certainly have to share co-authorship with John Williams, whom Lucas commissioned to write an original score for the film, and possibly the editors.[72] Interestingly, Lucas's claim even to joint authorship of

[67] See generally P. Kamina, *Film Copyright in the European Union* (Cambridge University Press, 2002).

[68] See, e.g., *Nottage* v. *Jackson* (1883) 11 QBD 627; *Evans* v. *E Hulton & Co. Ltd* (1924) 131 LT 534; *Springfield* v. *Thame* (1903) 89 LT 242.

[69] Pollock, *Skywalking*, pp. 141–4, 157.

[70] Moreover, Lucas was not named as one of the two authors of the screenplay for *The Empire Strikes Back*, and was only a joint author of *Return of the Jedi*. This is hardly grounds for romantic, solitary authorship.

[71] Although Harrison Ford became famous for saying to Lucas about the dialogue 'you can type this shit George, but you sure can't say it' (Pollock, *Skywalking*, p. 164), such that the actors were compelled to re-work the dialogue, it seems highly probable that large amounts of the original dialogue remain.

[72] *Code de la propriété intellectuelle*, art. L113-7.

the later movies under French law is tenuous.[73] As such, although the rules of various copyright systems that address film authorship may share parallels with the auteur-director model, they are probably best seen as independent legal rules that do not map easily onto the designation of Lucas as auteur-director.

Turning from film authorship to authorship of the franchise more generally, Lucas's alleged authorship of the franchise seems only to exacerbate tensions between legal and cultural conceptions of authorship. Two points of tension stand out. First, the 'expanded universe' comprises, in legal terms, any number of distinct copyright-protected productions – novels, comics, posters, toys (possibly sculptures, works of applied art), sequels, etc. – each with their own author. Whether any of them are sufficiently influenced by the creator of the concepts that they express, embody or develop, such as to make the concept-creator a co-author, is a matter of fact, but will depend on their close involvement in decisions over the form of the product. However, this only serves to highlight the second point of tension between legal and cultural conceptions of franchise authorship because, in general, a provider of an idea or concept does not make the right kind of contribution for authorship in law, and it is exactly this sort of general contribution to the 'story' or 'concept' behind *Star Wars* that is often said to warrant Lucas's status as 'franchise' auteur.

Quite apart from the difficulty of explaining how a contribution to the underlying concept behind *Star Wars* could be a contribution to authorship of the franchise, then, it is simply not possible to conceive of Lucas as the legal author of a franchising operation, precisely because a franchise relates to so many different goods or artefacts. A lawyer would want to know whether Lucas was the author of any given individual items. There is not space in this chapter to consider all the relevant items of the *Star Wars* franchise, nor all the relevant forms of protection (the variety of which has expanded significantly in Europe and the UK since the time when *Star Wars* was made). However, some further, brief remarks can be made to clarify this point of tension between legal and cultural notions of franchise authorship, focusing first on the novel *Star Wars* and secondly on the toy 'stormtrooper' figures.

The novel *Star Wars* that accompanied the release is attributed to 'George Lucas', and became a number one paperback bestseller.[74]

[73] In relation to *The Empire Strikes Back* it would seem to depend purely on his claim to authorship of 'the scenario', the other joint authors being Irvin Kershner (director), Brackett and Kasdan (co-authors of the screenplay) and Williams (composer).

[74] 'Paperback Best Sellers', *New York Times*, 28 August 1977, p. 255; Pollock, *Skywalking*, p. 195. According to the Judge Hill in *Twentieth Century-Fox Film Corp.* v. *MCA, Inc.*,

However, it was in fact ghost written by Alan Dean Foster.[75] From a legal standpoint, under British law, Foster is the author, not Lucas. The author in law is the one who composes the text, and the closest examples we find to cases of ghost authorship – involving, for example, the work of journalists who give concrete expression to general ideas[76] or writers who put an individual's oral memoirs 'into proper language'[77] – provide clear support for treating ghost authors as authors in law, even single authors of the works in question.[78] In the case of *Donoghue* v. *Allied Newspapers Ltd*, which concerned the written memoirs of jockey Steve Donoghue, the point was put as follows:

> Although many of the stories were told in the form of dialogue, and to some extent Mr Felstead no doubt tried to reproduce the story as it was told to him by the plaintiff, nevertheless the particular form of language in which those adventures or stories were conveyed to the public was the language of Mr Felstead and not the language of the plaintiff .[79]

Under US law, Lucasfilm Ltd might have been the 'author' if the work was a work-for-hire, but this seems unlikely as Foster was probably not an 'employee' and the second part of the definition of 'works for hire', which allows for agreements to be made as to authorship of commissioned works, only does so in relation to a limited set of categories of such works and does not apply to 'novels'.[80]

1980 WL 1184 (CD Cal, 1980): 'On about November 10, 1976 Star Wars Corporation ("SWC"), the predecessor in interest to Lucasfilm, published a novel entitled STAR WARS . . . SWC applied for and received a Certificate of Registration from the United States Register of Copyrights, identified as Number A845826, as the owner of the copyright in and to the novel STAR WARS': at [6]–[7].

75 See Pollock, *Skywalking*, p. 195; see also 'Interview with Alan Dean Foster', *SFF World* (online), 3 April 2000, at http://sffworld.com/interview/41p0.html (explaining how Foster was contracted). The Wikipedia entry for Foster, viewed on 1 December 2013, states: 'After two other writers had declined his offer of a flat fee of $5,000 for the work, Lucas brought to Foster the original screenplay, after which Foster fleshed out the backstory of time, place, planets, races, history and technology in such detail that it became canonical for all subsequent Star Wars novels. However, when asked if it was difficult for him to see Lucas get all the credit for *Star Wars*, Foster said "Not at all. It was George's story idea. I was merely expanding upon it. Not having my name on the cover didn't bother me in the least. It would be akin to a contractor demanding to have his name on a Frank Lloyd Wright house"': http://en.wikipedia.org/wiki/Alan_Dean_Foster.

76 *Springfield* v. *Thame* (1903) 89 LT 242.

77 *Evans* v. *E Hulton & Co. Ltd* (1924) 131 LT 534.

78 In keeping with these general principles, but refining them somewhat, in an Indian case in which the contribution of a ghost author was explicitly considered it was held that the ghost author was a co-author of the work, rather than its single author: *Heptulla* v. *Orient Longman Ltd* [1989] FSR 598.

79 [1938] Ch 106, 110 (Farwell J).

80 Lucasfilm was the copyright owner by the time the action was brought against MCA, Inc. in relation to *Battlestar Gallactica*, as the claim was based on Fox's copyright in the film and Lucasfilm's in the novel.

With respect to toy figures, we confine consideration to recent disputes in the USA and UK that offer some details of the facts surrounding the development of the Stormtrooper character (though the case law does not really deal with issues of authorship).[81] The disputes concerned infringement of copyright in drawings of the Stormtrooper characters made by Ralph McQuarrie (authorship and ownership of copyright in the drawings were not contested).[82] During the production of the film, two of McQuarrie's drawings depicting the Stormtroopers were provided to Nick Pemberton, a London-based artist, whom Lucas asked to produce a clay model of the helmet along with fifty plastic versions. Pemberton turned to a friend and neighbour Andrew Ainsworth for the latter task, and Ainsworth developed a prototype for the plastic helmets that in turn was approved by Lucas as the final design for the helmets in the film. Mr Ainsworth retained the moulds he had created after the film was made and, in 2004, began selling copies from the moulds, which brought about the infringement action.

In copyright terms, the process of producing the toy helmets involved at least four possible 'works': the two McQuarrie drawings, the clay prototype by Pemberton and the final helmet by Ainsworth.[83] For the infringement action,[84] Lucasfilm could rely on ownership of copyright in the drawings, as 'on any footing the Mr Ainsworth helmets were substantial copies of the McQuarrie drawings'.[85] But what is of interest for this chapter is who, in legal terms, is the author of these different works? Could Lucas claim authorship of the drawing, clay model or plastic finished artefact, in the sense required for franchise authorship? The trial judge found that:

81 *Lucasfilm Ltd* v. *Shepperton Design Studios Ltd*, 2006 WL 6672241 (CD Cal, 2006) (judgment in default against Shepperton and Ainsworth to the tune of US$20 million for infringement of copyright, trade mark and unfair competition). In the English proceedings, it was stated that Ainsworth admitted sales to a value of £14,500: *Lucasfilm Ltd* v. *Ainsworth* [2009] FSR 2, [86] (Mann J).

82 The complaint in the US action stated: 'Plaintiff's Stormtrooper characters are based upon drawings and artwork created as early as 1975 for the production of the 1977 *Star Wars* Film. Plaintiff owns all rights in and to those drawings and artwork, which are not only incorporated in Plaintiff's depiction of the Stormtroopers appearing in the 1977 *Star Wars* Film but also include artwork for which the US Register of Copyright issued Registration Certificate No. GU 59-037 on December 24, 1975 and artwork that appears in the book titled *The Art of Star Wars*, for which the Register of Copyright issued Registration Certificate No. TX 984-752': *Lucasfilm Ltd* v. *Shepperton Design Studios Ltd*, 2006 WL 6672241 (CD Cal, 2006), First Amended Complaint, [11].

83 The defendant's website can be viewed at http://sdsprops.com.

84 The main issue, under British law, turned out to be whether the helmets were 'sculptures'. Ultimately, the Supreme Court held they were not, meaning that Ainsworth was free to continue to make and sell copies of the *Star Wars* characters in the United Kingdom: *Lucasfilm Ltd* v. *Ainsworth* [2012] 1 AC 208.

85 *Lucasfilm Ltd* v. *Ainsworth* [2009] FSR 2, [37] (Mann J).

The original conception of the Star Wars films was that of the producer and director, George Lucas. *He plainly had many, and clear, views of how he wanted the film and its characters to look.*[86]

But McQuarrie did the drawings.[87] Merely offering instructions is insufficient to amount to authorship. In *Nottage* v. *Jackson*, the Court of Appeal emphasized the significance of presence or proximity during the act of creation:

Certainly [the author] is not the man who simply gives the idea of a picture, because the proprietor may say, 'Go and draw that lady with a dog at her feet, and in one hand holding a flower'. He may have the idea, but still he is not there.[88]

This might well be drawn on to substantiate the claim Lucas is not a co-author. At the same time, closer analysis of the facts could show that Lucas did more than merely offer ideas. According to the trial judge:

[The McQuarrie drawings] were arrived at after various drafts, and after careful consultation with Mr Lucas; and they embodied what Mr Lucas wanted so far as the appearance of the characters went (and indeed other matters). He specified the general look and approved the final drawings; it was he who specified that the armour and helmets should be white.[89]

Someone can be an author from the standpoint of copyright without literally putting pen to paper – a point Laddie J explained in the case of *Cala Homes (South) Ltd* v. *Alfred McAlpine Homes East Ltd*:

In my view, to have regard merely to who pushed the pen is too narrow a view of authorship . . . It is both the words or lines and the skill and effort involved in creating, selecting or gathering together the detailed concepts, data or emotions which those words or lines have fixed in some tangible form which is protected . . . It is wrong to think that only the person who carries out the mechanical act of fixation is the author.[90]

This move to relax the contribution requirement so as not to require literal penmanship might allow us to describe Lucas as co-author. The question would be whether his suggestions, corrections, etc. were sufficiently original and substantial contributions to the visual appearance

[86] *Ibid.*, [30] (emphasis added).
[87] Pollock, *Skywalking*, pp. 149–50. Lucas later recognized his appreciation by giving McQuarrie a share of the profits: see p. 197.
[88] (1883) 11 QBD 627, 632 (Brett MR).
[89] *Lucasfilm Ltd* v. *Ainsworth* [2009] FSR 2, [30] (Mann J).
[90] [1995] FSR 818, 835.

to justify recognizing him as a joint author – a claim that might be substantiated by further evidence of Lucas's creative control,[91] but is by no means certain or obvious.[92]

Closer analysis of how copyright law might understand 'franchise authorship' shows that, at best, Lucas is a joint author of some but no means all of the objects of the franchise. These two examples – ghost authorship and authorship of the toy helmets – illustrate that Lucas's claim to legal authorship of the novel is highly questionable, and that he is at best only a joint author of the toy helmets, and possibly not an author at all. And it hardly follows from seeing Lucas as a joint author of some of the works of the franchise that we should see him as a franchise author in the sense required by the above definition (see section 3, above) – indeed, such conceptions of franchise authorship usually speak of Lucas as *the* author of the franchise, rather than one out of many possible authors. And if the two specific items considered here make franchise authorship problematic, we need only think of the extent to which the franchise comprises merchandise ranging from 'dolls, toys, comic books, cookies, paper cups, watches, candles and even bubble bath'[93] to appreciate that it is very difficult to see how Lucas's claim to authorship of these disparate items under copyright law could be substantiated. Consideration of these difficulties might mean that a different legal model is needed to account for the cultural designation of Lucas as auteur: accordingly, we finish

91 As the trial judge noted: 'Mr Reynolds confirmed that the characters as depicted in the film had to be as Mr Lucas visualised them; Mr Lucas's overall involvement in set, props and costume design was, in his experience unusual. Other witnesses testified to the close involvement of Mr Lucas in design matters. This film was encapsulating his vision, and ideas were submitted to him for approval as they evolved': *Lucasfilm Ltd* v. *Ainsworth* [2009] FSR 2, [31] (Mann J). And, on the topic of the plastic helmets: 'a first version had been submitted to Mollo, who asked for changes and the final version was subject to the approval of Lucas himself: Mr Lucas, who was still exercising the close and detailed control that he had hitherto exercised, approved the helmet by 19th February and he and Mr Mollo said that they wanted 50 of them': at [39].

92 We might look, for example, at Ralph McQuarrie's description of the design process for the famous Darth Vader mask as follows: 'George asked me to create a guy with a cape that fluttered in the wind, with a wide-brimmed helmet like the headgear of a medieval samurai'. McQuarrie came up with the rest, and Lucas gave it his approval: M. Cotta Vaz and S. Hata, *The Star Wars Archives: Props, Costumes, Models and Artwork from Star Wars* (London: Virgin, 1995), p. 14. In the Foreword, Deborah Fine, the curator of the *Star Wars* Archive at Skywalker Ranch in Marin County, also acknowledges the creative input of the designers when she describes the *raison d'être* for the archive as being to preserve the 'products of the enormously talented designers and craftspeople who helped make the films'. See also Pollock, *Skywalking*, p. 149 (McQuarrie 'was free to invent whatever he thought appropriate, with George as his creative collaborator').

93 *Lucasfilm Ltd* v. *High Frontier*, 622 F Supp 931, 933 (DDC, 1985) (Gesell J) (refusing to enjoin defendant's use of 'star wars' to describe the Reagan Administration's strategic defence initiative, as the use was descriptive).

by considering the possibility that Lucas might be considered auteur from the standpoint of trade mark law; indeed, the various products referred to in the above quotation link back to Lucas precisely through the *Star Wars* trade mark. If an argument can be made linking Lucas's authorship of the franchise to his alleged authorship of the trade mark, it would turn out that this area of intellectual property law would offer the most promising avenue for aligning legal and cultural notions of authorship.

5.2 Authorship and trade mark law

The idea that Lucas could be 'author' of the Star Wars trade mark seems to connect to the view that Lucas is a brand-auteur (see 4.4). Indeed, this notion of brand authorship chimes with commentators who see copyright being supplanted by trade marks as the primary means of ensuring returns on investment in cultural production,[94] and with the increasing irrelevance of acts of creativity or novelty in defining authorship, such that all authorship is an act of signing or approving.[95] According to these commentators, the 'author function' has been subsumed by brand loyalty, and, because there is a degree of overlap between brands and trade marks – particularly in cases of dilution, where the trade mark owner is said to be harmed not by confusion regarding the origin of the goods, but by uses of the mark that damage its distinctiveness or the owner's reputation – authorship of trade marks seems tantamount to authorship of brands: the ongoing associations that consumers and users attach to the mark and to objects connected to the mark, which in turn connect back to the identity of the mark's producer as the individual who 'both invents and sustains the worth of the mark'.[96]

However, further reflection shows that the connection between brands, trade marks and authorship is far from straightforward. It is true that trade mark law is the proprietary nexus by which legal systems can offer protection to brands; however, trade marks are not themselves subjects of authorship in the sense of origination (indeed, authorship of graphic

[94] As Scott Lash and Celia Lury put it, 'trademark is as – if not more – important than copyright to the accumulation of capital in the global culture industry': Lash and Lury, *Global Culture Industry*, p. 150. See also J. Gaines, *Contested Culture: The Image, the Voice and the Law* (Chapel Hill, NC: University of North Carolina Press, 1991).

[95] C. Lury, 'Contemplating a Self-portrait as a Pharmacist: The Trade Mark Style of Doing Art and Science' (2005) 22 *Theory, Culture and Society* 93.

[96] S. Wilf, 'Who Authors Trademarks?' (1999) 17 *Cardozo Journal of Arts and Entertainment Law* 1.

works of art that become trade marks seem only to be a source of persistent problems). Trade marks are generally seen as commercial speech-acts that serve the functional purpose of product-identification, rather than individual speech-acts serving the expressive purpose of an authorial role under copyright law: as we saw, of 'natural persons' contributing to the 'expressive form of a work'. At the same time, naming an individual author – such as George Lucas – as the author of a commercial trade mark enables this key aspect of copyright's definition of authorship to be transplanted into trade mark law.[97] In referring to Lucas as the 'author of a brand', then, we see less the replacement of copyright with trade marks as the convergence of the two regimes into some sort of hybrid form. In that hybrid, the brand appears specifically as an 'intellectual creation' – an authored creation – albeit one that is instantiated in a multiplicity of different emanations.

At this point, however, we might wonder exactly how the 'author function' is being used in such locutions as 'brand authorship'. After all, 'trade marks' are signs that obtain their legally protected status through use and consequent *public* recognition as the origin of goods and services. Moreover, 'brands' include a whole panoply of associated values and emotions, often highly generalized and abstracted from the particular products in which they are instantiated. Even if legal systems seem willing to offer protection through trade mark law to these extended aspects of brand value, this does not in itself settle the question of who should be seen as the underlying 'author' of the brand. For one thing, using trade marks to guard against dilution rather than consumer confusion means that one aspect of the 'author function' – namely 'originality or authenticity in relation to a subject'[98] – seems to vanish: no longer are trade marks being used to designate origin or authenticity, but rather to control the ongoing process of communicating 'a whole range of associated values'[99] to the public.

If 'authorship' is the correct description of this phenomenon of trade marks being used to protect generalized brand values, which is questionable in itself, we need to take seriously the authorship status of all the

97 Another interesting comparison is J. K. Rowling's status as 'original author' with regards to infringement of copyright and trade mark in the 'Harry Potter universe' (Bowrey, 'The New Intellectual Property', 206). As Bowrey notes, *Warner Bros Entertainment, Inc.* v. *RDR Books*, 575 F Supp 2d 513 (SDNY, 2008) contained 'no substantive discussion of Warner's trade marks and associated claims, creating the false impression that the legal claims all revolved around the "original author"': at 208.

98 Lash and Lury, *Global Culture Industry*, p. 144.

99 M. Spence, 'The Mark as Expression/The Mark as Property' (2005) 58 *Current Legal Problems* 504.

potential *users* of the mark.[100] This is because brand values acquire their meaning after the creation of the mark not only through work expended by the trade mark owner through marketing, but also as a result of psychological associations in the minds of the public and the sharing of these associations.[101] Such changes of meaning are part and parcel of the dynamic nature of language and communication; to connect them all back to the speech-act of a 'trade mark author', and require extensive legal control over the use of the mark as a result, seems at best confused and at worst culturally dangerous.[102] As Scott Lash and Celia Lury put it:

> A trade-mark does not mark something as the work of an author, even a collective of distributed intelligence author . . . It is not the mark of something an advertiser or branding expert makes; it is something that is located inside and outside the production process: in the social imaginary of (and about) consumers.[103]

If brands are even partly dependent on the emotions and values of consumers in this sense, they cannot be said to be authored by trade mark owners – or the natural persons whose speech-acts are protected by trade marks – in any meaningful way. A proper appreciation of the 'author function' as applied to brand authorship, then, may bring us closer to the post-structuralist understanding of textual meaning as 'constructed by' an audience than the auteurist's search for an individual director's signature as somehow embodied in the film and all its related commercial franchise.

6 Conclusion

Our discussion has highlighted the tension between cultural and legal understandings of authorship in the age of the entertainment franchise. We have argued that the emergence of the entertainment franchise has exacerbated existing tensions between film authorship as a cultural phenomenon and film authorship from the standpoint of intellectual property law. On the one hand, authorship seems to be a key component of

[100] See Wilf, 'Who Authors Trademarks?' for an argument that the public's significance as a trade mark creator should be more widely recognized.

[101] For further discussion of this point in relation to Lockean justifications for trade marks, see D. Scott, A. Oliver and M. L. Pineda, 'Trade Marks as Property: A Philosophical Perspective', in L. Bently, J. Davis and J. Ginsburg (eds), *Trade Marks and Brands: An Interdisciplinary Critique* (Cambridge University Press, 2008).

[102] See D. Gangjee, 'Property in Brands: The Commodification of Conversation', in H. Howe and J. Griffiths (eds), *Property Concepts in Intellectual Property Law* (Cambridge University Press, 2013).

[103] Lash and Lury, *Global Culture Industry*, p. 197.

contemporary entertainment franchises; on the other hand, it is difficult to substantiate claims of 'commercial', 'franchise' or 'brand' auteurship from the standpoint of intellectual property law.

This discontinuity may, or may not, be troubling or surprising: after all, the factual, specific and case-sensitive nature of legal analysis seems a long way from the attempts of film scholars to provide a broader understanding of the practices through which agency, credit and evaluation operate in the context of the expanded universe of the entertainment franchise. Moreover, non-alignment of law and social practice may in some cases be desirable, particularly to the extent that intellectual property law has the potential to carve out an autonomous space for authorial recognition independently of the power dynamics of cultural industries or practices. At the same time, the non-alignment might seem troubling, particularly with respect to copyright law, which relies heavily for its operation on widespread acceptance of its legitimacy in promoting cultural flourishing and protecting artistic cultural activities that are deemed to warrant recognition, respect and reward. One question for legal scholars to consider in relation to the entertainment franchise, then, is the extent to which intellectual property law's potential to complicate matters of 'franchise authorship' might in fact *serve* copyright's legitimacy through challenging some of the expansive claims to authorship often made by the global entertainment industry.

3 Franchises, imaginary worlds, authorship and fandom

David Lindsay

Many of our best authors, from William Faulkner to J. R. R. Tolkien, understood their art in terms of world-creation and developed rich environments which could, indeed, support a variety of different characters.

H. Jenkins, 'Transmedia Storytelling',
MIT Technology Review (15 January 2003)

Everything I've written, nothing belongs to me.

Stan Lee, quoted in S. Howe, *Marvel Comics: The Untold Story*, p. 103

1 Introduction: the emergence of the author

The Church in medieval Europe operated the single greatest franchise in Western history, which included elements of what we might now refer to as an entertainment franchise. The franchise was based, to a considerable degree, on controlling the parameters of a timeless narrative of immense depth and richness. The cosmological drama of biblical stories, which was conveyed largely by a combination of word of mouth and often-melodramatic church images, created a totalizing context in which people positioned themselves and their actions in relation to an ostensibly single but, in fact, polysemous, transcendental truth. Personal meaning and identity were constructed largely against the background of this timeless narrative. Simultaneously, the power of the spiritual narrative created the conditions for the Church's accumulation of enormous temporal wealth.

Beginning in Renaissance Italy, the progressive loosening of control over the expression of a single timeless narrative framework eventually created the conditions for the emergence of a plurality of frameworks, of individualism, and of intellectual property. As the art historian Arnold Hauser put it:

> As long as art is nothing but the representation of the Divine and the artist only the medium through which the eternal, supernatural order of things is made visible, there can be no question of autonomy in art nor of the artist actually owning his work. The obvious suggestion is to connect the idea of intellectual property with the beginnings of capitalism, but to do so would only be misleading. The idea of

intellectual productivity and intellectual property follows from the disintegration of Christian culture. As soon as religion ceases to control and unite within itself all the spheres of spiritual life, the idea of the autonomy of the various forms of intellectual expression appears, and an art which bears its meaning and purpose within itself becomes conceivable.[1]

Moreover, as the meaning of stories and images ceased to be determined by reference to a purportedly single transcendental truth, the source of meaning came to be identified with individual authors and artists. Especially with the emergence of the novel, the figure of the author eventually came to dominate the creative work.

Critical practices, which involved the elucidation of the meaning of texts by reference to the privileged position of authors, formed the background for two of the most influential contributions to late-twentieth-century debates concerning authorship: Roland Barthes' essay, 'The Death of the Author'[2] and Michel Foucault's essay, 'What Is an Author?'[3] Under the influence of Friedrich Nietzsche (and pre-figuring Jacques Derrida), Barthes rejected attempts to ascribe a single unified meaning to a text by reference to the person of an author/God, famously claiming that texts consist of a plurality of meanings, determined both by other texts and by readers. Partly in response, Foucault argued that the consequences of the 'death of the author' needed to be explored in greater depth. The focus of his essay was on what he termed the 'author function', meaning those features of a text or discourse characterized by an author that set them apart from 'authorless' texts. In this respect, Foucault emphasized that the figure of the author performs a limiting or regulatory function, otherwise known as 'closure', which prevents an uncontrolled proliferation of meanings. Unlike Hauser, Foucault expressly associated the traditional ideology of the author as the source of meaning of a text with capitalism, stating that 'since the eighteenth century, the author has played the role of the regulator of the fictive, a role quite characteristic of our era of industrial and bourgeois society, of individualism and private property.'[4]

It has long been argued that the critique of authorship in literary theory has important implications for copyright law.[5] For example, it has been

[1] A. Hauser, *The Social History of Art: Renaissance, Mannerism, Baroque* (London: Routledge & Kegan Paul, 1951), vol. 2, p. 62.

[2] R. Barthes, 'The Death of the Author', in S. Heath (ed.), *Image, Music, Text* (New York: Hill and Wang, 1977).

[3] M. Foucault, 'What Is an Author?', in P. Rabinow (ed.), *The Foucault Reader* (New York: Pantheon Books, 1984).

[4] *Ibid.*, p. 119.

[5] See, e.g., the essays in M. Woodmansee and P. Jaszi (eds), *The Construction of Authorship: Textual Appropriation in Law and Literature* (Durham, NC: Duke University Press, 1994);

alleged that the romantic theory of the original author supported the ever-expanding scope of copyright law.[6] Another suggestion has been that the death of the author may be paralleled by a shift in emphasis in the protection of authors away from copyright and to other areas of the law, such as trade mark law and personality rights, which purportedly more accurately protect authorial interests in areas such as character merchandising.[7]

This chapter explores some problems relating to authorship and copyright in the context of the development of contemporary entertainment franchises, with a particular focus on the commercial exploitation of 'imaginary worlds' across multiple media platforms. First, it explains the difficulties faced by producers of information and entertainment products in marketing their products in the attention economy, and how a strong authorial reputation may assist in overcoming these obstacles. Secondly, it explains the central importance of establishing and controlling a viable imaginary world as a basis for a global entertainment franchise. In this respect, immersive imaginary worlds provide effective transmedia platforms both for franchise owners to launch new products, and for audiences and fans actively to engage with entertainment products. Thirdly, the chapter explores issues relating to the role of copyright in regulating the increasingly dynamic relationship between owners of a franchise based on an imaginary world and fan communities. Fourthly, the chapter examines the relationships between individual authors and franchises, and the complexities of the role of copyright law in mediating these relationships.

2 Attention economics, experience goods and the importance of reputation

In a market economy, information and entertainment products obviously must be marketed. In societies such as ours that are characterized by

see also L. Bently, 'Copyright and the Death of the Author in Literature and Law' (1994) 57 *Modern Law Review* 973.

[6] See, e.g., M. Rose, *Authors and Owners: The Invention of Copyright* (Cambridge, MA: Harvard University Press, 1993); J. Boyle, *Shamans, Software and Spleens: Law and the Construction of the Information Society* (Cambridge, MA: Harvard University Press, 1996); L. Hyde, *Common as Air: Revolution, Art, and Ownership* (New York: Farrar, Straus and Giroux, 2010).

[7] See, e.g., J. Gaines, *Contested Culture: The Image, the Voice and the Law* (Chapel Hill, NC: University of North Carolina Press, 1991); C. Lury, *Cultural Rights: Technology, Legality and Personality* (London: Routledge, 1993).

information overload, not information scarcity, there are obvious hurdles in attracting attention.[8]

Authors and publishers, just as other producers of products, must therefore be able satisfactorily to differentiate their products from those of their competitors. There are, however, specific problems that arise in the marketing of information products, such as novels and films, in the attention economy. The key problem is being able to communicate information about the quality of the product when this only becomes apparent after the product is consumed. In other words, information products are paradigmatic examples of what are referred to as 'experience goods'.[9]

Although almost every new product can be regarded as an experience good, as Carl Shapiro and Hal Varian point out, information is different in that it is an experience good each and every time it is consumed.[10] As a result of the absence of consumer information, producers must develop mechanisms for communicating information about the goods prior to purchase, including relying on the fame and reputation of individuals involved in their production. In this respect, in the film and publishing industries, attaching a 'name' with strong market recognition, such as a well-known actor, director or author, can make or break a product.[11]

This is hardly a new phenomenon. From the time that authors and artists have been able to operate relatively independently, establishing a strong reputation has been critical to economic independence. In Renaissance Italy, for example, artists were first able to break away from the medieval craft guilds, to achieve a limited degree of independence through the acceptance of commissions from wealthy patrons. While the conditions for this independence depended upon a strong demand for artistic works, an artist clearly needed first to establish a reputation to take advantage of this. Thus, many of the biographies in Vasari's *Lives of the Artists* deal, in part, with how a particular artist made a 'name' for

8 See, e.g., H. A. Simon, 'Designing Organizations for an Information-Rich World', in M. Greenberger (ed.), *Computers, Communication, and the Public Interest* (Baltimore, MD: Johns Hopkins University Press, 1971), pp. 40–1.

9 P. Nelson, 'Information and Consumer Behavior' (1970) 78 *Journal of Political Economy* 311.

10 C. Shapiro and H. R. Varian, *Information Rules: A Strategic Guide to the Network Economy* (Boston, MA: Harvard Business School Press, 1999), p. 5.

11 See, e.g., T. W. Wallace, A. Seigerman and M. B. Holbrook, 'The Role of Actors and Actresses in the Success of Films: How Much is a Movie Star Worth?' (1993) 17 *Journal of Cultural Economics* 1.

himself. Vasari, for instance, explains how Ghiberti's father persuaded him to compete for the commission for the famous bronze doors of the San Giovanni baptistery, saying that by making his genius known in this way he could avoid returning to more mundane craft work.[12] As Hauser explains, the emergence of biographies of the artists, such as Vasari's *Lives,* is a symptom of 'an unmistakable shift of attention from the works to the personality of the artist'.[13]

By building a reputation, successful Renaissance artists were able to establish themselves as masters with their own workshops. These were organized on the basis of the *collective* production of art works, which were then attributed to a celebrity artist (the role of assistants to the master artists rarely being expressly acknowledged).[14] This form of organization of artistic production was made possible only by the reputation of a famous artist whose name, as the emergence of the practice of signing works suggests, already acted as a type of brand. Although the market economy had yet fully to emerge, the competition for work between artists reinforced the importance of authorial reputation.

Just as the quality of an information product may be signalled, prior to consumption, by the reputation of an author, it may also be communicated by signalling its content, such as through samples or pre-release reviews. Messages about content are easier to communicate, or 'sell', when there is already some familiarity with the subject matter. Renaissance artists worked within a purportedly universal narrative tradition, using well-established iconography drawn from the biblical and classical traditions. There was no need to convince potential patrons of the importance of the content, which was already familiar and deeply resonant. Contemporary entertainment producers, on the other hand, face a more difficult task in selling 'content', as they confront a consumer market in which any shared meanings are derived from an ephemeral, fragmented popular culture. As the next section of this chapter explains, one of the best ways to 'sell' an experience good is to market a ready-made cosmology, which combines material that is familiar to an audience – both in

[12] G. Vasari, *The Lives of the Artists* (trans. G. Bull) (Ann Arbor, MI: University of Michigan Press, 1965), p. 107.

[13] Hauser, *The Social History of Art*, p. 58.

[14] These arrangements are made explicit, for example, in the bronze doors of St Peter's Basilica in Rome, where the sculptor, Filarete, incorporated an extraordinary signature, showing himself and his assistants linking hands in a dance: see C. King, 'Filarete's Portrait Signature on the Bronze Doors of St Peter's and the Dance of Bathykles and his Assistants' (1990) 53 *Journal of the Warburg and Courtauld Institutes* 296.

terms of its content and its 'authorial' reputation – with the potential for the generation of new meanings.

3 Entertainment franchises, imaginary worlds and the dialectics of fandom

It is striking that the vast majority of the most successful global entertainment franchises have been based on autonomous fictional worlds drawn from the genres of science fiction (such as *Star Wars* and *Star Trek*), fantasy (such as *Lord of the Rings*, *Harry Potter*, *Twilight* and *Game of Thrones*) or comics (such as *Batman*, *X-Men* and *The Avengers*). These imaginary worlds include strong elements of the transcendent or supernatural. Once the audience has been introduced to an imaginary universe, the task of marketing an experience good becomes easier, as the consumer is already familiar with, and hopefully identifies with, the universe of which an individual film, novel or piece of merchandise is merely a manifestation. In this sense, a successful transmedia entertainment franchise, including content-based products and merchandising spin-offs, can be built on the back of an imaginary universe.

The obvious initial hurdle in establishing a franchise such as this is first introducing unfamiliar audience members to the fantasy universe. Once a franchise is established, however, the challenge shifts to problems with managing the brand, which includes elements of the imaginary world that forms the basis for the content of the franchise. The imaginary world includes the main characters of the universe, but also the 'natural laws' of the universe and the moral world inhabited by the characters.[15] In managing the brand, the owners of a franchise must walk a tightrope between actively engaging consumers and fans, on the one hand, and retaining the authenticity of the universe and preventing the dilution of its distinctive qualities, on the other. As the power of the franchise is based upon the recognizably distinctive features of the imaginary world, control of this world becomes a key site of struggle between content owners and audiences. In effect, just like the medieval Church was threatened by alternative versions of the narrative that formed the source of its power, so entertainment franchises may feel threatened by a proliferation of discourses that can potentially dilute their distinctive brand. On the other

[15] In his recent book, Mark Wolf lists the elements of imaginary worlds as maps, timelines, genealogies, nature, culture, language, mythology, philosophy and narrative: M. J. P. Wolf, *Building Imaginary Worlds: The Theory and History of Subcreation* (New York: Routledge, 2013).

hand, audience members can be more rigorous in policing the authenticity of the universe than owners, at times even excoriating creators for real or imagined inconsistencies. In this respect, there is an ongoing dialectic between commodification and participation, or between world-building and world-sharing.[16]

What explains the power of imaginary worlds as a foundation for entertainment franchises? Much of the answer lies in the particular tension between closure and openness in discourses creating imaginary worlds. As far as closure is concerned, there is a need for some control over the discourse so as to ensure the authenticity and integrity of the imaginary world. This is essential if audiences and fans are to form an ongoing attachment to a franchise. In some respects, attachment or connection to imaginary worlds can create a sense of virtual community in dislocated, post-modern societies. As the sociologist Zygmunt Bauman has explained, we inhabit fragmented societies in which the complete erosion of traditional frames of reference results in existential anxieties about our uncertain identities, which must be continually re-invented.[17] The totalizing world view provided by detailed imaginary worlds offers some obvious respite from these anxieties.

In addition to retaining a degree of integrity and cohesiveness, however, imaginary worlds must also create the conditions for a proliferation of meanings or stories, over and above the polysemy of other texts. The objective in establishing a franchise is, after all, largely to establish a background universe against which a series of narratives may be acted out. In this regard, imaginary worlds seem to have a special status amongst authored texts. In 'What Is an Author?' Foucault distinguished authors of individual texts from 'transdiscursive' authors, pointing out that:

> It is easy to see that in the sphere of discourse one can be the author of much more than a book – one can be the author of a theory, tradition, or discipline in which other books and authors will in turn find a place.[18]

While Foucault went on to distinguish authors of religious texts or originators of literary genres from 'founders of discursivity', such as Marx and Freud, who make possible something much more than novelists, creators of fictional worlds must be distinguished from both Church

[16] On 'world-sharing' amongst franchise producers, and amongst producers and audience communities, see: D. Johnson, *Media Franchising: Creative License and Collaboration in the Culture Industries* (New York University Press, 2013).

[17] Z. Bauman, *Liquid Modernity* (Cambridge: Polity Press, 2000); Z. Bauman, *Liquid Times: Living in an Age of Uncertainty* (Cambridge: Polity Press, 2007).

[18] Foucault, 'What Is an Author?', p. 113.

fathers and 'founders of discursivity'. In particular, authors such as J. R. R. Tolkien, Jack Kirby, Stan Lee and George R. R. Martin are not merely interpreters of an established cosmology, but are responsible for establishing the parameters for a potentially endless proliferation of specific narratives.

The problems of marketing experience goods in the attention economy can therefore be addressed by attaching a well-known name, such as a celebrity author, to the product, or creating an immersive imaginary world which is attractive for audiences to identify with. A number of the most popular entertainment franchises have the potential advantage of both – 'J. K. Rowling' was as valuable a marketing device as the 'Harry Potter' brand, while 'Joss Whedon' is arguably as important to *The Avengers* franchise, at least for some fans, as the comic book characters themselves.[19] Whatever the case, once a franchise has imprinted itself on an audience, the owners of the franchise have the difficult task of controlling the distinctiveness (and therefore authenticity) of the brand, such as by exercising some control over the parameters of the imaginary world, while encouraging active engagement with the franchise.[20] The next sections of the chapter examine, in more detail, the role of copyright in regulating entertainment franchises based on imaginary worlds.

4 Copyright and entertainment franchises

As prominent entertainment franchises are commonly built around both a rich imaginary world, some elements of which will be protected by intellectual property, and 'authorial' reputation, it is important to analyse the role that copyright law plays in the exploitation of these franchises. This section of the chapter addresses two important issues. First, it explains and analyses the complex commercial and semantic relationships between owners of a franchise based on an imaginary world and audiences, and how copyright helps shape these relationships. Secondly, it examines the construction of 'authorship' of an imaginary world, and explains the contradictory role played by the ideology of copyright and authors' rights in both reinforcing and subverting the use of the authorial construct by franchise owners.

[19] See L. Bently and L. Biron, 'The author strikes back: mutating authorship in the expanded universe', in this collection.

[20] For a comprehensive analysis of struggles involving meaning and identity in fan texts, see C. Sandvoss, *Fans: The Mirror of Consumption* (Cambridge: Polity Press, 2005).

4.1 *Copyright, franchises and imaginary worlds*

A complex imaginary world or background universe comprises myriad interconnected elements, including maps, timelines, genealogies, natural laws and characters. Copyright law does not protect an imaginary world as such, nor even all elements of an imaginary world. Moreover, the elements of an imaginary world that are protected by copyright are not necessarily the most valuable, whether commercially or from the point of view of audience engagement. For example, the idea/expression dichotomy remains inextricably bound to copyright's textual past by privileging narrative structure over other elements of a work.[21] Yet, as argued in this chapter, the value of an imaginary world lies in the scope it provides for narratives to be enacted against an immersive framework, and not in the narratives per se.

Nevertheless, copyright in elements of imaginary worlds, such as characters that include a visual component,[22] clearly provides sufficient legal leverage for owners to exploit a franchise through licensing agreements, as well as potentially to police the integrity or authenticity of a world on which an entertainment franchise is based. In this, the essential issue is the limits to which licensees or an audience may go in using elements of an imaginary world. Problems invariably arise, as imaginary worlds are, as explained above, polysemous to a fault. As Derek Johnson has pointed out, franchises are 'over-designed', in the sense of the scope left for the elaboration of details of an imaginary world, which adds to the richness of a world by conveying the impression that things are happening 'off-page'.[23] This is clearly an invitation for others to fill in the gaps – which may be filled by authorized serial iterations of a franchise or by audience members ('fans') who, for better or worse, 'tell their own stories'.

'Over-design' of content is hardly a new phenomenon. In the Middle Ages, all of Christendom was engaged with the rich biblical narrative. Apart from the canonical texts, there were areas where blanks could be legitimately explored, such as in mystery plays, which often drew on apocryphal material. Heresy, on the other hand, was rigorously policed by the hierarchical structures of Church and state, but also by community norms. The line between legitimate exploration of biblical motifs and heresy, however, was labile. While heresy was (and is) an extraordinarily

[21] See, e.g., *Baigent* v. *Random House Group Ltd* [2007] FSR 24.

[22] On the distinction between the copyright protection of text-based characters and characters that include a visual component under US law, compare *Warner Bros Pictures, Inc.* v. *Columbia Broadcasting System, Inc.*, 216 F 2d 945 (9th Cir, 1954) ('Sam Spade') with *Walt Disney Productions* v. *Air Pirates*, 581 F 2d 751 (9th Cir, 1978) ('Mickey Mouse').

[23] Johnson, *Media Franchising*, pp. 119–22.

complex cultural phenomenon, the identification and punishment of heretics clearly played a central role in buttressing Church power, and the uncertain line between orthodoxy and heresy reinforced this power. What role, then, might be played by attempts of entertainment franchises to police, or legally control, the uses of imaginary worlds? It is instructive to examine the problem from the point of view of franchise owners, consumers and engaged fans.

Franchise owners face a complex exercise in determining the degree of control, if any, to exercise over an imaginary world. On the one hand, in the attention economy it is essential to engage and build an audience, and a proven way to do this is to permit fans to use imaginary worlds to build their own narratives and develop some sense of ownership of such worlds. As Henry Jenkins, Sam Ford and Joshua Green explain at length in *Spreadable Media*,[24] content owners are exploring a wide variety of strategies in attempts to harness the value of digital communities. For example, relying on the work of anthropologist Grant McCracken, they point to how audience members may generate value beyond their role as passive consumers, by acting as 'multipliers' of economic and social value, such as by sharing and distributing products, potentially value-adding meaning.[25] Following from this, Jenkins, Ford and Green contrast the old 'appointment-based' model of content distribution, where a consumer had essentially one point of contact with a producer, with the emerging 'engagement-based' model, where there are multiple points of contact, with committed fans performing valued roles as intermediaries between producers and audiences. As the authors point out, an essential feature of complex strategies of transmedia engagement is the development of 'immersive story worlds', which:

> are defined by large back-stories that cannot be neatly summarized; an ensemble of characters within the current narrative and across its larger history; substantial reliance on program history; a wide variety of creative forces over time; a serialized structure of storytelling; and a sense of permanence and continuity within the fictional universe.[26]

Further, borrowing from Derek Johnson, Jenkins, Ford and Green refer to the increasingly complex interactions between producers and audiences, which exist on a spectrum between passive consumption and active resistance, as a form of 'collaboration'.[27] This term effectively captures the extent to which fans, or digital communities, voluntarily subscribe to a cultural artefact, such as an imaginary world, yet seek to carve out their

[24] H. Jenkins, S. Ford and J. Green, *Spreadable Media: Creating Value and Meaning in a Networked Culture* (New York University Press, 2013).

[25] *Ibid.*, pp. 123–5. [26] *Ibid.*, p. 132. [27] *Ibid.*, pp. 172–3.

own space within that artefact, as well as potentially influencing it. The power relationship between producers and fans is therefore asymmetrical, but not unidirectional. As Jenkins, Ford and Green put it:

> Collaborators are complicit with the dominant regimes of power, yet they often use their incorporation into that system to redirect its energies or reroute its resources. At the same time, companies often have to tolerate behaviours that may have once been seen as resistant or transgressive if they want to court the participation of these networked communities.[28]

Intellectual property (and especially copyright), linked as it is with the market economy, plays a key role in establishing the parameters within which the dialectic between engagement and transgression is played out. Over and above this, however, mirroring the asymmetrical power relationship between owners and audiences, copyright is a driver in the very construction of fan communities. For example, as Karen Hellekson points out, the non-commercial nature of much fan-generated content is conditioned by fear of being sued for copyright infringement.[29] Just as the ambiguous line between orthodoxy and heresy played a policing role in the Middle Ages, *uncertainty* surrounding copyright infringement is essential in constructing the terms of the relationship between franchise owners and online communities.

While deep engagement is highly desirable, there are potential limits on the kinds of engagement that may be 'tolerated' by content owners. In his influential blog post from 2007, 'Transmedia Storytelling 101', Henry Jenkins referred to the importance of 'creating a unified and coordinated entertainment experience'[30] to effective transmedia storytelling. Following from this, most media franchises are not based on co-creation, which is difficult to co-ordinate, but on hierarchical licensing strategies, with subsidiary products referring to a 'master text'. Again, this is hardly a new dilemma. In the early 1970s, *Superman* comics were being produced by half a dozen different editors at DC Comics, each with their own view of how the character should develop, including competing views of Superman's powers. The co-ordination problems were such that DC necessarily abandoned the committee approach and appointed one editor, Julius Schwartz, to manage the franchise.[31] Similarly, in the late 1960s,

[28] *Ibid.*, p. 173.

[29] K. Hellekson, 'A Fannish Field of Value: Online Fan Gift Culture' (2009) 48 *Cinema Journal* 113.

[30] H. Jenkins, 'Transmedia Storytelling 101', *Confessions of an Aca-Fan: The Official Weblog of Henry Jenkins*, 22 March 2007, at http://henryjenkins.org/2007/03/transmedia_storytelling_101.html.

[31] M. Evanier, 'Afterward', in J. Kirby and M. Royer (eds), *Jack Kirby's Fourth World Omnibus* (New York: DC Comics, 2007), vol. 3.

Stan Lee told the writers at Marvel comics that the stories (and characters) should have only 'the illusion of change', so as not to interfere with cross-media licensing.[32] What is new, however, is the problem of grappling with fan communities that are producing and consuming their own content, in addition to a 'master text' controlled by the franchise owner.

In analysing this issue, it is important to appreciate the continued cultural significance of the distinction between canonical and non-canonical versions of an entertainment franchise. Owners of such a franchise naturally have a strong interest in being *a source* (although not necessarily *the sole source*) of canonical meaning, and in being perceived by a fan community as the responsible (and potentially responsive) guardians (or co-guardians) of canonical meaning. In other words, there must necessarily be some core, or 'authentic', meaning against which iterations of the universe can be played out. This is, amongst other things, a consequence of the need for a sense of permanence and continuity in an imaginary world, which is essential if a community is to identify with it. In order properly to capitalize on the meaning invested in an imaginary universe, the core canonical meaning must be strongly associated with the franchise owner.

Where audience members have invested a considerable amount of their identities, there is inevitably a struggle for control of core meaning. Suzanne Scott has analysed one aspect of this struggle by reference to the attempts of content owners to harness fans by means of 'ancillary content models', whereby official content is given away in the form, for example, of 'behind-the-scenes' video blogs, webisodes or podcasts.[33] As Scott explains, this form of 'transmedia extension' is an attempt to reroute and commercialize fan communities by means, in part, of an 'enclosure' of meaning. According to Scott:

> Whether or not ancillary content models are being actively deployed as a device to rein in and control fandom . . . they are pointedly offering a warped version of fandom's gift economy that equates consumption and canonical mastery with community.[34]

These sorts of criticisms of attempts by commercial content owners to 'enlist' fandom reflect fundamentally different views of 'authenticity': on the one hand, authenticity may be related to its source of origin in a

[32] S. Howe, *Marvel Comics: The Untold Story* (New York: Harper, 2012), p. 101.

[33] S. Scott, 'Repackaging Fan Culture: The Regifting Economy of Ancillary Content Models' (2009) 3 *Transformative Works and Cultures*, at http://dx.doi.org/10.3983/twc.2009.0150.

[34] *Ibid.*, [3.2].

franchise, as the authentic source of meaning, while, on the other hand, it is the meaning created by the community of fans that should be regarded as more authentic.

As Jenkins, Ford and Green point out, these competing views of authenticity are reflected within fan communities themselves, with an important distinction between 'affirmation fandom', which remains loyal to the text produced by a content owner, and 'transformation fandom', which alters the text, at least in part better to appeal to the interests of other fans.[35] This dichotomy draws attention to the significant role played by fan communities themselves in policing fans. Scott suggests that the motivations of the policing of meaning by franchise owners should be distinguished from the motivations of fan communities, with the latter being 'ultimately about protecting, rather than controlling, the ideological diversity of fannish responses to the text'.[36] Given the extent to which fan communities are based upon defining themselves against 'outsiders', largely by reference to the depth of knowledge (and loyalty to) canonical meaning, this is not a compelling interpretation of the motivations of such communities, which arguably have more to do with the politics of identity and exclusion than fostering diversity.

Moreover, activist fan communities increasingly seek to perform a role in policing the authenticity of franchise owners. For example, Jenkins, Ford and Green explain some of the complexities of producer/fan interactions by means of the activities of a fan activist group, known as 'Racebending', made up of fans of the animated series, *Avatar: The Last Airbender*.[37] As the authors explain, when the fan group discovered that a live-action film of the animation was set to cast all-white actors for the multi-ethnic characters, they initiated a cross-platform campaign, including producing their own videos, which had at least some effect on the film producers. In this instance, fans were disciplining the nascent film producers with the singular objective of preserving the integrity of a shared world – a clear illustration of the importance of core, canonical meaning for all concerned.

Much of the literature on digital culture, including fan fiction, extols the positive value, including the putative liberatory potential, of participation.[38] For example, Jenkins, Ford and Green quote from Mark Andrejevic's criticism of the metaphor of readers traversing 'fields they did not write':

[35] Jenkins, Ford and Green, *Spreadable Media*, pp. 150–1.
[36] Scott, 'Repackaging Fan Culture', [3.2].
[37] Jenkins, Ford and Green, *Spreadable Media*, pp. 171–2.
[38] See, e.g., Y. Benkler, *The Wealth of Networks: How Social Production Transforms Markets and Freedom* (New Haven, CT: Yale University Press, 2006).

> The metaphor breaks down in the transition from fields to texts: the consumption of crops is exclusive (or, as economists put it, 'rival'), the productive consumption of texts is not. Far from 'despoiling' the . . . texts through their practices, [fans on an online discussion group] enrich them, not just for themselves but for those who economically benefit from the 'added value' produced by the labor of viewers.[39]

The reality is, however, more prosaic and murkier. While the relationship between producers and audiences is not entirely rivalrous, neither is fan participation always necessarily mutually beneficial. As franchise owners have invested resources in creating and marketing franchise products, the expectation is that this will produce value for the corporation. Similarly, there is nothing at all remarkable in franchise owners seeking to harness audience participation into channels that maximize the value of their products, as it is equally unremarkable that there will be some resistance to this.

As we inhabit a commercial culture, the products produced by entertainment franchises are at once commodities and carriers of culture and meaning. This is conveyed by the subtitle of *Spreadable Media*, namely 'Creating Value and Meaning in a Networked Culture'. In analysing digital culture, however, cultural critics all too often slip into simplistic dichotomies between economic value and culture, between market and community. While presenting a more sophisticated picture than most, even Jenkins, Ford and Green tend to contrast the 'exclusionary' values of the market with the 'open' values of community participation. For example, in analysing media engagement, the authors distinguish a corporate conception of participation, which is based on 'a promise of making companies more responsive to the needs and desires of their "consumers"', from a political conception of participation, 'which focuses on the desire for us all to exercise greater power over the decisions which impact the quality of our everyday lives as citizens'.[40] Moreover, the book cautiously celebrates the digital empowerment of audiences via new tools of content creation and distribution by suggesting that 'these processes may hold the potential for social and cultural change'.[41]

While the emergence of digital communities through channels such as video-sharing sites and social networking is undeniably changing the shape of audiences and fan communities, claims that greater audience control of the circulation of content will somehow create a more participatory society may detract from more important issues. For example,

[39] Jenkins, Ford and Green, *Spreadable Media*, p. 174, citing M. Andrejevic, 'Watching Television without Pity: The Productivity of Online Fans' (2008) 9 *Television and New Media* 24, 42.

[40] Jenkins, Ford and Green, *Spreadable Media*, p. 156. [41] *Ibid.*, p. 294.

Jenkins, Ford and Green seem continually to contrast the role of audience members as passive consumers with their role as active members of a meaning-producing public.[42] At heart, however, this does not take us much further than Marxist-inspired dreams of liberation that draw on the dichotomy of exchange value and use value. To see content creation and distribution predominantly through the lens of the putative liberatory potential of technologies risks obscuring the complexity of the power dynamics at play: the contrast between franchise owners as over-zealous control freaks, and fans as the virtuous creators of socially valuable meaning, is superficial wishful thinking.

In a commercial culture, content is a commodity. The production and distribution of content on a large scale is a commercial activity, and producers must seek to maximize their return on investment. In doing so, they will respond to the demands of the market, and consumers, in various ways, will attempt to influence producers. Franchise owners are interested in producing products that the largest number of consumers will demand and consumers are interested in products that they want. In the sense that there is a relationship between producers and consumers, the relationship is necessarily asymmetrical, but still symbiotic, and no amount of content-related tools in the hands of consumers can alter that. Neither do new tools and applications for content creation and distribution alter the need for a degree of exclusivity, conferred by law, over content in order for that content to be commercialized. While there may be debates about the degree of exclusivity that is necessary, this is no more than the logic of the market.

Yet, entertainment franchise owners and audiences inhabit a shared universe of meaning. Within that universe, franchise owners must seek to ensure that those elements that define the franchise, such as an imaginary world, continue to have an association with the authorized brand. Insofar as the franchise is successful, audience members will be invested in the meaning generated by the franchise. The relationship between franchise owners and audiences is therefore not simply one of vendor and purchaser, not least because franchise owners wish to engage audiences in an ongoing exchange of meanings, and some audiences are more than willing to collaborate with this. But any system of meaning exists on a spectrum between closure and openness. For an entertainment franchise to have the depth needed for sustained audience attachment, distinctions must be maintained between authentic and inauthentic, between canonical and non-canonical. And, given the malleability of meaning, struggles

[42] *Ibid.*, pp. 165–7.

will occur over which versions are authentic and canonical and which versions are not.

From the point of view of a franchise owner, in order to keep audiences and fan communities engaged, it is not merely desirable but necessary for *struggles* over authenticity to occur. Moreover, from the point of view of fan communities, their very sense of self-definition depends upon *struggles* over authentic meaning. Just as, in the Middle Ages, the Church depended upon, and assisted in creating, heretics in order to reinforce a system of purportedly universal meaning, the creation of a coherent franchise based on an immersive imaginary world depends upon a degree of policing of the accepted boundaries of meaning. And, just as when the uniform Christian world view began to fray in the face of the proliferation of meanings spurred by the Reformation the Church developed institutions such as the Inquisition to police heretics, so, in the face of the proliferation of meanings through online fan communities, the *threat* of copyright infringement can be used by franchise owners to police meaning. The system of meanings that underpins an entertainment franchise is therefore both hierarchical and non-hierarchical, with the parameters of the relationship between franchise owners, audiences and fans shaped by the threat of an *uncertain* legal action. In other words, the threat posed by the existence of copyright laws plays a regulatory role in supporting the closure of meaning, which, ultimately, is necessary for the identities of franchise owners and fan communities alike. What this suggests is that rather than interpreting online fan communities as the harbingers of a liberating participatory culture it may be more productive to focus on the complex struggles over meaning engaged in by franchise owners, audiences and fans alike. In this, as the development of digital tools in the hands of digital communities alter the parameters of the struggle, it is important to avoid the temptation of identifying fans as the sole producers of socially valuable meaning, and understand that fandom is a complex phenomenon with its own power dynamics, including interests in exclusivity and the enclosure of meaning.

4.2 *Copyright, franchises and authorship*

From the mid-1980s, understanding of intellectual property, and especially copyright, has been influenced by literary critiques of the figure of the author.[43] Much of this literature has focused on the extent to which

[43] See M. Biagioli, P. Jaszi and M. Woodmansee, 'Introduction', in M. Biagioli, P. Jaszi and M. Woodmansee (eds), *Making and Unmaking Intellectual Property: Creative Production in Legal and Cultural Perspective* (University of Chicago Press, 2011).

the romantic theory of authorship has allegedly captured legal discourse, leading to an over-reach of copyright law.[44] Against this, it has been claimed that privileging the individualistic figure of the romantic author has obscured the more complex collective practices involved in producing texts and other creative works.[45] While no doubt true, at least to a degree, there is considerable over-simplification in this model.

As explained above, Hauser traces the emergence of the author in the West to the dissolution of a uniform, transcendental Christian world view. As further explained, this was associated with artists, and later authors, gaining a degree of independence for themselves, with the names of famous Renaissance artists already acting as a type of brand. With the development of the market, the figure of the author or artist came to operate as an organizing principle, in relation to both the marketing of creative products and the system of meanings associated with cultural production. The essential elements of these commercial and semantic systems were in place well before Edward Young's celebration of individual genius in his 1759 essay, 'Conjectures on Original Composition'.[46]

There are parallels between the organization of artists' workshops in the Renaissance and the collaborative production of some of the most significant imaginary worlds. Take, for example, the development of the Marvel universe in the early to mid-1960s. By their very nature, comic books require the collaboration of writers, artists, inkers and letterers, each making important, inter-related contributions. Although many of the most influential names in comic book history – including Jack Kirby, Steve Ditko and Roy Thomas, amongst others – contributed to the collaborative process, from the beginning the universe was most closely identified with Stan Lee.

In public perception, Stan Lee is regarded as the 'father' of the Marvel universe. Yet, although he was instrumental in the creation of the universe, Lee's greatest contribution may have been in marketing himself as an integral part of the franchise. As Lee, himself, put it:

> I guess I treated the whole thing like a big advertising campaign. . . . I wanted to give the product – which was Marvel Comics, and myself in a way – a certain personality.[47]

[44] See M. Woodmansee, 'The Genius and the Copyright: Economic and Legal Considerations of the Emergence of the Author' (1984) 17 *Eighteenth-Century Studies* 425; Boyle, *Shamans, Software and Spleens*, pp. 51–60.

[45] M. Woodmansee, 'On the Author Effect: Recovering Collectivity', in Woodmansee and Jaszi, *The Construction of Authorship*.

[46] See *ibid*., p. 16.

[47] As quoted in Howe, *Marvel Comics*, p. 90.

Lee's creative activities incorporated a fictional re-imagining, in the 'Bullpen Bulletins', of the collaborative production process, in which he depicted the artists as working in a 'utopian workplace', known as the bullpen, in which they happily shared jokes and work.[48] The reality was far different, with many of the artists, including Jack Kirby, working independently from home.

The extent to which the 'Stan Lee' authorial construct obscured the creative contributions of others is perfectly illustrated by the tensions between Lee and Kirby regarding a 1966 *Herald Tribune* article.[49] In the article, which focused on a plotting session between Lee and Kirby for a forthcoming clash between the Thing and the Silver Surfer, Lee appeared as a creative genius, with Kirby as little more than a glorified assistant. In fact, not only was Kirby the sole creator of the Silver Surfer, he customarily completely transformed the ideas discussed at plotting meetings, such as that involving the Thing and Silver Surfer story-line, so that they barely resembled the agreed outline. Following this incident, the credits for *Fantastic Four* were altered to read 'A Stan Lee and Jack Kirby Production', but the ill-feeling generated by the article formed part of the background to Kirby's decision to leave Marvel for DC in 1970.

The history of comics is littered with examples of disputes between artists and creators, on the one hand, and publishers, on the other. The two main sources of contention have been creative control over characters and rights to merchandising revenue streams. For example, apart from Jack Kirby's claims over characters such as the Silver Surfer, there have been significant disputes regarding Jerry Siegel and Joe Shuster's rights to Superman, Joe Simon's rights to Captain America and Carl Burgos's rights to the Human Torch.[50] Moreover, one of the factors for Kirby leaving Marvel was the denial of any share of merchandising revenue, while he was producing most of the images for the merchandising spin-off, *Marvelmania*, without remuneration.[51]

A more recent dispute between the popular fantasy author Neil Gaiman and Todd McFarlane, one of the founders of Image Comics, illustrates some of the complexities. Gaiman initially achieved fame largely as a result of his 'authorial' role in the 1980s cult graphic novel series, *Sandman*. Although significant contributions were made to the series by artists including Dave McKean, Sam Keith, Mike Dringenberg

[48] *Ibid.*, p. 44. [49] *Ibid.*, pp. 64–6.

[50] The definitive history of these disputes has yet to be written, but many of them are referred to in Sean Howe's history of Marvel Comics, *ibid*. For the recent dispute between the estate of Jack Kirby and Marvel Comics, see *Marvel Worldwide, Inc.* v. *Kirby*, 777 F Supp 2d 720 (SDNY, 2011).

[51] Howe, *Marvel Comics*, pp. 101–2.

and Malcolm Jones III, the *Sandman* series came to be identified with Gaiman as the sole author, in a manner reminiscent of Stan Lee's identification with the Marvel universe, with the work of other contributors being comparatively obscured.[52]

Image Comics was formed in 1992, after a dispute with Marvel over creative control, which focused on the unremunerated use of artwork on merchandising. The two key provisions of Image's charter were:

- Image does not own a creator's work; the creator does.
- No Image partner would ever interfere, creatively or financially, with any other's work.[53]

One of the first, and most enduringly popular, of the Image comics is the *Spawn* series, which Todd McFarlane commenced publishing in 1992. While the early issues featured striking artwork, the scripts were uninspiring. As a result, McFarlane engaged four well-known writers, including Gaiman, to write the scripts for special issues of the comic. After being assured by McFarlane that Image would treat him 'better than the big guys', Gaiman agreed to write the script for *Spawn* No. 9.[54]

The agreement between McFarlane and Gaiman was oral, with no express terms other than the promise made by McFarlane. In the absence of any written assignment, Gaiman remained the owner of the copyright in any material he produced pursuant to the agreement. In the script, Gaiman introduced three new characters, known as 'Medieval Spawn', 'Angela' and 'Count Cogliostro', for which he was paid $100,000.[55]

McFarlane's strategy proved successful, and *Spawn* No. 9 received widespread acclaim. Given the popularity of the characters, McFarlane started producing and marketing *Spawn*-related merchandise, including action figures and paperback books, which proved highly remunerative. Following this, McFarlane paid Gaiman a further $20,000. Subsequently, a dispute arose over ownership of the characters, with McFarlane presenting Gaiman with a 'take-it-or-leave-it' offer, in which, while acknowledging Gaiman's rights to 'Angela', he denied that Gaiman had any rights to 'Medieval Spawn' and 'Cogliostro'.[56]

Unhappy with the offer, in 2002, Gaiman commenced an action claiming royalties as a result of co-ownership of the copyright in 'Medieval Spawn' and 'Cogliostro'. By that stage, the characters had become part

[52] C. Smith, 'Get Gaiman?: PolyMorpheus Perversity in Works by and about Neil Gaiman' (2008) 4 *ImageTexT: Interdisciplinary Comics Studies*, at http://english.ufl.edu/imagetext/archives/v4_1/smith/.

[53] S. Rhoades, *Comic Books: How the Industry Works* (New York: Peter Lang, 2008), p. 177.

[54] *Gaiman* v. *McFarlane*, 360 F 3d 644, 649 (7th Cir, 2004) (Posner J).

[55] *Ibid.*, p. 651. [56] *Ibid.*, p. 652.

of the burgeoning *Spawn* franchise, featuring in extensive derivative works and merchandising, including trading cards, video games and a 1997 motion picture that had grossed over US$80 million. In the Seventh Circuit Court of Appeals, Judge Posner found in favour of Gaiman, essentially concluding that, although his contributions in terms of purely textual descriptions of the characters were insufficient to be copyrightable in themselves they amounted to a sufficient contribution to the expression of the characters for Gaiman to be a co-author.[57]

While the precise facts in the Gaiman case may be unusual, including that Gaiman's contributions were not subject to the US 'work-for-hire' doctrine, they do serve to illustrate the inherently contradictory nature of copyright and authorship in market-based societies. On the one hand, copyright and the image of the individual creative author perform the functions of organizing principles and regulators of commercial and semantic relations. In this sense, copyright and the ideology of individual creative authorship are mutually reinforcing, and obscure the myriad collaborations needed to produce complex cultural artefacts, such as imaginary worlds. On the other hand, however, the ideology of copyright and authors' rights legitimizes the claims of those who make significant contributions to cultural products to be identified as authors and to be properly remunerated for creative work. The legal claims of comic book authors and artists, such as Jack Kirby and Neil Gaiman, although not always successful, would simply have been impossible to make in a Renaissance artists' workshop. And, in part, this is because an author of an artefact such as an imaginary world is regarded as a significant autonomous creator, not merely one amongst many contributors to an essentially collective process.

The critique of the ideology of authorship has effectively moved the focus of analysis away from the creative work of individual authors to the relationships between copyright owners, readers or audiences, and non-authorial collaborators. In doing so, it risks missing something important. The history and analysis of franchises built on imaginary worlds is not merely about struggles over control and meaning between franchise owners and audiences, or the extent to which the ideology of romantic authorship masks collaborative production. To focus solely on these aspects of the creative process is to lose sight of the real role of individual creators in producing socially valuable meaning. Although it is far from popular to say so, there are some individuals who justifiably deserve recognition as creators of genius. And, to the extent that literary and cultural criticism

[57] *Ibid.*, pp. 660–2.

undervalues the role of creative geniuses, it may perpetuate incipient cultural tendencies that increasingly privilege collectivism over individuality. By this, I mean, in part, that the creative process, and the relationship between authors and audiences, is necessarily asymmetrical: it remains the case that authors create and audiences consume (although both, of course, do much more than this); and that consumption is not production. Moreover, in the networked society, everyone may be a creator, but that does not mean that everyone is equally creative. While the ideologies of copyright and authorship no doubt obscure power relations that are mediated through commerce and meaning, so too do the ideologies of audiences, fandom or readers as 'creators'.

One of the strongest impressions from an unbiased reading of the history of imaginary worlds is the emotional attachment authors feel for their creations. In the past, authors like Jack Kirby felt betrayed when their creations, such as the Silver Surfer, were used by other employees of a franchise in ways that the author felt to be 'inauthentic'.[58] In the contemporary context, some authors have expressed similar views about the use of their work in fan fiction. In May 2010, for example, George R. R. Martin, the author of the *Game of Thrones* series, posted a blog entry controversially arguing against fan fiction.[59] In the post, which expressly acknowledged arguments on both sides of the debate, Martin emphasized the importance of respect for the creator of an imaginary world, essentially arguing that the decision of an author either to consent to, or to refuse to consent to, the use of characters and/or the imaginary world should be respected. Referring to the *Wild Cards* shared world, which he deliberately created to allow collaboration between multiple authors, Martin pointed to the importance of a shared world being a 'controlled environment', with characters not acting contrary to type. Over and above this, Martin explained his own personal attachment to his characters, conveying his sense of violation where someone uses one of his characters without permission.[60] Yet, as Martin readily acknowledged, there are many authors, including fantasy and science fiction authors, who actively encourage fan fiction.

[58] Stan Lee's effective 'appropriation' of the Silver Surfer in 1968 was yet another factor in Kirby's discontent with Marvel: Howe, *Marvel Comics*, pp. 90–1.

[59] G. R. R. Martin, 'Someone is Angry on the Internet', *Not a Blog*, 7 May 2010, at http://grrm.livejournal.com/151914.html.

[60] Martin has continued in this vein, telling an Australian audience that he 'would rather [fans] make up their own characters and their own stories and not just borrow my world' and that fan fiction was 'lazy': N. Bochenski, 'George R. R. Martin: Hands Off My Characters', *Sydney Morning Herald* (online), 8 November 2013, at www.smh.com.au/entertainment/books/george-rr-martin-hands-off-my-characters-20131108-2x6fb.html.

The reason Martin's comments, which are by no means unique,[61] are referred to here, is not to enter into the increasingly tendentious debates over the pros and cons of fan fiction. Rather, it is to emphasize the complex and contradictory roles played by authorship and copyright in the contemporary entertainment franchise ecosystem. On the one hand, Martin's opposition to fan fiction can be seen as reinforcing the policing of the semantic boundaries of the *Game of Thrones* corporate franchise. As such, however, this might be at odds with the attitudes of some corporate stakeholders in the franchise, who may well wish to encourage some forms of fan fiction in order to promote deep engagement and 'spreadability'. On the other hand, the comments are a genuine expression of the strength of the relationship felt by a creator for his creations. If this attitude were expressed by an author towards the bowdlerization of her or his creation by a corporate producer or publisher, which also characterizes comic book history, our sympathies would most likely lie with the author. Why, then, should our attitudes differ when it is digitally empowered fans that may be responsible for the bowdlerizing?

What this suggests is that the relationships between franchise owners, authors and audiences are best seen as the sites of ongoing struggles over values and meanings, in which no one party has self-evidently better claims to higher normative ground.[62] While, as Foucault suggested, the author function performs a regulatory or enclosing role on texts, to claim that somehow 'liberating' texts from authors is possible, let alone desirable, seems as delusional as the claim that the emergence of engaged networks of fans presages the emergence of a more fully participatory society. In fact, in a cultural environment dominated by the increasingly strategic relations between corporate franchises and networked communities, the interposition of claims by individual authors, which may admittedly sometimes support corporate franchise owners, may also sometimes have a highly desirable disruptive effect. By this, I mean that the interests of individual authors are by no means identical to the interests of either franchise owners or fans, and that the recognition of these claims can play an important role in revealing the full extent of the power relations at issue. Copyright law plays a role in constructing and regulating these power relations, but it is simplistic to regard it as invariably supporting the interests of corporate owners and repressing the expressive activities of fan communities.

61 See, e.g., the response of Brian Grazer to a mash-up of his film *8 Mile* with the film *Napoleon Dynamite*, as reported in Jenkins, Ford and Green, *Spreadable Media*, p. 187.

62 Although particular parties may have higher normative claims in particular contexts.

5 Conclusion

Rich imaginary worlds and author/creators are central to attempts at creating and maintaining entertainment franchises in the attention economy. An 'over-designed' imaginary world provides multiple points of contact between the content produced by a franchise and audiences, with the potential for deep engagement. At the same time, a certain enclosure of meaning is necessary to maintaining the identity of both the franchise and fan communities. In part, this guarantees the ongoing debates about canonical and non-canonical content, and authentic and inauthentic content, which sustain a franchise. In this, the uncertain threat of copyright infringement plays a significant role in constructing and regulating both franchise content and fan communities.

The identification of a unitary author/creator with an imaginary world can perform an important role in marketing an entertainment franchise. In doing so, however, this can obscure the creative contributions of other collaborators. The ideology of copyright and authors' rights may reinforce the social construction of 'authorship', which, in turn, supports the economic and semantic control exercised by franchise owners. On the other hand, copyright may support the claims of authors over their creations, against franchise owners and fans alike. In this sense, claims made by individual creators can disrupt the dialectic between franchise owners and fandom, each of which may seek to harness the social construction of authorship for their own ends. The figure of an author can therefore perform functions in both closing and opening the meanings of the texts produced and marketed by an entertainment franchise.

4 Digital sampling and music industry practices, re-spun

*Johnson Okpaluba**

1 Introduction

Digital sampling in hip-hop music continues to be a source of fascination for legal and cultural scholars. After a flurry of writing in the music press[1] and law journals[2] in the mid- to late 1980s during hip-hop's 'golden age', and a key US court decision in 1991 that is thought to have settled the issue of the legality of sampling, the subject continues to generate wide interest today. Part of the reason is that claims about the value of sampling are now bound up in broader, ongoing debates about 'remix culture',[3] namely the extent to which the law should be more responsive to those seeking to make creative use of others' copyright works in the digital environment.[4] As Kembrew McLeod and Peter DiCola state in *Creative License*, their wide-ranging legal and ethnographic study of sampling in hip-hop:

* Thanks go to Jennifer Lena for kindly providing copies of her unpublished work, as well as to Kathy Bowrey for inspiring the topic at the outset and her helpful editorial contributions. Special thanks also to Michael Handler for reading and discussing earlier drafts of this chapter and for his invaluable comments, contributions and editorial skills, without which this chapter would not have made this volume.

1 See, e.g., S. Dupler, 'Digital Sampling: Is It Theft? Technology Raises Copyright Questions', *Billboard*, 2 August 1986, pp. 1, 74; B. Holland and S. Dupler, 'Digital Technology May Violate Copyright Law: Experts Doubt the Legality of Sampling', *Billboard*, 9 August 1986, pp. 4, 84; S. Alvaro, 'What Is Musical Property? The Ethics of Sampling', *Keyboard*, October 1986, pp. 10, 157; R. Hoffman, 'Digital Sampling – Lawyers Debate the Legal Realities of an Emerging New Art Form', *Back Stage*, 27 October 1989, p. 34.

2 See, e.g., Note, 'Digital Sound Sampling, Copyright and Publicity: Protecting Against the Electronic Appropriation of Sounds' (1987) 87 *Columbia Law Review* 1723; J. C. Thom, 'Digital Sampling: Old-Fashioned Piracy Dressed up in Sleek New Technology' (1988) 8 *Loyola Entertainment Law Journal* 299; R. M. Wells, 'You Can't Always Get What You Want But Digital Sampling Can Get What You Need' (1989) 22 *Akron Law Review* 691; J. S. Newton, 'Digital Sampling: The Copyright Considerations of a New Technological Use of Musical Performance' (1989) 11 *Hastings Communications and Entertainment Law Journal* 671.

3 See, e.g., L. Lessig, *Remix: Making Art and Commerce Thrive in the Hybrid Economy* (London: Bloomsbury, 2008).

4 See D. E. Long, 'Dissonant Harmonization: Limitations on "Cash n' Carry" Creativity' (2007) 70 *Albany Law Review* 1163, 1166.

The disputes that have arisen over sampling implicate many issues of broad importance, such as achieving creativity within economic and legal constraints; artistic control and moral rights; appropriation and sequential innovation; fair compensation for intellectual property; and freedom of expression.[5]

What is particularly striking about this issue is the way that an orthodox narrative has developed about the relationship between law on the one hand and the practice of sampling and, more generally, creativity in hip-hop on the other hand. The conventional view of copyright and sampling is that the former acts exclusively as a constraint on the latter. More specifically, it is suggested that during a period of legal uncertainty in the 1980s, unauthorized sampling was widespread and creativity in hip-hop blossomed. Things are said to have fundamentally changed in late 1991 once the US District Court for the Southern District of New York in *Grand Upright Music Ltd* v. *Warner Bros Records, Inc.*[6] determined that sampling constituted copyright infringement. The decision is said to have resulted in the development of new, reactionary industry practices, where reliance on copyright law and associated licensing fees and conditions for the use of samples formed significant barriers to creativity in the hip-hop community. Proponents of this view often use this narrative to make broader, normative claims that copyright law must therefore be recalibrated so as to encourage and protect creative conduct involving the use and recoding of others' copyright works.

One of the clearest expressions of this narrative is in the work of Siva Vaidhyanathan. He claims that:

> Until 1991, no one in the rap or licensing businesses knew what the guidelines for digital sampling were . . . the industry was waiting for a court to weigh in so there could be some predictability and stability in the system.[7]

When the court did weigh in, in the *Grand Upright* case, it made it 'safe to assume that any sample of any duration used for any purpose must be cleared',[8] and that from this point in time 'a new industry emerged – the industry of sample clearances'.[9] Vaidhyanathan asserts that the decision 'removed from rap music a whole level of communication and meaning' and makes the empirical claim that hip-hop since 1991 has been 'marked

[5] K. McLeod and P. DiCola, *Creative License: The Law and Culture of Digital Sampling* (Durham, NC: Duke University Press, 2011), p. 267.

[6] 780 F Supp 182 (SDNY, 1991).

[7] S. Vaidhyanathan, *Copyrights and Copywrongs: The Rise of Intellectual Property and How it Threatens Creativity* (New York University Press, 2001), pp. 140–1.

[8] *Ibid.*, p. 143.

[9] S. Vaidhyanathan, quoted in the documentary film *Copyright Criminals* (dir. B. Franzen, 2009).

by a severe decrease in the amount of sampling'.[10] McLeod and DiCola take a similar approach, considering *Grand Upright* to have 'effectively ended the "Wild West" period for sampling',[11] and citing with approval the opinion of an independent label owner who considered that 'the ambiguous legal environment during the "golden age" produced more creativity than the current environment'.[12] Similarly, Joanna Demers contends that *Grand Upright* caused some artists to abandon sampling altogether, and that sampling only persisted amongst artists who were wealthy enough to afford licences or obscure enough to risk unauthorized sampling.[13] More recently, other cultural scholars have made qualitative claims about the law–creativity nexus, linking the decline in levels of sampling with a decline in the political content and potency of hip-hop.[14]

In an important recent contribution, Thomas Joo has sought to challenge this orthodox narrative as part of his broader critique of the argument that facilitating the recoding of copyright works necessarily enhances semiotic democracy.[15] Joo's argument is that clear industry standards controlling the use of sampling based on established copyright norms had in fact emerged in the 1980s and that *Grand Upright*, rather than representing the imposition of law on otherwise unregulated cultural practices, merely confirmed existing industry practices. He also questions some of the assumptions that are made about the impact of the decision on sampling and on creativity in hip-hop more generally. In doing so, he suggests that the orthodox narrative ascribes too much force to the role of the formal law (in the form of court decisions) in driving creative practice, while at the same time failing to recognize the standards that had emerged that regulated sampling. Joo's article provides a corrective to the idea that law operates only as a restriction in this space in arguing that sampling 'developed in the presence of copyright law and reached accommodation with it'.[16] However, like the scholarship that relies on the conventional narrative, it tends to engage in a degree of generalization in order to make its broader, more polemical case, and tends to gloss over

[10] Vaidhyanathan, *Copyrights and Copywrongs*, p. 143.

[11] McLeod and DiCola, *Creative License*, p. 132. James Boyle expresses similar views, acknowledging the influence of Vaidhyanathan and McLeod: see J. Boyle, *The Public Domain: Enclosing the Commons of the Mind* (New Haven, CT: Yale University Press, 2008), pp. ix, 146–7.

[12] McLeod and DiCola, *Creative License*, pp. 138–9.

[13] J. Demers, *Steal This Music: How Intellectual Property Law Affects Musical Creativity* (Athens, GA: University of Georgia Press, 2006), p. 97.

[14] E. Nielson, 'Did the Decline of Sampling Cause the Decline of Political Hip Hop?', *Atlantic*, 18 September 2013, at www.theatlantic.com/entertainment/archive/2013/09/did-the-decline-of-sampling-cause-the-decline-of-political-hip-hop/279791/.

[15] T. W. Joo, 'Remix Without Romance' (2011) 44 *Connecticut Law Review* 415.

[16] *Ibid.*, p. 420.

some of the more complex industry dynamics at play, both before and after the *Grand Upright* decision, and the cultural significance of them.

This chapter seeks to mediate this scholarly debate by focusing more closely on the interplay between legal (un)certainty, industry practice and creativity in hip-hop production and, in particular, the ongoing importance of extended notions of authorship in hip-hop. The chapter starts by exploring the various forms that sampling took in the 1980s, showing that there was at that time a degree of justifiable uncertainty about the legality of at least some types of sampling. It then engages with the question of how such uncertainty was managed in practice, showing that it is a mistake to attribute an absence of law as the primary driver of creativity. It also shows how the more interesting dynamic at this time was how publishers and record companies started to realize that sampling afforded the opportunity to exploit the franchise-like potential of their back catalogues – that is, that in licensing samples they were doing more than permitting the re-use of fragments of mere sound, but rather were extracting ongoing value from the reputations of the artists being sampled (importantly, only some of whom were authors of the sampled works for copyright purposes). In this way, sampling opened up new revenue streams for composers, publishers and record companies, not only by ensuring that old authors were credited as authors of new hip-hop hits, but also by introducing sampled artists to new audiences and helping to facilitate the re-release of old recordings. Recognizing this helps to explain why the major labels were so determined to develop internal strategies for managing sampling and to avoid litigation. This provides the context for a further re-evaluation of *Grand Upright*. The case is most interesting because it reveals another aspect of the franchise-like qualities of sampling, namely the interest that copyright owners might have in seeking to control authorial reputation by *denying* a sample licence.[17] The case is also significant, not because of its legal outcome, but because of its symbolic value, in that it fortified many participants in the industry to strengthen their sampling management practices and develop new techniques to exploit authorial reputation. The chapter concludes with reflections on Joo's critique of claims that *Grand Upright*, and the intervention of formal copyright law that the case was said to usher in, 'stunted' creativity in hip-hop,[18] causing a decline in both the quantity and quality of sampling. Such a view is based on a romanticized notion of old school hip-hop and sampling, in that it treats certain sample-heavy

[17] The chapter draws on archived court records from the *Grand Upright* litigation, obtained from the National Records and Archives Administration, Missouri.

[18] Cf. McLeod and DiCola, *Creative License*, p. 29.

albums as both paradigmatic examples of sampling and the apex of creativity in hip-hop. It overlooks how sample-based hip-hop has continued to flourish since the early 1990s, as well as factors wholly unrelated to copyright law that have served to influence the production of hip-hop music.

2 Unpacking the relationship between law, creative freedom and music industry practice in the 1980s

How is it that some commentators can assert that the 1980s was a lawless time for hip-hop, where unlicensed sampling was the norm,[19] whereas others can assert that 'the hip-hop community, from its earliest days, generally understood the obligation to obtain and pay for permission to use samples'?[20] What industry practices were in place in the 1980s, how were these applied and what impact did lawsuits over sampling in the early 1990s have? Addressing these questions requires a careful understanding of the relationship between law, music industry practice and artistic freedom – a relationship forged at the very beginnings of recorded hip-hop.

The first commercially available hip-hop records were released in 1979,[21] with 'Rapper's Delight' by The Sugarhill Gang being the first major hip-hop hit. It is part of hip-hop's origin story that 'Rapper's Delight' featured string stabs, bass and guitar lines copied from 'Good Times', a very recent US number one pop and R&B hit for Chic, written by Bernard Edwards and Nile Rodgers. The bass and guitar lines were recreated by a studio band, but Sugar Hill Records did not obtain a licence for use of the musical composition.[22] The writers of 'Good Times' objected to the recording featuring such a prominent and unlicensed portion of their popular song and threatened to sue for copyright infringement. The dispute was eventually settled out of court, with Edwards and Rodgers each receiving a co-writing credit on the track.[23]

[19] *Ibid.*, p. 132. [20] Joo, 'Remix Without Romance', 422.

[21] The first recorded hip-hop record, 'King Tim III (Personality Jock)' by the Fatback Band, was released in March 1979.

[22] Nile Rodgers claims that the strings that were used in 'Rapper's Delight' were copied directly from 'Good Times' either by scratching the segment of sound directly into the new recording or by recording the strings on tape and overdubbing it onto the new recording: see 'The Story of Rapper's Delight by Nile Rodgers', POPBOXTV (2007), at www.youtube.com/watch?v=t-SCGNOieBI.

[23] Interestingly, Rodgers claims that when he approached the CEO of his record label for support in the suit against Sugar Hill Records, the CEO declined: see N. Rodgers, *Le Freak: An Upside Down Story of Family, Disco and Destiny* (London: Sphere, 2011), pp. 172–5.

This particular outcome is said by some to show that, from its very inception, there was a clear recognition that licences were required for sampling in hip-hop,[24] which is then used to make the argument that the idea that hip-hop was somehow a law-free zone throughout the 1980s is a convenient myth. However, the situation was far more complex than this. Even 'Rapper's Delight' itself is illustrative of this complexity. It is rarely noted that the song in fact opens with, and uses as its break, a Latin percussion sound that is copied from 'Here Comes That Sound Again' by Love De-Luxe, a 1979 US number one dance hit.[25] There is no record of legal action being pursued in relation to this borrowing and, unlike the more substantial borrowing from 'Good Times', it is unclear that the taking would have been considered more than *de minimis* and would have needed permission at all. In addition, the fact that many early hip-hop recordings involving similar borrowings from earlier compositions were released on small, independent labels to niche audiences meant that the question of copyright on original rhythm tracks was often ignored, at least until copyright owners of the original compositions raised the issue post-release.[26] This might well explain the release of tracks like Mr Q's 'DJ Style' in late 1979, which was based on a recreation of the rhythm track of Michael Jackson's October 1979 number one single 'Don't Stop 'Til You Get Enough',[27] or Funky Four Plus One More's 'Rappin' and Rockin' the House', which contained an interpolation of Cheryl Lynn's January 1979 number one dance hit 'Got to Be Real'.[28] Hip-hop label credits from the time indicate that the composers of original rhythm tracks upon which hip-hop songs were based were not routinely credited.[29]

A major change in the creation of hip-hop records occurred in the mid-1980s with the development of relatively cheap digital sampling technology. This technology enabled producers to capture fragments of sounds from sound recordings, such as individual beats, short snatches

[24] See, e.g., Joo, 'Remix Without Romance', 428.

[25] See www.whosampled.com/sample/22794/Sugarhill-Gang-Rapper%27s-Delight-Love-De-Luxe-with-Hawkshaw%27s-Discophonia-Here-Comes-That-Sound-Again/.

[26] D. Toop, *The Rap Attack: African Jive to New York Hip Hop* (London: Pluto Press, 1984), p. 106.

[27] See http://hiphoponwax.blogspot.co.uk/2006/09/mr-q-dj-style.html.

[28] See www.whosampled.com/sample/17400/Funky-4-%2B-1-Rappin%27-%26-Rockin%27-the-House-Cheryl-Lynn-Got-to-Be-Real/.

[29] Label credits clearly show that Sugar Hill Records were selective about the composers they credited. For instance, while both 'Apache' by The Sugarhill Gang and West Street Mob's 'Break Dance Electric Boogie' prominently feature the main hook from the track 'Apache', written by Jerry Lordan, only the West Street Mob track features a label credit for Lordan. Equally, on the Treacherous Three album *Whip It* (1983), only two out of the six tracks feature full credits.

of vocals or horn blasts, rather than having to rely on stock sounds pre-loaded with their equipment.[30] Digital sampling (or 'sampling' as it is commonly referred to) can therefore be seen to be related to other practices of music quotation or borrowing that span historical periods and musical traditions,[31] but it differed from the sort of borrowing described in the previous paragraph in a key aspect. In addition to involving copying elements of a musical composition, sampling also involved the copying of part of another work, namely the sound recording, the copyright in which would most likely have been owned by a record company. Much of the difficulty in assessing the linked questions of the legality of sampling and industry practice in relation to sampling throughout the latter part of the 1980s relates to the heterogeneity of the concept of 'sampling' itself. Sampling did not take a particular, consistent form over this time, something the literature on the topic often glosses over in choosing to privilege one type of sampling over another. As digital sampling technology evolved, its 'potential . . . to go beyond the simple replication of deejaying techniques led to an increasingly sophisticated aesthetic for hip-hop music'.[32] A wide variety of possible uses for samples emerged, differing as to their lengths, the types of sounds taken, the extent of any distortion or manipulation of those sounds and the contexts and purposes of their re-use.[33] This is not to say that the early practice of copying popular rhythm tracks disappeared in the 1980s. On the contrary, the two biggest global hip-hop hits of 1990 relied on this model: MC Hammer's 'U Can't Touch This' is based on the sampled and looped rhythm track of Rick James's 'Super Freak' (a US number one dance hit in 1981), and Vanilla Ice's 'Ice Ice Baby' sampled the distinctive bass line from Queen and David Bowie's 'Under Pressure' (a UK number one in 1981).[34] However, far more sophisticated types of sampling emerged during the latter half of

[30] Marley Marl claimed to be the first person to use drum samples on a record when he produced a record called 'The Bridge' by MC Shan in 1986: P. Hewitt, 'Licensed to Chill', *New Musical Express*, 12 March 1988, pp. 12, 46.

[31] See J. P. Burkholder, 'The Uses of Existing Music: Musical Borrowing as a Field' (1994) 50 *Notes* 851.

[32] J. G. Schloss, *Making Beats: The Art of Sample-Based Hip-Hop* (Middletown, CT: Wesleyan University Press, 2004), p. 39.

[33] See D. Sanjek, '"Don't Have to DJ No More": Sampling and the "Autonomous" Creator' (1992) 10 *Cardozo Arts & Entertainment Law Journal* 607, 612–15; see also J. Okpaluba, 'Digitisation, Culture and Copyright Law: Digital Sampling, A Case Study', PhD thesis, King's College London (2000), pp. 69–76. For a musicological analysis, see A. Sewell, 'A Typology of Sampling in Hip-Hop', PhD thesis, Indiana University (2013), pp. 26–67.

[34] As seen in nn. 108–9, and accompanying text, this type of sampling has never left hip-hop: there is an obvious commercial benefit to be gained by relying on a prominently used sample from a recent hit.

this decade, with some producers developing techniques of layering slivers of barely recognizable sound samples to create dense aural collages, a method best exemplified by landmark hip-hop albums such as the Beastie Boys' *Paul's Boutique* (1989)[35] and Public Enemy's *It Takes a Nation of Millions to Hold Us Back* (1988) and *Fear of a Black Planet* (1990).[36]

In addition, artists' reasons for choosing to sample particular sounds varied greatly. In some cases, a sample might have been used to provide little more than an association with a well-known hit. At other times, the sample might have involved a more transformative use of the source material. Other hip-hop artists used samples from soul and R&B artists from the 1960s and 1970s to identify themselves as the inheritors of an African-American musical legacy.[37] This took on a life of its own, with particular drum breaks, such as those from James Brown's 'Funky Drummer' and 'Funky President', The Winstons' 'Amen, Brother' and the Honey Drippers' 'Impeach the President', each being sampled on dozens of separate occasions during the 1980s. Some hip-hop acts sampled widely from a diverse group of artists. Notably, De La Soul's *3 Feet High and Rising* (1989), which celebrated eclecticism and openness, included samples from funk and soul icons such as James Brown, Funkadelic and Otis Redding, and white rock, pop and variety acts such as Steely Dan, Hall and Oates, and Liberace. What is particularly noteworthy about a good deal of the sampling from this time is that it can be argued that it did not simply involve artists playing with undifferentiated sounds for their own sake, but rather involved an active reliance on, and engagement with, the reputations of the artists and authors responsible for those sounds.[38]

Understanding the variety of forms that sampling took and the range of aesthetic and cultural choices that samplers made helps to explain some of the difficulties faced in the mid- to late 1980s in managing digital sampling. Judged purely in terms of the formal law, it could not always be determined in advance whether a licence would be needed for a particular sample. Many samples, particularly those involving only fragments

[35] According to Adam Yauch of the Beastie Boys, the group's artistic intention was 'to go completely over the top and sample everything [and make the album] the nail in the coffin for sampling': D. LeRoy, *Paul's Boutique* (New York: Continuum, 2006), p. 47.

[36] See R. L. Doerschuk, 'Bomb Squad Leader Declares War on Music', *Keyboard*, September 1990, pp. 81, 83; M. Dery, 'Public Enemy: Confrontation', *Keyboard*, September 1990, pp. 81, 92.

[37] Heavily sampled soul, R&B and funk artists from this time included James Brown, Sly & the Family Stone, Curtis Mayfield, Isaac Hayes, Marvin Gaye, Kool & the Gang and Parliament/Funkadelic. Notably, Public Enemy combined samples from African-American artists with samples from political speeches from figures such as Malcolm X and Jesse Jackson. See further McLeod and DiCola, *Creative License*, pp. 99–100; see also J. Demers, 'Sampling the 1970s in Hip-Hop' (2003) 22 *Popular Music* 41.

[38] Schloss, *Making Beats*, pp. 144–50.

of sound, might have involved *de minimis* uses of sound recordings and underlying musical compositions, and there was particular doubt about whether taking a drum break (as distinct from, say, a snippet of melody or a synthesizer or guitar riff) would be infringing. If the sample was treated or distorted, there might have been an issue over whether the source material and sample were substantially similar. There might have been doubts over whether the sample was a 'fair use' of the source material, given the nature of its recontextualization.[39] There were no formal industry-wide precedents in place,[40] nor were there sampling-specific court decisions that were able to provide clear, *ex ante* answers to these questions.

The legal issues were undoubtedly complex. However, it is a mistake to assume that because of these legal uncertainties the industry by and large had no response to digital sampling until it started threatening to bring lawsuits.[41] Similarly, it is a mistake to assume that the lack of litigation at this time was simply the result of fear, namely that if one label sued it would increase the likelihood of one of its artists being sued in return.[42] Such an approach gives too much credence to the role of formal law – in particular, the absence of specific legislative rules and court decisions – as an organizing principle that drives creative decision-making. Contrary to claims by Vaidhyanathan and others, there is evidence that as hip-hop became more commercially successful and artistically creative in the latter half of the 1980s some major publishers and record companies developed detailed internal guidelines to promote and regulate the licensing of samples. Importantly, these guidelines did not map on to the contours of the formal law, but rather tended to take a more pragmatic approach, in which permission for the use of samples (of whatever length, used for whatever purpose) was routinely given in exchange for the right price and conditions. Significantly, what this practice also demonstrates

39 For a summary of the formal legal issues, see R. Kravis, 'Does a Song by Any Other Name Still Sound as Sweet?: Digital Sampling and its Copyright Implications' (1993) 43 *American University Law Review* 231, 250–62.

40 Attempts to set uniform royalty rates or to establish an industry-wide protocol governing payments and clearances proved unsuccessful: see S. R. Gordon and C. J. Sanders, 'The Rap on Digital Sampling: Is It Theft or Merely Innovation?', *New York Law Journal*, 28 April 1989, pp. 5, 6.

41 Cf. McLeod and DiCola, *Creative License*, pp. 25–6 (claiming that hip-hop artists had 'a small window of opportunity to run wild with the newly emerging sampling technologies before record labels and lawyers started paying attention').

42 See, e.g., S. R. Gordon and C. J. Sanders, 'Roadblocks to Legal Protection in Sampling', *New York Law Journal*, 19 May 1989, p. 5. Cf. N. George, *Hip Hop America* (New York: Viking Penguin, 1998), pp. 94–5 (suggesting that one of the reasons for the lack of litigation was that many of the old R&B artists who were being sampled were simply not aggressive enough to pursue action, or were just used to being ripped off).

is the industry's lack of interest in stifling sampling, and instead its recognition of the extra forms of value that could be extracted via managing sampling.

Detailed evidence of industry practices from the late 1980s is difficult to obtain. But some of the best evidence of such practices was provided in the course of the 1991 *Grand Upright* litigation – the irony here being that this case is so often presented as ending the good-time sampling free-for-all and bringing about the music industry's intervention in sampling.[43] Fredrick Silber, Vice-President of Business Affairs at EMI Music Publishing, who had been responsible for sample clearance at Zomba Records in 1988 and at EMI since July 1989, gave evidence that he had been involved in around 100 to 120 claims by EMI artists that had been sampled and about fifteen or twenty claims where EMI artists had been accused of sampling.[44] Silber indicated that industry practices had developed gradually, as sampling had not come into its own until around 1988, and when digital sampling was first practised it was generally discovered only after the record had been released, but as sampling became prevalent the industry policed itself and copyright owners were approached prior to the actual release of the record. Despite this, Silber stated that in 20 per cent to 30 per cent of cases where EMI granted a licence the record had already been released.[45] In evaluating samples, the approach of EMI under Silber's guidance had been to acquire either a financial interest or copyright ownership interest in the new song.[46] EMI's interest in the new song was determined by the prominence and length of the sample, with the copyright-ownership percentage ranging from 100 per cent, for obvious, recognizable samples, to 5 per cent or 10 per cent, or a nominal buyout for $500 or $1,000, for a *de minimis* use.[47] Silber testified that EMI had rarely refused to grant a licence, and had only done so where the new song was particularly obscene or politically objectionable.[48] Another expert witness, Jane Peterer, a copyright administrator who in the previous three years had negotiated the use of about 250 samples, gave evidence that essentially corroborated that of Silber, including that she had never refused to grant a sample licence

[43] See nn. 10–13, and accompanying text.

[44] *Grand Upright*, Transcript of Hearing, 26 November 1991 (Examination of Fredrick Silber), pp. 122–5 (copy on file with author).

[45] *Ibid.*, p. 126. [46] *Ibid.*, p. 128.

[47] *Ibid.* On early business practices in relation to digital sampling in the music industry, see M. Ashburne, *Sampling in the Record Industry* (Oakland, CA: Law Offices of Michael Ashburne, 1994).

[48] *Grand Upright*, Transcript of Hearing, 26 November 1991 (Examination of Fredrick Silber), pp. 129–30. See also McLeod and DiCola, *Creative License*, pp. 119–20.

following a request.[49] Other literature from this time shows that such practices were starting to develop in the industry more widely.[50]

It thus appears that well before *Grand Upright*, and at a time of great creativity in hip-hop in the late 1980s, at least some major players in the industry had effectively determined that 'any sample of any duration used for any purpose must be cleared'.[51] What is also revealing about the evidence above is the licensing condition that sampled authors be given songwriting credits on the new tracks. This shows a recognition of how sampling was controlled so as to open up new revenue streams for publishers and record companies: by ensuring that old authors were credited as authors of new hip-hop tracks, such parties became entitled to additional royalties whenever those tracks were themselves reproduced, broadcast or licensed to film or television. Further, it is entirely unlikely that EMI would have been able to behave as it did (that is, in creating a market for the licensing of samples whose boundaries were not determined by the scope of the copyright in the sampled works)[52] in isolation. Other major labels would have recognized the similar value in being able to license samples from their own catalogues, which would, in turn, explain why they would pay fees to EMI and give songwriting credits for the use of samples.[53] This also helps explain the paucity of litigation throughout the late 1980s and early 1990s: there was simply no incentive for the major players to disrupt a set of practices they had developed for their mutual benefit, certainly not when the prospect of litigation might open up difficult, formal legal questions such as whether a sample involved *de minimis* taking or constituted fair use.[54]

There is other evidence from this time that the music industry started to recognize the broader, 'franchise-like' value in commercializing the reputations of the artists being sampled. Managing sampling helped promote a new awareness of and commercial interest in the back catalogues of sampled artists, which spurred many labels to re-release old recordings. For instance, in 1986, Polydor Records cashed in on the popularity

49 *Grand Upright*, Transcript of Hearing, 26 November 1991 (Examination of Jane Peterer), pp. 130–7.

50 See, e.g., Gordon and Sanders, 'Roadblocks to Legal Protection in Sampling', p. 6; and Note, 'Current and Suggested Business Practices for the Licensing of Digital Samples' (1991) 11 *Loyola Entertainment Law Journal* 479.

51 Cf. Vaidhyanathan, *Copyrights and Copywrongs*, p. 143.

52 Cf. Joo, 'Remix Without Romance', 446 (asserting that the contracting was 'clearly based on the legal entitlements' set out in copyright legislation).

53 *Ibid.*, p. 443.

54 See further M. Africa, 'The Misuse of Licensing Evidence in Fair Use Analysis: New Technologies, New Markets, and the Courts' (2000) 88 *California Law Review* 1147, 1172–3 (on why artists were prepared to pay for uses where, in strict legal terms, they might not have been required to do so).

of James Brown samples by reissuing previously deleted or unreleased recordings, including a stripped-down version of James Brown's 'Funky Drummer' that included only the drum break.[55] Even artists who were not entitled to songwriting royalties recognized some of the flow-on benefits of sampling: Bobby Byrd, a former member of James Brown's band, along with other singers from James Brown's roster of artists, openly acknowledged the debt that they and other singers from the 1950s, 1960s and 1970s owed hip-hop for revitalizing their careers.[56]

Of course, this is not to say that every label or publisher had come to recognize the value in entering a market for samples. A good deal of hip-hop throughout the 1980s and early 1990s was recorded on independent labels, with small budgets and limited resources, meaning that producers were often more inclined to invest money in the production of the record than clearing samples,[57] especially when such labels did not themselves own a back catalogue of records that could be sampled in return. Risks were clearly taken on the basis that if an uncleared sample were to be discovered after a recording had been released, a licence fee

[55] *In The Jungle Groove*, a compilation of James Brown recordings between 1969 and 1971, was released in August 1986. The success of this album led to the release in 1988 of another James Brown compilation, *Motherlode*, which focused on the same era of James Brown's funk recordings.

[56] D. Snowden, 'Sampling: A Creative Tool or License to Steal? The Controversy', *Los Angeles Times*, 6 August 1989, p. 61. In 1986, Polydor released the first of three compilation albums, *James Brown's Funky People*, featuring James Brown-associated artists such as Bobby Byrd, Lyn Collins, Marva Whitney and Vicki Anderson, all of whose tracks were popular with hip-hop artists. The approach of George Clinton of Parliament/Funkadelic to digital sampling can be contrasted with the less embracing approach of James Brown. From an early stage, Clinton was very pragmatic about sampling. Clinton claimed that he loved sampling, despite the fact that of the 500 hip-hop songs that had sampled his works, bringing him to the attention of a new generation of consumers, he had only been paid for about twenty-five of them: see H. Weinger, 'Sampling Amok', *Rolling Stone*, 14 June 1990, pp. 103, 104. Not only did Clinton embrace sampling of his records and record sample CDs for licensing, he worked with many hip-hop artists. Arguably, this might have been for several reasons. For instance, after releasing his final solo album for Capitol Records in 1986, Clinton was without a record label until he was signed to Paisley Park Records, and he did not release another solo album until 1989. In addition, Clinton had financial difficulties and disputes with his record company and publishing company during this time; see J. Alexis, 'George Clinton: "We Never Minded Them Sampling"', *Red Bull Music* (online), 14 May 2013, at www.redbull.com/us/en/music/stories/1331590648362/george-clinton-on-samples-youtube-and-youth; see also The Company Man, 'George Clinton Explains Saving Hip Hop Artists on Samples, Recalls Early Days of Dr. Dre, Afrika Bambaataa, Eminem', *HipHopDX* (online), 10 January 2012, at www.hiphopdx.com/index/news/id.18253/title.george-clinton-explains-saving-hip-hop-artists-on-samples-recalls-early-days-of-dr-dre-afrika-bambaataa-eminem.

[57] See T. Rose, 'Contracting Rap: An Interview with Carmen Ashurst-Watson, Former President of Def Jam Records', in M. Forman and M. A. Neal (eds), *That's The Joint: The Hip-Hop Studies Reader* (New York: Routledge, 2004), pp. 541, 546.

could be negotiated at that time. Industry practice was, on the whole, much messier than commentators such as Joo have made it out to be.[58] What is perhaps more interesting though is that it appears that the fact that recordings were released with uncleared samples in the late 1980s by major labels was more the result of a failure by artists and/or labels to have fully developed sampling protocols, or to follow the protocols that were in place, than of a lack of engagement with copyright issues. For example, while debate still rages about the extent to which the hundreds of samples on the Beastie Boys' *Paul's Boutique* were cleared and the costs that were involved,[59] it is instructive to note a comment from Tim Carr from Capitol Records that drums were not seen as being part of sample clearance at that time, and only the samples that needed to be cleared were cleared.[60] De La Soul and Tommy Boy Records were sued in 1989 by two former members of the band The Turtles over the use of a few seconds of the recording of The Turtles' 'You Showed Me', which had been distorted and looped into De La Soul's track 'Transmitting Live From Mars' on its *3 Feet High and Rising* album. The case settled out of court with a settlement in favour of the members of The Turtles.[61] However, the reason clearance for the sample was not sought was most likely due to an internal miscommunication, with Tommy Boy Records claiming that the sample was not on the list of those given to them by the group to be cleared.[62]

58 Cf. Joo, 'Remix Without Romance', 435–9.

59 Mario Caldato, the engineer on the album, claimed in an interview to *Tape Op* magazine in 2002 that the Beastie Boys paid US$250,000 in sample clearance fees: LeRoy, *Paul's Boutique*, pp. 46–7. However, the Beastie Boys' attorney, Ken Anderson, is said to have cleared some 400 or so samples at little or no cost: see J. H. Marcus, 'Don't Stop That Funky Beat: The Essentiality of Digital Sampling to Rap Music' (1991) 13 *Hastings Communications and Entertainment Law Journal* 767, 768. See further n. 101, and accompanying text, on current litigation involving samples from *Paul's Boutique*.

60 See LeRoy, *Paul's Boutique*, p. 46. See also S. Rule, 'Record Companies Are Challenging "Sampling" in Rap', *New York Times*, 21 April 1992, p. C13 on uncertainty over whether licences were required for drum breaks.

61 The members of The Turtles reportedly offered to drop the suit if De La Soul recorded a collaboration with them: McLeod and DiCola, *Creative License*, p. 132. While the idea was rejected, in 2009 De La Soul announced an intention to re-record some of the songs on *3 Feet High and Rising* with the artists sampled, as a way of allowing the album to be re-released: E. Serpick, '"3 Feet High and Rising": De La Soul's Track by Track Guide to Groundbreaking 1989 LP', *Rolling Stone* (online), 3 June 2009, at www.rollingstone.com/music/news/3-feet-high-and-rising-de-la-souls-track-by-track-guide-to-groundbreaking-1989-lp-20090603.

62 B. Coleman, *Check the Technique: Liner Notes for Hip-Hop Junkies* (New York: Villard Books, 2007), p. 153. De La Soul later claimed that they gave all the information to Tommy Boy, who made the decision that some samples were not worth clearing because the album was only expected to sell a couple of thousand copies: Serpick, '"3 Feet High and Rising"'.

3 Rethinking the significance of *Grand Upright* for the music industry

If by the early 1990s clear industry practices regulating sampling had started to emerge, why was the litigation in *Grand Upright* brought, and why has the decision been interpreted as such a significant intervention in hip-hop? The case was, in many respects, an entirely unremarkable copyright infringement action. At issue was the unauthorized sampling by Biz Markie of the opening eight bars of Gilbert O'Sullivan's 1972 US number one hit 'Alone Again (Naturally)'.[63] The sample was clearly recognizable and was looped so that it played continuously throughout Biz Markie's track, 'Alone Again', released by Cold Chillin' Records and distributed by Warner Bros Records.[64] Most commentators focus only on the outcome of the case – that the plaintiff was successful – and on that basis hold up the decision as marking a turning point in the history of hip-hop, where the courts finally determined that sampling constituted infringement, from which substantially negative consequences flowed. However, a careful reading of the decision and the material on the court file sheds an entirely different light on the case.

The litigation did not in fact involve a contested dispute over whether the sample was infringing. It was not brought, as Jeff Chang has claimed, to 'make an example' out of a rapper,[65] suggesting that the purpose of the litigation was to send an industry-wide message about sampling. Nor did it involve a fight over licensing fees and conditions. Rather, the case was brought to *prevent* the release of a recording that the defendants admitted contained a prima facie infringing sample, with the only issue in dispute being whether the plaintiff was in fact the copyright owner. After having recorded 'Alone Again', lawyers for Biz Markie had sent a cassette copy of his album to O'Sullivan Music, Inc. (OSM) to secure consent for the use of the sample,[66] and had also warned Cold Chillin' Records to delay releasing the album until the sample had been cleared.[67] OSM indicated that it did not generally grant permissions for the type of use requested.[68] Biz Markie then offered a 50 per cent publishing interest

[63] *Grand Upright*, Plaintiff's Post-Hearing Memorandum, Preliminary Statement.

[64] Drawing attention to the sample further, Biz Markie sang the words 'alone again, naturally' six times in 'Alone Again'.

[65] J. Chang, quoted in the documentary *Copyright Criminals*.

[66] See *Grand Upright*, Letter from Mayer, Katz, Baker & Leibowitz, PC (MKBL) to OSM, 24 July 1991. OSM was the publisher of Grand Upright Music Ltd, the owner of copyright in the composition and recording of 'Alone Again (Naturally)'.

[67] *Grand Upright*, Letter from MKBL to Leonard Fichtelberg, President, Cold Chillin' Records & Video, Inc., 12 August 1991.

[68] *Grand Upright*, Letter from OSM to MKBL, 6 October 1991.

and a penny per record for use of the master recording,[69] an offer that OSM rejected, demanding instead that 'Alone Again' be deleted from the album.[70] The album was, however, released containing the unauthorized sample. OSM requested the album be immediately withdrawn,[71] and sought a preliminary injunction against ten defendants, including Biz Markie, Cold Chillin' and Warner Bros. Crucially, the defendants did not seek to argue at the hearing that the sample was not infringing (for example, because it involved *de minimis* taking or constituted fair use).[72] They admitted that they needed a licence to use it[73] and, mindful that the court could refer the matter to the US Attorney for prosecution, were keen to provide the court with evidence on the issue of wilfulness.[74] To the extent the defendants initially sought to avoid the grant of the injunction, it was on the sole basis that the plaintiff did not in fact own copyright in the composition and recording of 'Alone Again (Naturally)'.[75] In a terse judgment, Judge Duffy granted the preliminary injunction, having found clear evidence of the plaintiff's ownership.[76]

In light of the testimony from industry participants such as Fredrick Silber and Jane Peterer that licences for samples were routinely granted, as outlined in section 2, above, OSM's decision to refuse permission outright was unusual.[77] In that sense, the case is something of an outlier. At the same time, what is noteworthy about the facts of the case is that in refusing to grant permission for use of the sample the copyright owner was merely exercising another aspect of its rights, but for broadly similar

69 *Grand Upright*, Transcript of Hearing, 26 November 1991 (Examination of Theodore Weis), p. 86.

70 *Grand Upright*, Letter from OSM to MKBL, 12 October 1991.

71 *Grand Upright*, Letter from OSM to MKBL, 18 October 1991.

72 It is interesting to compare this approach with that taken in *Acuff-Rose Music, Inc.* v. *Campbell*, 754 F Supp 1150 (MD Tenn, 1991), where 2 Live Crew and its record label Luke Skyywalker Records had successfully argued that the parodic use of a pre-existing copyright work constituted fair use.

73 *Grand Upright*, Transcript of Hearing, 26 November 1991, pp. 144–50.

74 *Ibid.*, pp. 65–6, 77.

75 Having failed to show that the ownership of the copyrights by the plaintiff was defective, the defendants consented to an injunction under 'judicial compulsion' on the second morning of the hearing: see *Grand Upright*, Transcript of Hearing, 26 November 1991, pp. 150–2.

76 As Joo has noted, claims that the decision suffered from 'inadequate legal reasoning' and represented a missed opportunity to clarify this area of the law (see, e.g., Kravis, 'Does a Song by Any Other Name Still Sound as Sweet?', 269; McLeod and DiCola, *Creative License*, pp. 132–3) mischaracterize the limited issues at stake: Joo, 'Remix Without Romance', 431, 433.

77 It was not, however, unique. Biz Markie had during the course of clearing samples for his album been denied consent to use the Eagles' composition 'Hotel California' on his track 'Buck Wild', and the sample was removed: see *Grand Upright*, Transcript of Hearing, 26 November 1991 (Examination of Theodore Weis), p. 87.

purposes as if it had sought to grant a licence. That is, rather than seeking further to commodify the reputation of the artist being sampled by way of a licence and a new assignation of authorship, it was choosing to safeguard the commercial value of that artist's reputation, so that that reputation could continue to be exploited, but on different, more closely guarded terms. In the course of giving evidence, Gilbert O'Sullivan claimed that 'Alone Again (Naturally)' was the most valuable song in his repertoire and had only been licensed for uses consistent with the song's serious content. He testified that use of the sample would damage his reputation in the music industry because no artist would allow a popular, serious song to be used in that way, and that people in the industry would assume that the sample had been authorized, thereby damaging the original's credibility and the song's potential for use in other media, such as commercials and films. O'Sullivan also claimed that radio station DJs would be dissuaded from playing the original, leading to a reduction in performance revenues from the song.[78] While some of these beliefs might have been counter-intuitive, what is interesting about them is that they show the awareness that existed at the time of the link between controlling sampling (whether by choosing to license a sample, or choosing *not* to license a sample) and the commercial exploitation of an artist's reputation.

Beyond this, the narrow compass of the legal issues at stake in *Grand Upright*, and especially the fact that the issue of whether the sample in question infringed copyright was conceded by the defendants, raise the question of why the case has been characterized as a turning point for hip-hop. This requires looking at two, related issues. In the remainder of this part we will consider some of the industry responses in the aftermath of the case. In the next part we will consider the more qualitative claims that the decision caused a decline in the quantity and quality of sampling.

In looking at the issue of industry responses to *Grand Upright*, the decision might not have broken any new legal ground, but it can be seen to have been of highly symbolic importance. It may well be the case that certain aspects of the decision that suggest a more general judicial disapproval of the entire practice of sampling have been taken out of context by commentators claiming that copyright law has restricted sampling – for example, Judge Duffy's opening words 'Thou shalt not steal', his scathing comments about the defendants' attempt to argue that weight should be given to the fact that other players in the industry released recordings with uncleared samples, or his tone of barely concealed contempt for the defendants' conduct.[79] But an argument can be made

[78] *Grand Upright*, Transcript of Hearing, 25 November 1991 (Testimony of Gilbert O'Sullivan), pp. 17–23.

[79] Joo, 'Remix Without Romance', 434–5.

that these ideas were internalized within the industry more widely after *Grand Upright*. In some cases they served to embolden some smaller players to take a more aggressive stance in relation to past sampling from their back catalogues.[80] More pertinently, they served to fortify the internal pre-release clearance practices that had been developing since the late 1980s and provided new commercial opportunities for record companies.

After the decision, many labels implemented additional safeguards to prevent unauthorized samples from appearing on their recordings.[81] These ranged from merely paying closer attention to existing guidelines to adding a buffer zone between the artist and the label by sending written reminders to producers that the responsibility of seeking clearances for samples was theirs.[82] EMI was reportedly keen to educate its hip-hop artists with seminars on the creative and legal side of sampling, while encouraging them to use samples from EMI's music catalogue.[83] It was estimated that whereas prior to the *Grand Upright* decision around 80 per cent of samples had been unlicensed pre-release, a year later 80 per cent of samples were cleared in advance.[84]

Over the course of the 1990s, publishers began to acknowledge that sampling was not as much of a problem as it had been previously, as it became widely accepted by hip-hop producers and record labels that they had to clear samples in advance.[85] Most record companies set up their own departments to deal with sample clearance, and during this decade a large number of third-party firms dealing with sample clearance for

[80] For instance, shortly after the *Grand Upright* decision, Salsoul Records, the premier disco label in the mid-1970s, one of whose major hits, Loleatta Holloway's 'Love Sensation', had been frequently sampled without authorization, placed the following notice in *Billboard*: 'Salsoul Records for many years has been the victim of wanton sampling of all of its catalog. Now that the law has finally been clarified that it is illegal to sample songs without the owner's written consent, Salsoul is vigorously pursuing its rights against producers, mixers, record companies or anyone else involved or benefiting from these illegal acts. We have commenced lawsuits and have retained a law firm with six full-time attorney litigators to prosecute all those who have sampled our music': *Billboard*, 16 May 1992, p. 85.

[81] Some record companies had made changes to their sampling policies before the *Grand Upright* decision. For instance, Capitol Records instituted a contractual change in July 1991, under which Capitol artists were asked to deliver a schedule of samples and a list of original artists and song publishers to the label. Delivery of an album was deemed to occur only when all samples had been cleared: see M. Newman and C. Morris, 'Sampling Safeguards Follow Suit: Biz Markie Ruling Prompts Labels Action', *Billboard*, 23 May 1992, pp. 1, 80.

[82] *Ibid.* [83] *Billboard*, 16 May 1992, p. 85.

[84] See J. McAdams, 'Clearing House: EMI Music Uses Sampling Committee', *Billboard*, 30 January 1993, pp. 1, 85.

[85] See J. Bessman, 'Sampling's Big Score', *Billboard*, 14 June 2003, p. 43 (quoting Dag Sandsmark, VP of Copyright Administration and Sampling, EMI Music Publishing and David Hirshland, Executive VP, Bug Music).

smaller labels and publishers were established.[86] Publishers even started to target hip-hop producers by sending them works from their catalogues to sample.[87] As this market for samples developed during the 1990s, there is evidence to suggest that, at a general level, samples increased in cost from some of the figures provided in the *Grand Upright* litigation.[88]

In addition, the industry continued to develop new, 'franchise-like' techniques for extracting value from authorial reputation through sampling. For example, the growth in the market for licensed samples led to the development of a secondary market for 'bespoke' samples. George Clinton of Parliament/Funkadelic, whose songs had been much sampled in the 1980s and early 1990s, produced his own series of 'sample CDs' containing snippets of music featuring isolated instrument and vocal parts that could be licensed for use in new compositions.[89] When UK act NW1 sampled the Blue Note Records jazz standard 'Sookie Sookie' on a bootleg single, it came to the attention of Capitol Records. Instead of suing, Capitol offered the group a recording contract and free rein to sample from the jazz label Blue Note's catalogue, the rights to which were owned by Capitol. After changing their name to Us3, the resulting album, *Hand on the Torch* (1993) became Blue Note's first ever million-selling album, featuring licensed samples from Blue Note recordings by Herbie Hancock, Art Blakey and the Jazz Messengers and Lou Donaldson.[90] As part of a general renewed interest in jazz music because of jazz samples being used in hip-hop, Blue Note began reissuing records from its back catalogue for this new market.[91]

Another new business model that emerged involved companies purchasing rights to the back catalogues of other labels in order to license samples and bring infringement proceedings in relation to uncleared samples from those catalogues, which has led to such companies being

[86] P. Théberge, 'Technology, Creative Practice and Copyright', in S. Frith and L. Marshall (eds), *Music and Copyright*, 2nd edn (Edinburgh University Press, 2004), p. 147.

[87] Bessman, 'Sampling's Big Score', p. 46.

[88] For an indication of the rise in sampling clearance costs from the perspective of various hip-hop artists, see M. Newton, 'Is Sampling Dying', *Spin* (online), 21 November 2008, at www.spin.com/articles/sampling-dying/; K. McLeod, 'How Copyright Law Changed Hip Hop: An Interview with Public Enemy's Chuck D and Hank Shocklee', at www.alternet.org/story/18830/how_copyright_law_changed_hip_hop; see more generally McLeod and DiCola, *Creative License*, pp. 158–63.

[89] *Sample Some of Disc – Sample Some of DAT, Vols 1–3* were released on AEM Records between 1993 and 1994. See S. Jacobs, 'Hey Man . . . Smell My Sample', *Wired*, August 1994, at www.wired.com/wired/archive/2.08/clinton_pr.html.

[90] See K. Grow, 'Biddy Biddy Bop: The Oral History of Us3's Bold Jazz-Rap Breakthrough "Cantaloop (Flip Fantasia)"', *Spin* (online), 24 October 2013, at www.spin.com/articles/us3-cantaloop-flip-fantasia-herbie-hancock-lou-donaldson/.

[91] C. Morris, 'Repeat Beat: "Acid" Heads and Thirsty Collectors Feel a Reissue Frenzy', *Billboard*, 1 July 1995, p. 54.

labelled 'sample trolls'.[92] One example is Bridgeport Music, Inc., which purportedly acquired the rights to much of George Clinton's catalogue.[93] About 95 per cent of Bridgeport's revenues since the 1990s have come from sample licences.[94] It has also been an aggressive litigator. In May 2001, it filed an action in the District Court of the Middle District of Tennessee alleging almost 500 acts of infringement against around 800 defendants.[95] It achieved a remarkable success in 2005 in relation to one of those actions when the Sixth Circuit Court of Appeals held that a sample of a fraction of a second from a Funkadelic recording constituted an infringement of copyright, on the basis that the Copyright Act 1976 (US) did not allow scope for consideration of whether a taking from a sound recording was a *de minimis* use.[96] While the Court's interpretation of the Act is deeply problematic,[97] claims that the decision would have a negative impact on sampling have proven to be wide of the mark, as the decision was largely consistent with sampling clearance practices since the late 1980s where *de minimis* uses had routinely been subject to licences.[98] A similar company to Bridgeport is Tuff City Records, a hip-hop and R&B label that has acquired the rights to other labels' compositions and recordings, and through various related companies has vigorously pursued litigation over the past twenty years, particularly over uncleared samples of drum beats.[99] It has continued to bring actions to the present day, often in relation to records released in the mid- to

[92] See, e.g., T. Wu, 'Jay-Z Versus the Sample Troll', *Slate* (online), 16 November 2006, at www.slate.com/articles/arts/culturebox/2006/11/jayz_versus_the_sample_troll.html.

[93] The ownership of rights in songs written by George Clinton have been in dispute for many years, with Clinton claiming that the rights were fraudulently obtained by Bridgeport: see A. Keyes, 'George Clinton Fights for His Right to Funk', *The Record: Music News from NPR* (online), 6 June 2012, at www.npr.org/blogs/therecord/2012/06/06/154451399/george-clinton-fights-for-his-right-to-funk; see also McLeod and DiCola, *Creative License*, pp. 93–4.

[94] S. Hunter, 'B.I.G. Song May Cost Diddy', *Billboard*, 1 April 2006, p. 7.

[95] *Bridgeport Music, Inc.* v. *11C Music*, Civ. No. 3:01-0412 (MD Tenn., 2001).

[96] *Bridgeport Music, Inc.* v. *Dimension Films*, 410 F 3d 792, 798–802 (6th Cir., 2005).

[97] For scholarly criticism, see, e.g., D. Nimmer (ed.), *Nimmer on Copyright* (Newark, NJ: LexisNexis, looseleaf), vol. 4, para. 13.03; J. R. R. Mueller, 'All Mixed Up: *Bridgeport Music* v. *Dimension Films* and De Minimis Digital Sampling' (2006) 84 *Indiana Law Journal* 435. For judicial criticism, see, e.g., *Saregama India Ltd* v. *Mosley*, 687 F Supp 2d 1325, 1338–41 (SD Fla., 2009). The *Bridgeport* view is contrary to the views of other Circuit Courts on the issue: see *United States* v. *Taxe*, 540 F 2d 961, 965 (9th Cir., 1976); *Leigh* v. *Warner Bros, Inc.*, 212 F 3d 1210, 1214 (11th Cir., 2000); it is also inconsistent with *Newton* v. *Diamond*, 388 F 3d 1189 (9th Cir., 2004) (three-note sample from a musical composition held to be *de minimis* and therefore non-infringing).

[98] Joo, 'Remix Without Romance', 442.

[99] See, e.g., *Tuff 'N' Rumble Management, Inc.* v. *Def Jam Recordings, Inc.*, 91 Civ 8637 (SDNY, filed 21 December 1991) (over samples of the drum break from the Honey Drippers' 'Impeach the President', in tracks by LL Cool J and EPMD); but cf. *Tuff 'N' Rumble Management, Inc.* v. *Profile Records*, 42 USPQ 2d 1398 (plaintiff unable to

late 1980s, as technological advances have enabled the identification of fragments of sampled beats that had been treated or distorted.[100] However, the limitations of this strategy have recently been exposed, with defendants having some success in persuading courts that the particular samples in question constituted *de minimis* uses of both the original compositions and sound recordings.[101]

4 Reassessing the law–creativity nexus after *Grand Upright*

The chapter now turns to the other issue relating to the characterization of *Grand Upright*, namely that the decision led to a reduction in the volume and the quality of sampling, best encapsulated by Vaidhyanathan's assertion that by the late 1990s what sampling that did occur 'was non-transgressive, nonthreatening, and too often clumsy and obvious'.[102] Such quantitative and qualitative claims are problematic. The difficulty with much of the scholarship seeking to make the case that *Grand Upright* and the subsequent rise of the sample clearance industry were responsible for a decline in the quality of hip-hop is that it sets up the dense, layered sampling seen in the late 1980s albums of the Beastie Boys and Public Enemy as the paradigm of sampling. It is argued that because it became prohibitively expensive to clear hundreds of samples for a single album in the 1990s, albums like *Paul's Boutique* and *It Takes a Nation of Millions to Hold Us Back*, featuring 'tricky, playful, transgressive sampling',[103] could no longer be made.[104] It is a short step from that to say that, to the extent sampling continued, it was in a compromised form, and necessarily of a lower quality.[105] But to suggest that albums like *Paul's Boutique* and *It Takes a Nation of Millions to Hold Us Back* were somehow representative of how samples were deployed in hip-hop before

provide sufficient evidence that it in fact owned copyright in the sound recording and composition of 'Impeach the President').

[100] For example, in May 2012, TufAmerica, an imprint of Tuff City Records, sued the Beastie Boys in relation to a number of uncleared samples on their 1980s albums *Licensed to Ill* and *Paul's Boutique*. Audio analysis was required to determine the presence of the samples. TufAmerica had acquired the relevant rights as exclusive administrator and copyright licensee in 1999.

[101] *TufAmerica, Inc.* v. *Diamond*, 968 F Supp 2d 588 (SDNY, 2013).

[102] Vaidhyanathan, *Copyrights and Copywrongs*, p. 143; see also A. Said, *The Art of Sampling: The Sampling Tradition of Hip Hop/Rap Music and Copyright Law* (Brooklyn, NY: Superchamp Books, 2013), p. 76; Demers, *Steal This Music*, p. 97.

[103] Vaidhyanathan, *Copyrights and Copywrongs*, p. 144.

[104] See, e.g., McLeod and DiCola, *Creative License*, p. 29.

[105] See J. Okpaluba, '"Free-Riding on the Riddim"? Open Source, Copyright Law and Reggae Music in Jamaica', in L. Bently, J. Davis and J. Ginsburg (eds), *Copyright and Piracy: An Interdisciplinary Critique* (Cambridge University Press, 2010), p. 384, n. 52, and accompanying text.

Grand Upright overlooks the heterogeneity of sampling that was discussed in section 2. These albums, with their hundreds of samples, were outliers – much of the hip-hop in the late 1980s and early 1990s in fact relied on far fewer samples per album.[106] Further, the idea that the sort of heavy sampling seen on these albums represents an artistic peak rests on little more than a subjective aesthetic value judgement. It also fails to engage with how sampling and creativity continued to thrive in the wake of *Grand Upright*. And, even if the assertion that mainstream hip-hop became more homogenized in the 1990s is accepted, there would appear to be a range of non-copyright-related factors that might explain this, which further complicates the idea that the law has operated as a restriction in hip-hop.

As discussed above, securing licences for samples did become more expensive in the 1990s.[107] Some hip-hop artists made aesthetic mileage out of the costs involved in securing licences. For example, successful 1990s acts like Puff Daddy,[108] who sought to promote an image of entrepreneurialism and conspicuous consumption, reinforced their reputations by using prominent samples from major hits by established artists such as The Police and Led Zeppelin in their tracks.[109] This type of deployment of samples in 'luxury rap' can still be seen today.[110] But this is not to suggest that sampling only became a practice for the wealthiest artists on major labels after *Grand Upright*. Despite the assertions to the contrary, empirical evidence suggests that there was not in fact a decline in overall levels of sampling that can be attributed to *Grand Upright*. Jennifer Lena has conducted research on hip-hop songs that appeared on the weekly Top 100 R&B *Billboard* charts from 1979 to the end of 1995, finding that the number of songs featuring samples rose year on year from 1979 to 1989, dipped substantially in 1990, rose back to 1989 levels by the end of 1991 when *Grand Upright* was decided, increased by almost 50 per cent up to the end of 1993, and then dipped back to 1991 levels

[106] For instance on albums produced in this era by artists such as Eric B and Rakim, Big Daddy Kane, EPMD and Boogie Down Productions, the number of recognizable samples ranges from about ten to thirty: see the information on these artists at http://samplesetindex.hiphopisread.com/.

[107] See n. 88, and accompanying text.

[108] In 1997 alone, songs on Puff Daddy's label Bad Boy Records comprised 39 per cent of the number one records on the *Billboard* Hot 100: D. Charnas, *The Big Payback: The History of the Business of Hip-Hop* (New York: New American Library, 2010), p. 501.

[109] See, respectively, 'I'll Be Missing You' (1997) and 'Come With Me' (1998). Puff Daddy oversaw the production of records on Bad Boy, which often featured prominent looped samples from R&B and pop hits.

[110] See, e.g., Kanye West and Jay-Z's 'Otis' (2011), based on a lengthy sample from Otis Redding's recording of 'Try a Little Tenderness'.

by the end of 1995.[111] Such a snapshot suggests that the orthodox view about the impact of *Grand Upright* on levels of sampling is simplistic.

After 1991, it is fair to say that much of the most influential and highly regarded hip-hop relied on fewer samples than acts like the Beastie Boys and Public Enemy had in the late 1980s. Yet, even if it is accepted that the increased cost of clearing samples was a factor in this,[112] there is nothing to suggest that this led to a decline in creativity. On the contrary, rather than being stifled by the law, many producers innovated during this decade by developing new sampling techniques aided by advances in technology, and used samples in a range of novel ways and often relied on live instrumentation.

For instance, early 1990s hip-hop was dominated by a laid-back sound called 'G-Funk', pioneered by Dr Dre on his album *The Chronic* (1992). G-Funk relied on samples from stalwarts such as Parliament/Funkadelic and Leon Haywood, but involved studio musicians recreating the sounds of those recordings on synthesizers and live instruments.[113] Dr Dre claimed to find samples limiting, and said that he would only use a sample of a recording if it could not be replayed by musicians.[114] Speaking before the release of *The Chronic*, hip-hop producer Sir Jinx said that the G-Funk sound was 'gonna revolutionize, just change everything . . . because [it's] showing that we don't need the samples'.[115] Later in the 1990s, a style known as 'dirty south' rose to prominence, which involved the use of drum machines, sequencers and other instruments to create original backing tracks, rather than relying on samples for these purposes.[116] The most influential hip-hop act to come out of the south at this time was the duo OutKast, whose music blended soul, gospel, jazz and R&B and whose style and aesthetic shifted wildly from album to album in the

111 See J. C. Lena, 'Meaning and Membership: Samples in Rap Music, 1979–1995' (2004) 32 *Poetics* 297, 302–3. For a visual representation of sample usage, see J. Kriss, 'The History of Sampling v. 1.3', at http://jklabs.net/projects/samplinghistory/. Cf. Amanda Sewell, who has conducted research on the music of the Beastie Boys, De La Soul, Public Enemy, Salt 'n' Pepa, and A Tribe Called Quest before and after *Grand Upright*, over approximately ten years. While Sewell concluded that these artists sampled less and included different types of samples in their music, they modified certain elements of their musical styles without necessarily abandoning every defining feature of their sample-based musical styles: see Sewell, 'A Typology of Sampling in Hip-Hop', pp. 189–238.

112 See n. 88, and accompanying text.

113 A. Krims, *Rap Music and the Poetics of Identity* (Cambridge University Press, 2000), p. 74.

114 See www.dr-dre.com/info/interview_scratch_dr_dre.php; see also Said, *The Art of Sampling*, p. 79.

115 K. McLeod, *Owning Culture* (New York: Peter Lang, 2001), p. 83.

116 See M. Miller, *Bounce: Rap Music and Local Identity in New Orleans* (Amherst, MA: University of Massachusetts Press, 2012), p. 136.

course of their broader exploration of modern African-American identity. Of their album *Aquemini* (1998), Jeff Weiss said: 'Samples are sparse. It's not old music being re-interpreted; it's old ideas being reincarnated.'[117] Even those who had engaged in heavy sampling in the 1980s acknowledged how sampling had changed as an art form. Speaking in 2004, Mike D of the Beastie Boys said:

> We can't just go crazy and sample everything and anything like we did on *Paul's Boutique*. It's limiting in the sense that if we're going to grab a two-bar section of something now, we're going to have to think about how much we really need it. But then the flip side is that it pushes us to be creative. We have to look for stuff to sample that is maybe more low-profile. And take what we find and manipulate and recontextualize it in a way that makes it sound totally new.[118]

A further factor that complicates the orthodox narrative is that it is possible to point to albums after *Grand Upright* that relied on a much larger number of samples than late 1980s albums such as *Paul's Boutique*. A notable early example is DJ's Shadow's album *Entroducing*... (1996), a digital collage consisting of possibly thousands of samples[119] from all genres of music, most of them heavily treated, which, as the liner notes suggest, 'reflect a lifetime of vinyl culture'. According to the liner notes, only seven samples were cleared before release. Part of the reason these and other collage-like albums have been able to be released may well have been because of a commercial calculation undertaken by their labels: that the samples are so unlikely to be detected that the costs of seeking clearance are outweighed by the commercial benefits of releasing the album.[120] In addition, Joseph Schloss has argued that producers came to recognize the purely reputational value in creating sample-heavy records that went unreleased.[121] A major factor in this regard is that hip-hop has a ready outlet for these types of recordings through the distribution of mixtapes or online distribution,[122] designed to allow for degrees of experimentation while also boosting an artist and/or producer's reputation. Even where copyright owners object, such as in the case of EMI preventing the distribution of Danger Mouse's *The Grey Album* (2004), a mash-up of Jay-Z's *The Black Album* and The Beatles' *White Album*, it is arguable that the notoriety of the legal intervention creates greater

[117] J. Weiss, 'Weird Storms in the Wrong Season', *Pitchfork* (online), 5 November 2013, at http://pitchfork.com/features/articles/9253-outkast/.

[118] E. Steuer, 'The Remix Masters', *Wired*, November 2004, at www.wired.com/wired/archive/12.11/beastie.html.

[119] G. Rule, 'DJ Shadow + AKAI MPC = History', *Keyboard*, October 1997, p. 51.

[120] Joo, 'Remix Without Romance', 443–4.

[121] Schloss, *Making Beats*, p. 180.

[122] See also McLeod and DiCola, *Creative License*, pp. 196–200.

interest in the new work and sampling artist than would otherwise be the case.[123]

The final point worth considering in this part is that even if one accepts the argument that mainstream hip-hop (that is, the sort of hip-hop that has achieved mass popular appeal) has become more homogenous since the early 1990s, there would seem to be better explanations for this than the *Grand Upright* decision or the tightening in the market for sample clearances. A more convincing explanation might relate to the buying up of independent hip-hop record labels by major record labels in the 1990s. To recoup their investments, major labels backed fewer artists in the hope of receiving bigger returns. While some artists benefited, it has been suggested that this resulted in a narrowing of voices made available through the majors' distribution channels and a decrease in the diversity of sounds.[124] In a 2007 study of the *Billboard* pop charts from 1990 to 2005, a period in which independent hip-hop labels began to be bought out by the major record labels, Letrez Myer and Christine Kleck examined the relationship between legal ownership, commodification and commercialization of hip-hop and rap music.[125] They considered that a danger of major record labels having control over smaller independent record labels was that the major labels would quash the cultural and diverse aspects of the genre, which they said was illustrated by a 'decrease in creativity in rap with the same artists topping the charts consecutively'.[126] They concluded that vertical integration of the music industry has resulted in hip-hop morphing into mainstream culture and that 'rap music loses the value of its messages, social urgency, and authenticity as it gets watered down and formulaic with corporate control'.[127] Similarly, it has been argued that the consolidation of radio stations, following the enactment of the Telecommunications Act 1996 (US), had a profound effect on the hip-hop industry.[128] As broadcast

[123] That is, it could be argued that the fact *The Grey Album* remained a bootleg bolstered Danger Mouse's reputation as a cutting edge producer, leading to further commissions (such as on Gorillaz' *Demon Days* (1995) (on Parlophone/EMI, no less) and him being signed to a major label as part of the duo Gnarls Barkley: *ibid.*, p. 198.

[124] J. Chang, *Can't Stop Won't Stop: A History of the Hip-Hop Generation* (London: Ebury Press, 2007), pp. 444–5. See also T. Rose, *The Hip Hop Wars* (New York: Basic Books, 2008), pp. 14–18.

[125] L. Myer and C. Kleck, 'From Independent to Corporate: A Political Economic Analysis of Rap *Billboard* Toppers' (2007) 30 *Popular Music and Society* 137.

[126] *Ibid.*, p. 146. [127] *Ibid.*, p. 147.

[128] See, e.g., A. N. Folami, 'The Telecommunications Act of 1996 and the (Over)Development of Gangsta Rap', in L. King and R. Schur (eds), *African-American Culture and Legal Discourse* (New York: Palgrave Macmillan, 2009); Rose, *The Hip Hop Wars*, pp. 18–25. More generally, the Future of Music Coalition has criticized the merger and acquisition frenzy that followed deregulation, assessing that ownership consolidation led to format consolidation and shorter playlists, depriving citizens of the opportunity to hear a wide range of music: see P. DiCola *et al.*, 'Radio Deregulation: Has

companies recouped investments and chased advertising revenue, there was a consolidation of playlists within and across formats, higher levels of repetition of record industry-chosen songs and more homogenized (in some cases, automated) programming. This resulted in less room for local, non-record-industry-sponsored artists, as commercially established major label stars were able to be readily packaged for a national audience and dominate playlists nationwide.[129] After the passage of the Act, numerous independent labels, unable to compete with the expenses required to secure radio play for their acts, either closed down or were bought out.[130]

Despite the clear merit of these arguments, some of them can be challenged for at times relying too heavily on the same aesthetic value judgements and selective use of examples as the scholarship on the impact of copyright law on hip-hop creativity. For example, Myer and Kleck, who view hip-hop as an outlet to express social, political and economic struggles within the African-American community, contrast what they see to be the political and challenging content of Jay-Z's debut album *Reasonable Doubt* (1996) with his more 'listener friendly' and 'diluted' second album after his label started doing corporate deals.[131] Conversely, Jennifer Lena has recently made a detailed case that authenticity and industrial production do not necessarily exist in an antagonistic relationship, and that, as major record labels came to own more and more hip-hop music, artists adjusted their sound and image to infuse it with legitimacy and authenticity. Lena's work reveals that 'authenticity' is not a stable attribute but it is redefined as fans and artists face shifting social conditions.[132] Attributing changes in perceived degrees of creativity to copyright law oversimplifies the complex interplay of personal, social and economic factors in play in the music industry. Political hip-hop thrived throughout the 2000s, with acts as diverse as Nas, Common, dead prez, Killer Mike and, most recently, Kendrick Lamar producing arguably political and challenging content on major labels. This is a further illustration of the problems in assuming that law – whether in the form of copyright, or in its facilitation of corporate consolidation – necessarily imposes restrictions on creativity that result in a loss of artistic quality.

It Served Citizens and Musicians?' (November 2002), at www.futureofmusic.org/sites/default/files/FMCradiostudy.pdf.

129 Rose, *The Hip Hop Wars*, p. 18.

130 A. N. Folami, 'From Habermas To "Get Rich or Die Tryin'": Hip Hop, The Telecommunications Act of 1996, and the Black Music Sphere' (2007) 12 *Michigan Journal of Race & Law* 235, 300–1.

131 Myer and Kleck, 'From Independent to Corporate', 146–7.

132 J. C. Lena, 'Authenticity and Independence in Rap Music and Other Genre Communities', in S. T. Horsfall, J-M. Meij and M. D. Probstfield (eds), *Music Sociology: Examining the Role of Music in Social Life* (Boulder, CO: Paradigm Publishing, 2013).

5 Conclusion

Nothing that has been said in this chapter should detract from the fact that there are clearly serious problems with the sample clearance industry, and with some of the copyright rules underpinning it. McLeod and DiCola have shown that there are numerous inefficiencies and transaction costs in the licensing system that impact disproportionately harshly upon smaller artists and labels.[133] Some suggest there is scope for change here, such as the potential development of best-practice fair-use guidelines to promote greater awareness of the extent of samplers' rights to act without licences.[134] There are also problems with some of the fundamental principles of copyright law that underpin the sampling economy. For example, it strikes as problematic that many of the performers on records sampled (such as drummers) are not entitled to publishing royalties, even though only their contributions, and not elements the law recognizes as going towards authorship of the work, were sampled.[135] However, the concern in this chapter has been with a different set of issues, namely the broader claims that tend to be made for the purpose of driving reform, that the law has operated primarily as a restriction on creativity in hip-hop. The relationship between law and culture is far more complex than the traditional narrative holds. Not only has it been shown that both sampling and creativity have thrived since the advent of recorded hip-hop, albeit in shifting ways over time, but such creativity has frequently been enabled by contractual regulation. In addition, the legal regulation of sampling has allowed for the ongoing exploitation of the reputation of older artists, in the form of new royalty streams and in the generation of new levels of interest for older recordings and new audiences. The idea that hip-hop culture was in the past and would be in the present stronger and richer in the relative 'absence' of the law, both overclaims the restrictive role that the law has played and continues to play in this space and sentimentalizes a particular moment in hip-hop's history at the expense of embracing its diversity and resilience. Whether hip-hop music is alive and well clearly depends on whom you ask.

[133] McLeod and DiCola, *Creative License*, ch. 5.

[134] See generally P. Jaszi and P. Aufderheide, *Reclaiming Fair Use: How To Put Balance Back In Copyright* (University of Chicago Press, 2011).

[135] See D. S. Bloch, '"Give The Drummer Some:" On the Need for Enhanced Protection of Drum Beats' (1997) 14 *Entertainment & Sports Law Review* 187.

Part III

Managing authorship

5 Building and rebuilding reputations

Reflections on the role of defamation law in the life of a celebrity

*David Rolph**

1 Introduction

Celebrities are great litigators. The impetus for the recent developments in privacy law in the UK has been the volume of litigation brought by a diverse range of celebrity plaintiffs.[1] Notoriously, celebrities, as well as their families, friends, managers and agents, were the victims of phone hacking by the *News of the World*, and, to a lesser, proven extent, other newspapers, and they have responded by suing those media outlets.[2] Celebrities, though, are not only protective of their privacy. They are also concerned with their image, their public perception, their reputation. One of the other legal avenues available to celebrities to protect their reputations is defamation law. Celebrities have not been averse to suing for defamation.

The central legal interest protected by the tort of defamation is reputation. Celebrities are people too, so they have a right to reputation. However, what is actually meant by 'reputation' is somewhat problematic. For centuries, defamation law has protected reputation highly without being

* The author wishes to thank Simon Bensley and Patrick Caldwell for their useful comments, and Joanna Connolly and Jackson Wherrett for their excellent research assistance.

1 The privacy jurisprudence in the United Kingdom is large and burgeoning. Some of the important and interesting cases include *Douglas* v. *Hello! Ltd* [2001] QB 967; [2003] EWHC 786 (Ch); [2006] QB 125; [2008] 1 AC 1 (*sub nom OBG Ltd* v. *Allan*) (film stars, Michael Douglas and Catherine Zeta-Jones); *Campbell* v. *MGN Ltd* [2004] 2 AC 457 (supermodel, Naomi Campbell); *McKennitt* v. *Ash* [2008] QB 73 (singer, Loreena McKennitt); *Murray* v. *Express Newspapers plc* [2009] Ch 481 (author, J. K. Rowling); *Terry* v. *Persons Unknown* [2010] EWHC 119 (QB) (footballer, John Terry); *Ntuli* v. *Donald* [2011] 1 WLR 294 (pop singer, Howard Donald, member of Take That); *Ferdinand* v. *MGN Ltd* [2011] EWHC 2454 (QB) (footballer, Rio Ferdinand).

2 See R. Greenslade, 'Phone Hacking: News International Faces More than 60 Claims', *Guardian* (online), 5 October 2011, at www.guardian.co.uk/media/2011/oct/05/phone-hacking-news-international-60-claims?CMP+twt_gu; J. Halliday, 'Phone Hacking: News International Settles with Victims', *Guardian* (online), 19 January 2012, at www.guardian.co.uk/media/2012/jan/19/phone-hacking-news-international-settles. See also *Coogan* v. *News Group Newspapers Ltd* [2013] 1 AC 1; *Gulati* v. *MGN Ltd* [2013] EWHC 3392 (Ch).

especially reflective about what reputation actually is. Recent defamation scholarship has begun critically to analyse the concept of reputation, suggesting that reputation is a complex legal interest.[3] Influenced by Robert Post's taxonomy of reputation, defamation scholars have recognized that reputation can be viewed as a social construct (reputation as honour and dignity),[4] an economic construct (reputation as property)[5] and, as has been more recently suggested, a media construct (reputation as celebrity).[6] Obviously, not every view of reputation will be present in every defamation proceeding. However, where a celebrity is the plaintiff, the complexity of the reputational interests involved is amplified.

Recourse to defamation law is not the only way in which celebrities can protect and manage their reputations. Indeed, the number of defamation cases litigated to final judgment is small. The importance of celebrities' defamation trials cannot be assessed numerically, though. A celebrity's defamation trial has an impact on the celebrity and his or her place in the media, social or cultural landscape, given the profile of the plaintiff and the attendant publicity. Even if a celebrity does not sue to final judgment, the threat of defamation litigation and the well-known 'chilling effect' of defamation law may be sufficient to alter the way in which the celebrity is publicly portrayed.

This chapter highlights the complexity of the reputational interests involved in a celebrity's defamation trial. More importantly, it examines the legal and non-legal ways in which a celebrity can attempt to protect and manage his or her reputation. A non-legal strategy for managing reputation, available to celebrities of all types but not often available to ordinary people, is the commercially published memoir. The celebrity memoir is a well-established genre in publishing. Celebrities from all fields of endeavour are regularly contracted to write their life stories (with or without the assistance of a ghost writer). It is not unusual for celebrities who have sued for defamation to discuss their defamation trials in their

[3] D. Rolph, 'Dirty Pictures: Defamation, Reputation and Nudity' (2006) 10 *Law Text Culture* 101; L. McNamara, *Reputation and Defamation* (Oxford University Press, 2007); D. Rolph, *Reputation, Celebrity and Defamation Law* (Aldershot: Ashgate, 2008); K. H. Craik, *Reputation: A Network Interpretation* (Oxford University Press, 2008); D. S. Ardia, 'Reputation in a Networked World: Revisiting the Social Foundations of Defamation Law' (2010) 45 *Harvard Civil Rights-Civil Liberties Law Review* 261; B. Tarantino, 'Chasing Reputation: The Argument for Differential Treatment of "Public Figures" in Canadian Defamation Law' (2010) 48 *Osgoode Hall Law Journal* 595; L. A. Heymann, 'The Law of Reputation and the Interest of the Audience' (2011) 52 *Boston College Law Review* 1341.

[4] R. C. Post, 'The Social Foundations of Defamation Law: Reputation and the Constitution' (1986) 74 *California Law Review* 691, 699–719.

[5] *Ibid.*, pp. 693–9.

[6] Rolph, *Reputation, Celebrity and Defamation Law*, pp. 171–84.

memoirs.[7] Some do this incidentally, some do this at length, depending upon the perceived importance of the defamation trial to their lives and their public profiles.

This chapter explores the place of the defamation trial in a celebrity's reputation through an examination of Jason Donovan's libel proceedings against *The Face* magazine in the early 1990s and his extensive reflections upon the impact of that case almost two decades later in his memoirs, *Between the Lines: My Story Uncut*, including his downward spiral into extensive drug use with a particular emphasis on cocaine.[8] Donovan sued *The Face* over allegations that he was homosexual and was successful in court. However, the victory was a hollow one, which alienated key audiences and ultimately and paradoxically harmed his reputation. Donovan's autobiography is centrally concerned with his court case and its impact on his life and his celebrity. This chapter does not assume that Donovan's proceedings and their aftermath are representative of all celebrities' experience of defamation law, nor does it purport to provide definitive answers about the role of defamation litigation in the management of celebrity. Rather, it uses Donovan's defamation trial and his memoirs as a starting point to interrogate the implicit assumptions of defamation law about reputation and to invite critical reflection upon the various legal and non-legal ways in which celebrity is protected and managed, particularly focusing on the role of the celebrity memoir as a means of rebuilding a damaged reputation.

2 Jason Donovan's libel proceedings against *The Face* magazine

Jason Donovan is an Australian actor who came to prominence playing Scott Robinson between 1986 and 1989 in the long-running soap opera, *Neighbours*, which screened on Network Ten in Australia and in numerous countries around the world, including the United Kingdom. His character's relationship with Charlene Mitchell, played by Kylie Minogue, which culminated in a much-watched wedding, formed one of the crucial storylines in the early years of *Neighbours* and was one of the main reasons for its immense international popularity. In 1988, Minogue left *Neighbours* to pursue her singing career and the following year Donovan

[7] For some noteworthy Australian examples, see J. Bjelke-Petersen, *Don't You Worry About That!* (Sydney: Angus & Robertson, 1990), pp. 208–12; B. Harrigan and D. Lane, *Harrigan* (Sydney: Hodder Headline Australia, 2003), pp. 351–5; K. Fitzpatrick, *Name Dropping* (Sydney: Harper Collins, 2004), pp. 245–58; J. Marsden, *I Am What I Am: My Life and Curious Times* (Camberwell, Vic.: Penguin, 2004).

[8] J. Donovan, *Between the Lines: My Story Uncut* (London: HarperCollins, 2007).

did likewise. Donovan relocated to London, where he worked with music producers Stock, Aitken and Waterman, who were responsible for Minogue's output at the time. Donovan released a number of hit singles and albums between 1988 and 1991. In 1991, he was cast in the leading role in a West End revival of Andrew Lloyd Webber's *Joseph and the Amazing Technicolor Dreamcoat*. Still in his early twenties, Donovan was enjoying considerable professional success.

Things soured rapidly. In the northern summer of 1991, a group of gay activists calling itself FROCS ('Faggots Rooting Out Closet Sexuality') devised a campaign promising to 'out' approximately 200 high-profile 'closeted' homosexuals. As a forerunner of the campaign, posters of Donovan wearing a T-shirt with the words 'Queer as Fuck' superimposed on it were put up on walls and bus stops around London.[9] The campaign itself never eventuated. Indeed, the action appeared to have been designed to expose the hypocrisy of mainstream media outlets, which were critical of the practice of 'outing', but would turn up to FROCS' press conferences in the expectation that high-profile figures would be 'outed'. However, FROCS' activities had already attracted the attention of *The Face* magazine, a sophisticated publication covering style, fashion and music. *The Face* published an article on the practice of 'outing' in which it reproduced the poster. Donovan was highly offended by the posters. Initially, he gave press interviews, asserting his heterosexuality and categorically denying the rumours that he was a closeted homosexual.[10] He went further, deciding to sue *The Face* for libel. As an entity that voluntarily disseminated the arguably defamatory matter, *The Face* could be held liable as a publisher for the purposes of defamation law. Although it is the publication, so defined, not the composition, of defamatory matter that constituted the wrong, it was a forensic mistake on Donovan's part to pursue *The Face* rather than the people responsible for the FROCS campaign, as he himself later admitted.

The trial, which was held in 1992, attracted substantial media coverage.[11] Ultimately, Donovan succeeded, with the jury awarding him £200,000 damages. Donovan was also awarded costs.[12] Having won his court case, Donovan should have experienced the vindicating of his

[9] *Ibid.*, pp. 172–3.

[10] See, e.g., C. Iley, 'Jason: Not "Outed"... Just Outraged', *Herald Sun* (Melbourne), 3 August 1991, p. 19.

[11] See, e.g., R. Borrill, 'TV Star Sues Magazine over "Outing" Poster', *Independent*, 31 March 1992, p. 2; A. Millington, 'Musical Star Tells of Disgust over Gay Slur', *Guardian*, 31 March 1992, p. 2.

[12] See, e.g., R. Borrill, 'Donovan Awarded £200,000 Damages for "Queer" Libel', *Independent*, 4 April 1992, p. 1; R. Clancy, 'Donovan Wins Damages of £200,000 for Gay Slur', *The Times*, 4 April 1992, p. 3.

reputation that is supposed to follow from such a victory. In fact, he experienced the opposite: his reputation was damaged by the proceedings he took to protect his reputation and his success in them. This paradoxical outcome, and Donovan's defamation trial, and its aftermath more generally, stimulate some reflections about defamation law and its protection of reputation, particularly for the celebrity plaintiff.

3 Creating a reputation

Reputation has long been recognized as an important common law right. An individual does not have a right to a good reputation, only a right to the reputation he or she deserves.[13] More recently, reputation has been recognized as a fundamental human right, part of the innate dignity of the individual.[14] As both a common law right and a human right, reputation is somewhat unusual. There is a formal equality in individuals' entitlement to assert a right to reputation but the substance of the right varies from person to person. Reputation is radically subjective and purely personal; no two people's reputations can be the same.[15] Yet, defamation law is not particularly reflective about how a plaintiff acquired the reputation he or she has. It largely assumes that the plaintiff has the reputation he or she presents in court, usually as established in evidence relevant to the assessment of damages late in the proceedings, and generally inquires no further.

What is submerged by defamation law is how reputations are created. Although defamation law recognizes an innate right to reputation, reputation itself is created, often self-consciously, by individuals. Individuals have an agency in how they present themselves in social interactions, professional contexts, in the media. They have a degree of control over how others perceive them. Individuals then participate, in varying degrees of activity or passivity, in the creation of their own reputations. For celebrity plaintiffs, there is an additional, franchise-like element to their active engagement in the creation of their reputations. For celebrity plaintiffs, their reputations are not purely personal and professional manifestations of themselves, for which they are wholly responsible. Their reputations

[13] *M'Pherson* v. *Daniels* (1829) 109 ER 448, 451 (Littledale J); *Rofe* v. *Smith's Newspapers Ltd* (1924) 25 SR(NSW) 4, 21–2 (Street ACJ); P. George, *Defamation Law in Australia*, 2nd edn (Chatswood, NSW: LexisNexis Butterworths, 2012), [19.1].

[14] See, e.g., International Covenant on Civil and Political Rights, opened for signature 16 December 1966, 999 UNTS 181 (entered into force 23 March 1976), art. 17(1); Universal Declaration of Human Rights, GA Res 217A (III), UN Doc A/RES/217A (III) (10 December 1948), art. 12.

[15] *Rogers* v. *Nationwide News Pty Ltd* (2003) 216 CLR 327, 349 (Hayne J).

are created, cultivated and finessed by a range of what Rojek describes as 'cultural intermediaries': 'agents, publicists, marketing personnel, promoters, photographers, fitness trainers, wardrobe staff, cosmetics experts and personal assistants'.[16] Their reputations are collaborative efforts, to which often significant resources are directed. They are also conscious products, deliberately created and maintained to appeal to particular audiences. Their reputations extend beyond the activities for which they might be said to be primarily famous, and can be spun off in the form of endorsements of goods and services, personal appearances at public events and further forms of 'creativity' such as fashion lines, fragrances, merchandising and books.

Donovan's memoirs are instructive about the ways in which celebrity is created, developed and sustained, and the range of people involved in the process of its production. Donovan was fortunate to have been born the son of two prominent television personalities: his father, Terence, is an actor, notable for starring roles in the successful Australian television series *Division 4*, *Cop Shop* and, after his son's departure, *Neighbours*. His mother, Sue McIntosh, from whom Donovan is estranged, is an actress, television presenter and newsreader.[17] His family connections assisted him to get parts in television programmes *Skyways* (in which he made his first appearance playing opposite Kylie Minogue) and *I Can Jump Puddles*,[18] and in securing him the opportunity to audition for the part of Scott Robinson in *Neighbours*.[19] Once on *Neighbours*, Donovan recounts the instrumental role played by Channel Ten's then Director of Publicity, Brian Walsh, in establishing *Neighbours* as a brand and Donovan as a household name.[20] He identifies the programme launch as a key function for engaging the interest of the television industry and particularly critics. More importantly, Donovan identifies the extensive personal appearances he and other cast members undertook as crucial to the success of *Neighbours*, generating a buzz about the programme and allowing fans opportunities to engage with the characters outside of the confines of viewing alone, augmenting their experience and giving them purchase in the franchise.[21] He details the broad range of merchandising opportunities which flowed from *Neighbours* – fanzines, merchandise, board games – some authorized, some unauthorized. Donovan notes the personal and professional benefits of celebrity, which led to a range of interview opportunities for him, as well as invitations to a wide range of exclusive functions where he met other influential people from all walks

[16] C. Rojek, *Celebrity* (London: Reaktion Books, 2001), p. 9.
[17] Donovan, *Between the Lines*, p. 11. [18] *Ibid.*, pp. 28–30.
[19] *Ibid.*, p. 41. [20] *Ibid.*, pp. 56–9. [21] *Ibid.*, pp. 72–4.

of life.[22] He writes about how the producers, the directors and the scriptwriters developed the relationship between Scott and Charlene in response to positive feedback from audiences.[23] When Donovan and Minogue began dating in real life, they discussed with the show's producers and the network's publicity how to handle their relationship in media interviews, both to protect their privacy and to avoid alienating their teenage fan base. Unsurprisingly, they claimed merely to be 'really good friends'.[24] When the tabloid newspaper, *The Truth*, purported to reveal their relationship, Donovan was told to direct all media inquiries to Channel Ten's publicity department, which would 'keep 'em guessing', to generate further interest.[25] In relation to his music career, Donovan relates how he signed with his manager Richard East,[26] who, in turn, arranged Donovan's signing with Mushroom Records.[27] Launching his career in the United Kingdom, Donovan worked with writer-producers Stock, Aitken and Waterman, who were responsible for his musical output.[28] According to Donovan, Mushroom Records devised the idea for his duet with Minogue, 'Especially For You', in order to capitalize on both singers' musical success and their on-screen and off-screen relationship, as well as to try to secure the coveted Christmas number one position in the UK.[29] When his relationship with Minogue ended, his manager and the managing director of his record label were on the spot to console him.[30] As his fame increases, Donovan introduces other people who were responsible for his career, including his agent and concert producers and promoters with whom he worked.[31] Ultimately, Donovan summarizes his celebrity at its peak thus:

> My success was due to a combination of factors – the popularity of *Neighbours*, the fact that I was accessibly but not threateningly good-looking, and a team of highly skilled producers.[32]

Donovan's memoirs make clear the disjunction between, on the one hand, who he really was, how he thought about himself and what he was interested in, and, on the other hand, his celebrity persona. Having established himself as a soap opera actor and a pop star, Donovan wanted to try to reposition himself as a serious rock musician, which was more consistent with his own personal preferences. However, his manager thought the natural progression for Donovan, at that point in his

[22] *Ibid.*, p. 95. [23] *Ibid.*, pp. 70–1. [24] *Ibid.*, p. 90. [25] *Ibid.*, pp. 91–2.
[26] *Ibid.*, pp. 115–20. [27] *Ibid.*, p. 120. [28] *Ibid.*, pp. 122–3.
[29] *Ibid.*, pp. 126–7. Cruelly, Cliff Richard's 'Mistletoe and Wine' prevented this song from taking the coveted Christmas number one position in the UK singles chart in 1988. It did manage to top the charts for three weeks in January 1989.
[30] *Ibid.*, p. 140. [31] *Ibid.*, p. 150. [32] *Ibid.*, p. 147.

career, was to move into musical theatre.[33] Reflecting upon this period of his career, Donovan observed that:

> I didn't want to be the squeaky-clean boy-next-door any more – for I wasn't that person in real life. I was a dope-smoking twenty-two-year old who in his spare time liked to party.[34]

In *not* exploring how reputations are created and in not recognizing the extent to which reputations can be self-conscious commodities created by or contributed to by many people, defamation law arguably limits its own efficacy in protecting celebrities' reputations. Defamation law proceeds on the implicit assumption that a celebrity's reputation is an extension or an amplification of his or her underlying self. It does not countenance the possibility that a celebrity's professional reputation might be substantially or wholly different from his or her personal reputation. By overlooking the processes by which a person's reputation can be commercialized and propertized, defamation law is unable or unwilling to recognize that it might be the case that a celebrity's public profile differs markedly, if not completely, from the view formed by people who actually interact with him or her. If the reality of a celebrity's reputation is that it is complex, commodified and comprised of disparate or discrete elements, the question arises as to what reputation is in fact protected and vindicated in a defamation trial. Is it the whole of the plaintiff's reputation or only some aspects of it? How real then is the reputation protected by defamation law?

4 The dynamic nature of reputation

There is another aspect of defamation law that is largely unexamined but warrants attention, namely the nature of the interest in reputation. Is it static or dynamic? Again, defamation law is not overly reflective about this issue. Defamation law views itself as a means by which reputations can be altered. Thus, if a person has enjoyed an undeserved good reputation and the defendant tells the truth about him or her, the defendant commits no wrong and defamation law operates to recalibrate that person's reputation down to the lower level at which it belongs.[35] Given that reputation is undertheorized, it is unsurprising that defamation law does not provide a fuller account of how reputations can and do change. Indeed, to the extent that it theorizes the nature of reputation, defamation law

[33] *Ibid.*, pp. 156–7. [34] *Ibid.*, p. 156.

[35] *M'Pherson* v. *Daniels* (1829) 109 ER 448, 451 (Littledale J); *Rofe* v. *Smith's Newspapers Ltd* (1924) 25 SR(NSW) 4, 21–2 (Street ACJ); George, *Defamation Law in Australia*, [19.1].

characterizes reputation as a relatively stable interest. For example, in *Dingle* v. *Associated Newspapers Ltd*, Holroyd Pearce LJ stated that:

> A man's reputation in the sense in which the word is used in civil or criminal courts does not alter daily as good or bad deeds are ascribed to him. It is the judgment of his fellows on his general life over a period of time.[36]

Implicit in this reasoning is an acceptance that reputation as protected in the courtroom might differ from reputation experienced outside the courtroom. His Lordship's observations here also recognize that reputations outside the courtroom can change markedly in a short period of time but suggests that the reputations with which defamation law is concerned are the stable, underlying, enduring ones. Again, this seems to indicate that defamation law is implicitly concerned with protecting and vindicating some, not all, reputations, or some, not all, aspects of reputation. This is reinforced by Lord Denning's observations in *Plato Films Ltd* v. *Speidel* to the effect that the reputation which defamation law should protect is that

> which is built upon the estimate of those who know him. No other reputation is of any worth. The law can take no notice of a reputation which has no foundation except the gossip and rumour of busybodies who do not know the man.[37]

The protection afforded by defamation law to reputations as they exist and are experienced outside the courtroom then might be limited in its efficacy.

A consideration of reputation as celebrity can provide a useful counterpoint. Post's tripartite taxonomy of reputational interests – reputation as property; reputation as honour; and reputation as dignity – are all founded upon the notion that a good reputation is an economic and a social good, that it is deserved, either as a product of one's labour, a consequence of one's social standing or an aspect of an individual's innate dignity. Yet, in contemporary media culture, an individual can acquire a widespread and lucrative profile readily, often without the need for a particular skill or the exertion of labour. International television franchises have been established around formats that allow ordinary people to be transformed into celebrities overnight. Social media platforms allow users to create and disseminate content, thereby facilitating users' development of their own profiles. A reputation can be created through the media. Such a reputation can then be viewed as a media construct – reputation as celebrity. The self-referential nature of such a reputation was recognized early in the academic literature on celebrity: as Daniel Boorstin famously defined it, '[t]he celebrity is a person who is known for

36 *Dingle* v. *Associated Newspapers Ltd* [1961] 2 QB 162, 181.
37 *Plato Films Ltd* v. *Speidel* [1961] AC 1090, 1138.

his well-knownness'.[38] The media play a crucial role in creating and sustaining this type of celebrity. Another characteristic of celebrity as a form of reputation is that it is often fleeting and ephemeral. Just as celebrity can be rapidly acquired or created, it can also be rapidly lost. The fact that some reputations can be lightly acquired and lightly dispensed with challenges the assumptions about the importance defamation law ordinarily ascribes to a good reputation. It also questions the stability of reputation as a legal interest and suggests that reputation might be more dynamic than defamation law allows.

The dynamism of celebrity is illustrated by Donovan's account of his career. Donovan's memoirs trace the development of his celebrity, from its initial phase from 1986 to 1989 as a soap opera actor, then his transition in 1988 to being a pop singer. They chart the internationalization and intensification of his fame, culminating in his status as the biggest-selling musical artist in the United Kingdom in 1989.[39] They follow his progression into musical theatre. Following the release of his second album, *Between the Lines*, which had not been as successful as his debut album, *Ten Good Reasons*, Donovan's manager began exploring other opportunities. The major one that presented itself was the leading role in a revival of *Joseph and the Amazing Technicolor Dreamcoat*. In his memoirs, Donovan discusses this period thus:

> And yet, even though my career as a pop singer was going well, Richard [Donovan's manager] was starting to think ahead of the game. He realised how fickle the music industry was and knew that with the type of music I was producing and the image I was projecting, I didn't have long in that world. My appeal lay with the teenage girl market and, as lucrative as that could be, he was only too aware of the fact that in time they would come of age and move on to something else. He didn't want me to fade out of the charts, he wanted me to capitalise on my success and use it as a bargaining tool to get me somewhere else.[40]

This is not the only reference in Donovan's memoirs to the fickleness of fame and not the only recognition of the possibility of his celebrity being 'in danger of having a very short shelf-life'.[41] As shall be seen, his memoirs also chart the steep decline in his popularity and profile after his success in his libel proceedings against *The Face*. What emerges clearly, though, from Donovan's memoirs, is the variability of his celebrity throughout his career.

No reputation is entirely static; every reputation changes over time as the person or entity interacts with others. The issue then is how slowly

[38] D. Boorstin, *The Image: A Guide to Pseudo-Events in America* (New York: Vintage Books, 1992), p. 57.

[39] Donovan, *Between the Lines*, p. 146. [40] *Ibid.*, pp. 155–6. [41] *Ibid.*, p. 146.

or rapidly reputations change. Some reputations change little over time; some are more dynamic. There is, of course, no single trajectory for celebrity reputations. Many celebrity reputations change more rapidly than those of private individuals, or the changes are more noticeable because of their prominence. For a celebrity like Jason Donovan, his public profile had to change to keep his fans engaged and entertained, to mirror their tastes, to exploit opportunities available to him while they lasted, to negotiate changes in tastes. The changes to Donovan's celebrity then were motivated in part by Donovan's own interests and by his perception of his fans' and his potential audiences' interests. His celebrity was predicated upon an interdependence of his own interests and those of his fans and his potential audiences. Few celebrities, though, are able to sustain their public profiles for long periods of time; few are able to negotiate, defy or transcend changes in taste. Many celebrities will, like Donovan, have periods of time during which they are popular, sometimes immensely so. Their popularity wanes with periodic resurgences or revivals or transmutations. The management of a celebrity's public profile then can involve the sometimes conscious construction of a narrative that seeks to integrate and explain these fluctuations in prominence.

Celebrities can and do sue for defamation and, as Donovan demonstrates, do so successfully (or, at least, they win in court). If the reality of a celebrity's reputation is that it is dynamic and often ephemeral, though, and defamation law privileges stable reputations, how useful then is defamation law as a means of protecting and vindicating a celebrity's reputation (and managing a celebrity's public profile), particularly when the time delay between the allegedly defamatory publication and the trial itself is not uncommonly several years when the celebrity's prominence might already have begun to fade?

5 The role of audiences

A celebrity needs an audience. There is no fame without fans. Indeed, a celebrity needs, and successful ones have, multiple audiences. For any given celebrity, there is no single, monolithic, undifferentiated audience. There are necessarily multiple, sometimes overlapping, audiences, each with their own interests, preferences and desires. A celebrity's relationship with his or her audiences, actual and potential, is complex, dynamic and interdependent, as Donovan's example demonstrates. This reality contrasts sharply with defamation law's reductive approach to a plaintiff's interaction with his or her hypothetical audience, 'the ordinary, reasonable reader'. The example of Donovan's celebrity illustrates starkly the way that defamation law, as a strategy for protecting reputation, can cut across the other diverse strategies for cultivating, targeting, managing and negotiating a celebrity's various audiences. This disparity between the principles of defamation law and the reality of celebrity reputations suggests that a defamation suit may not be a very effective strategy for attempting to control or manage a reputation.

It is useful to start by examining defamation law's own account of the relationship between the plaintiff and 'the ordinary, reasonable reader'. Defamation is fundamentally a relational tort, protecting a relational interest. Reputation, being in essence what other people think of the plaintiff,[42] posits a relationship between the plaintiff and third parties. Post's concepts of reputation identify the market as the medium through which reputation as property occurs, with the participants in the market being the third parties forming a view about the plaintiff, and society as the medium through which reputation as honour and dignity occur, with members of that society being the third parties forming a view about the plaintiff. The concept of reputation as celebrity rests upon the notion that the media are the mechanism by which the plaintiff is connected to the audience, which forms its opinion about the plaintiff's reputation. At this level of abstraction, the concepts of 'the market', 'society' and 'the media' seem monolithic, homogeneous and undifferentiated. This is consistent with the principles of defamation law, which are placed on the objective footing of reasonableness and purport to be of universal application, but embody an artificial view of how reputations are in fact experienced.

Notwithstanding the fact that different people acting reasonably can understand the same matter to mean different things, defamation law has long proceeded on the basis that there is a single meaning to be ascribed to the published matter, which would be the sense in which the ordinary, reasonable reader would understand it.[43] Furthermore, whether that meaning was defamatory is assessed by reference to whether the ordinary, reasonable reader would tend to think less of the plaintiff or would otherwise be led to shun and avoid the plaintiff or view the plaintiff in a ridiculous light[44] and, in assessing this, a uniform

[42] *Plato Films Ltd* v. *Speidel* [1961] AC 1090, 1138 (Lord Denning).

[43] *Slim* v. *Daily Telegraph Ltd* [1968] 2 QB 157, 171–2 (Diplock LJ); *Reader's Digest Services Pty Ltd* v. *Lamb* (1982) 150 CLR 500, 506 (Brennan J); *Ajinomoto Sweeteners SAS* v. *Asda Stores Ltd* [2011] QB 497, 502 (Sedley LJ).

[44] *Radio 2UE Sydney Pty Ltd* v. *Chesterton* (2009) 238 CLR 460, 466–7 (French CJ, Gummow, Kiefel and Bell JJ).

moral or social standard is applied.[45] As the hypothetical referee by which defamatory meaning is assessed, the ordinary, reasonable reader is imbued with a range of characteristics. The ordinary reasonable reader:

> is a person of fair, average intelligence . . . who is neither perverse . . . nor morbid or suspicious of mind . . . nor avid for scandal . . . This ordinary reasonable reader does not . . . live in an ivory tower. He can, and does, read between the lines, in the light of his general knowledge and experience of worldly affairs . . . [T]he ordinary, reasonable reader is a layman, not a lawyer, and . . . his capacity for implication is much greater than that of the lawyer.[46]

The construction of the 'ordinary, reasonable reader' as a monolithic, objective standard erases the actual diversity of potential responses to the levelling of a defamatory allegation against a plaintiff.

Donovan's experience of his fame demonstrates the complex reality of a celebrity's audiences in contrast to the reductive approach of defamation law. There was no single audience for Donovan's celebrity. As with many celebrities with an international profile, Donovan's audience was potentially people of all ages across the world. The reality, of course, was that his principal audience were pre-teen and teenage girls. Other audiences might have been and, as shall be seen, were interested in Donovan's career but young girls were the principal audience to which his acting and singing career was directed. In his memoirs, Donovan makes clear that he and those responsible for developing and managing his career were acutely aware that this was his target audience[47] and that the needs and expectations of that audience had to be satisfied. He describes 'Jason-mania', where '[g]irls screamed, cried and fainted' with ambulances on standby.[48] The catering for his young audiences went further:

> Only too aware of how young this market was, those shows were staged for late afternoons so that the kids could be home in bed on time, and [the promoter] persuaded them to turn up with the promise of free soft drinks and burgers.[49]

When discussing his transition from pop music into musical theatre, Donovan identifies the predicted response of his principal audience as the crucial determinant. His teenage fans would not accept his transition to a serious rock musician, which was his own personal preference, but

45 *Reader's Digest Services Pty Ltd* v. *Lamb* (1982) 150 CLR 500, 506 (Brennan J).

46 *Farquhar* v. *Bottom* [1980] 2 NSWLR 380, 386 (Hunt J) (references omitted). See also *Amalgamated Television Services Pty Ltd* v. *Marsden* (1998) 43 NSWLR 158, 165 (Hunt CJ at CL).

47 Donovan, *Between the Lines*, pp. 136–7 and 155–6.

48 *Ibid.*, p. 137. 49 *Ibid.*, pp. 136–7.

could accept a less threatening, less commercially risky transition into a musical theatre performer.[50]

The audiences for a celebrity are not always the ones he or she consciously targets and cultivates. Audiences can decide to appropriate a celebrity for themselves, to ascribe their own meaning and value to that celebrity, reinforcing the agency of the audiences in the creation of celebrity. In Donovan's case, he became popular amongst gay men. This was not an audience he had consciously sought. It was an audience that was alienated by Donovan's decision to sue *The Face*. Tellingly, Donovan's memoirs minimize references to the specific impact of his trial on his appeal to gay men. The impact was immediate and vocal: it began with protesters outside the courtroom.[51] Donovan did not immediately grasp the need to rehabilitate his reputation with this audience. His desire to distance himself from the issues in the trial led him to turn down the role of one of the drag queens in the film *The Adventures of Priscilla, Queen of the Desert*, which was ultimately played by fellow *Neighbours* alumnus, Guy Pearce.[52] This opportunity might have led to greater career success for Donovan, providing him with an entry into Hollywood film-making, as it did for Pearce. It might also have helped Donovan more readily rehabilitate his reputation in the eyes of his gay fans. Subsequently, Donovan did try to re-engage his gay audience, hosting events at gay nightclubs[53] and giving interviews to the gay press.[54] Notwithstanding his attempts, Donovan was never really able to reclaim this audience.

The 'ordinary, reasonable reader' seeks to embody a uniform reaction to the plaintiff yet, for a celebrity like Donovan, there was no such uniform response. His celebrity was consciously cultivated so as to engage a particular audience. Obviously, not every member of that target audience was engaged. Equally, other people who were outside of that target audience might have been fans, notwithstanding the fact that the efforts to promote Donovan might not have been directed to those people. The reality of diverse audiences for a celebrity, with diverse reactions – such as engaged fandom, mild interest, indifference or a complete lack of awareness – contrasts with the artificial, universal response of 'the ordinary, reasonable reader' in defamation law. Defamation law proceeds

[50] *Ibid.*, pp. 155–6.
[51] A. Mitchell, 'Gays Turn on Jason', *Sun Herald* (Sydney), 29 November 1992, p. 28.
[52] Donovan, *Between the Lines*, pp. 212–13.
[53] B. Corbett, 'Jase Dressed for Gay Abuse Contest', *Daily Telegraph* (Sydney), 29 May 1996, p. 13.
[54] M. Gow, 'In Bed with Jason', *(Not Only) Blue* (Sydney), November 1996, p. 44.

on the basis that the plaintiff already has a single, captive audience. Celebrity is in fact dependent upon the identification and exploitation of new audiences, while cultivating, consolidating and maintaining existing ones.

A focus on the audiences for a celebrity can also help illuminate how celebrity is produced and developed. On one view, celebrity is a form of property, a commodification of an individual's persona, or some aspects of it. These need not be central aspects of the individual's persona. So commodified, celebrity may have a lot or only a little to do with the actual person upon whom it is dependent, as Donovan discovered. Part of the purpose then of celebrity is to maximize the return on it from potential, diverse audiences while it lasts, which, as Donovan recognizes, might not be long for some forms of celebrity. Yet celebrity should not be conceived of in purely economic terms and it does not simply entail the economic exploitation of audiences. Celebrity is not merely property and the dynamics that produce it are nuanced. Audiences can be engaged in the production and development of celebrity. A celebrity like Donovan does not simply lay before his target audiences his acting or his music and ask them to consume or to reject it. Part of the process involves predicting what will and will not be acceptable to fans, as well as cultivating or moulding the tastes of fans. In turn, fans will signal their reactions back to the celebrity. A celebrity wanting to maintain his or her fame will seek to respond to and accommodate the reactions of fans. Celebrity then is not produced or developed unilaterally. There is an important, dynamic interdependence between the celebrity and his or her audiences, which is responsible for creating and sustaining the celebrity. So produced, celebrity is not purely economic, but can also be a distinct cultural artefact with its own discursive power. The celebrity himself or herself is not wholly responsible for this and is not totally in control of it. Audiences have control over celebrity. They can give value and meaning to celebrity, including value and meaning not ascribed to or even desired by the celebrity himself or herself. This is clear from Donovan's example: Donovan's celebrity was clearly directed at young girls, yet Donovan acquired, not intentionally, a significant gay following. It is perhaps unsurprising – Donovan was young, handsome and clean-cut and made infectious pop music. Donovan's celebrity demonstrates that there can be divergent audiences for the same celebrity, some of which are cultivated, some of which are not, each of which imbues the celebrity with their own meanings and expectations. Managing a celebrity with divergent audiences and differing expectations, then, becomes a difficult task, as Donovan discovered.

6 The efficacy of defamation in protecting reputation and the role of the defamation trial

Whether a defamation suit is in fact an effective means of managing a celebrity reputation and competing audience expectations is ultimately the question that needs to be asked. Donovan's defamation trial and its aftermath should cause celebrities considering suing for this cause of action to think carefully before proceeding. Donovan's trial, its aftermath and his own reflections upon its impact on his celebrity in his memoirs highlight the disparity between the claims that defamation law makes for itself about its effectiveness in protecting reputations and the actuality and raises questions about the efficacy of defamation proceedings as a strategy for managing celebrity reputation.

The implicit justification defamation law provides for itself is that it facilitates the protection of reputation. Like other torts, defamation is concerned with compensating plaintiffs for harm unlawfully done to the legal interest it protects, namely reputation.[55] The compensatory impulse of tort law, though, takes on a particular form in relation to defamation, reflecting the impossibility of precisely compensating a plaintiff for a damaged reputation in monetary terms, because money and reputation are incommensurable. Compensating a plaintiff by an award of damages for defamation serves the additional purposes of being 'a vindication of the plaintiff to the public and as consolation to him of a wrong done'.[56] Like other torts, defamation law seeks to adjudicate reputations on a final, once-and-for-all basis. The dynamic nature of reputation has already been remarked upon, yet defamation law proceeds on the basis that a verdict of substantial damages to the plaintiff at the end of a trial, calculated on a once-and-for-all basis, comprehending all past and future losses, allowing the plaintiff to 'nail the lie' or to be able to point to the baselessness of the charge levelled against him or her, will provide a complete remedy.[57] This gives primacy then to the defamation trial as the means of securing the protection and vindication of a plaintiff's damaged reputation. In its own terms, defamation law necessarily assumes the efficacy of its own determinations.

It is instructive to examine the stated motives of litigants who sue for defamation to compare and contrast these reasons with the principled

[55] *Uren* v. *John Fairfax & Sons Pty Ltd* (1966) 118 CLR 119, 149 (Windeyer J).

[56] *Ibid.*, 150 (Windeyer J). See also *Carson* v. *John Fairfax & Sons Ltd* (1993) 178 CLR 44, 60–1 (Mason CJ, Deane, Dawson and Gaudron JJ); *Rogers* v. *Nationwide News Pty Ltd* (2003) 216 CLR 327, 347–9 (Hayne J).

[57] *Australian Consolidated Press Ltd* v. *Uren* (1966) 117 CLR 185, 205 (Windeyer J); *Rigby* v. *Associated Newspapers Ltd (No 2)* [1969] 1 NSWR 729, 743; *Broome* v. *Cassell & Co Ltd* [1972] AC 1027, 1071 (Lord Hailsham of Marylebone LC).

rationale of defamation law. In his memoirs, Donovan records the complex reasons why he pursued his libel proceedings against *The Face*. In significant measure, he was concerned to 'nail the lie'.[58] He insists that the imputation of homosexuality was not the problem, as he did not view it as insulting, but rather the imputation that he had lied about his sexual orientation.[59] Donovan was also concerned that public discussion of his sexuality intruded upon his privacy.[60] He reflected, though, that he might have invited attention and heightened scrutiny by lying to the media about his earlier relationship with Kylie Minogue.[61] Donovan's decision to sue was ultimately his own but there was input from those supporting and advising him. Donovan states that he was not concerned with being awarded damages, but those around him 'huffed and puffed' about the damage to his career and emphasized Donovan's entitlement to remuneration for future loss of income.[62] Those who were dependent upon his celebrity for their own economic well-being were more concerned, according to Donovan's account, with the economic impact of *The Face* article than he was.

Donovan also indicates that suing *The Face* was a step not taken lightly and that other non-litigious means of protecting and managing his reputation were first taken. He claims that he did not object to the circulation of rumours about his sexuality because there was effectively nothing that he could do to stop mere rumours, but that the posters were a step too far, particularly given their prominent placement around the West End. When he and his friends took down the posters themselves, even more went up to replace them. Donovan realized that FROCS, as an underground group, would be difficult to sue.[63] *The Face* magazine gave the posters, and therefore the rumours, a wider prominence than they otherwise would have had. It also presented the issue in the form of a 'straightforward piece of reportage'; it did not, in Donovan's view, sufficiently disavow the suggestion that he was gay.[64] For these reasons, then, Donovan decided to sue, and decided to sue *The Face*.

The lived experience of celebrity reputations and their encounters with defamation law casts doubt upon the efficacy of defamation law in protecting and vindicating reputations. Tellingly, Donovan's chapter dealing with the aftermath of his libel proceedings against *The Face* is called 'Close Every Door to Me' – a play on one of the more famous songs from *Joseph and the Amazing Technicolor Dreamcoat*. The title encapsulates his actual experience following his defamation case, which was the opposite of what the principles of defamation law suggested should happen.

[58] Donovan, *Between the Lines*, pp. 174 and 178. [59] *Ibid.*, p. 174. [60] *Ibid.*, p. 173.
[61] *Ibid.*, p. 174. [62] *Ibid.*, p. 186. [63] *Ibid.*, p. 175. [64] *Ibid.*, p. 178.

Donovan describes how, after his success in court, he was turned away from nightclubs, asked to leave clothes shops, spat at in the street and had his car damaged.[65] He felt that he had become 'the social pariah of London, the person it seemed that everyone wanted to hate'.[66] He recognized the 'irony' that by suing to protect his reputation he in fact ruined it.[67] As Donovan describes it:

> By taking on *The Face* all I had ever set out to do was to restore my reputation and stand up for myself, and at the time I believed that was the right thing to do, but in the days that followed the verdict it quickly became clear that I had made the biggest mistake of my life and had completely misjudged the situation.[68]

Reflecting on his reasons for suing and the effect of the trial on his reputation, Donovan observes:

> I had been vindicated in the eyes of the law, but for me it was a hollow victory. I had never wanted things to go that far as it was; all I had ever set out to do was to get an apology from the magazine, a public acknowledgement that I was neither a liar nor a hypocrite.[69]

Beyond the potential disparity between the stated purpose and the actual effect of a defamation trial on a celebrity's reputation, there is the additional point that the defamation trial itself – the very fact of it, the attendant media coverage, its outcome and its aftermath – become part of the celebrity's reputation. In seeking to protect and vindicate a plaintiff's reputation, a defamation trial publicizes the defamatory allegations against a plaintiff, often to a much wider audience than the original publication. For a celebrity, his or her defamation trial is newsworthy and the publicity cements both the allegations and the celebrity's denial of them as part of the celebrity's reputation. As Donovan notes, his defamation trial received extensive international media coverage, reflecting the international reach of his celebrity.[70] The verdict in the case was not the end of the trial. Because reputation is a dynamic interest, Donovan's defamation trial became integrated into his reputation. In the succeeding two decades, no profile of Donovan has been complete without reference to it. As recently as 2012, when the Australian *Good Weekend* magazine profiled Donovan leading up to his debut as a judge on reality television programme *I Will Survive* (a talent contest to find a male performer to feature in the Broadway production of *The Adventures of Priscilla, Queen of the Desert*), journalist Jack Marx focused his piece around Donovan's libel proceedings against *The Face* and its adverse

[65] *Ibid.*, p. 188. [66] *Ibid.* [67] *Ibid.* [68] *Ibid.*, p. 185.
[69] *Ibid.*, p. 184. [70] *Ibid.*, p. 183.

impact on his celebrity.[71] This has been a consistent theme of media coverage of Donovan's career since his victory against the magazine.[72] According to the implicit account of defamation law, the defamation trial is the venue at which a plaintiff's reputation is adjudicated upon, a formal and neutral occasion on which competing views on a plaintiff's reputation are presented. The reality for a celebrity plaintiff is that his or her defamation trial is not a detached, objective event at which his or her reputation is finally settled but rather another event in the dynamic narrative of a celebrity life.

7 Rebuilding reputations: some concluding thoughts

Analysing how Donovan's celebrity was created, finessed then damaged, the variable effect of Donovan's success in his defamation proceedings and its impact on his audiences, the ways in which Donovan's celebrity has transformed over his career and how Donovan himself reflects upon these issues in his memoirs (these being another commercial extension of his reputation), provides insights into the complexity of reputation and celebrity in legal and non-legal contexts. It reinforces that defamation law is only one of many strategies available to a celebrity for the purpose of protecting and managing his or her public profile. Indeed, defamation law may be one of the least efficacious means of securing these ends.

There are other means available to celebrities to protect and manage their reputations. The celebrity memoir is one of them. The celebrity memoir can serve multiple functions. It can act as a (self-selected) record of the celebrity's public and sometimes private life. It can help construct or develop a narrative of a celebrity's life. It can integrate or obscure or minimize or highlight aspects of a celebrity's life. It can simultaneously perform the function of reflecting upon celebrity and participating in its

[71] J. Marx, 'Jason's Technicolour Life', Good Weekend, *Sydney Morning Herald*, 4 August 2012, p. 32.

[72] See, e.g., P. Wilmoth, 'Jason, Seriously', Agenda, *Sunday Age* (Melbourne), 23 April 1995, p. 1; V. Trioli, 'Fallen Idol', *Age* (Melbourne), 8 June 1996, p. 21; S. Hattenstone, 'Prisoner of his Fame', *Guardian*, 5 October 1996, p. 6; W. Leith, 'Jason Donovan: The Amazing Technicolour Nightmare', *Observer*, 17 November 1996, p. 6; C. Jardine, 'Narcissism Drove Me to Drugs Hell', *Sun Herald* (Sydney), 3 May 1998, p. 56; C. Manly, 'Jason is a New Man', *Sunday Telegraph* (Sydney), 18 April 1999, p. 24; S. Vincent, 'Pills and Soap', *Guardian*, 22 May 1999, p. 24; C. Sullivan, 'Jason Gets Sorted', *Guardian*, 19 October 2000, p. 6; M. Curtis and S. Wilson, 'Wise Guy – Jason Donovan Earns a Little Respect – Don't Look Back in Anger', *Sunday Telegraph* (Sydney), 4 May 2003, p. 1; D. Ross, 'Fame and Misfortune', *Independent*, 12 January 2004, p. 2; R. Hardy, 'Love and Redemption for the Boy Next Door', *Daily Telegraph* (Sydney), 24 January 2004, p. 4; S. Button, 'Jason Donovan – "I Don't Regret my Career Going Off the Rails"', *Sunday Mirror*, 1 February 2004, p. 38.

production, reinforcement and development. It produces a rich resource for how the celebrity thinks about his or her own public life. It is an opportunity for reputation management that is ordinarily available only to the famous. It serves as a reminder of how limited and artificial the protection of defamation law is in the face of contemporary celebrity.

6 Dramatic copyright and the 'Disneyfication' of theatre space

*Brent Salter and Kathy Bowrey**

1 Introduction

The existing legal theorization of theatre is preoccupied with discussion of the rights of authors to texts and, in particular, the competing ownership claims of playwrights, directors and producers. This focus draws our attention away from consideration of a much more radical change in the entertainment landscape – the 'Disneyfication' of theatrical experience. Disneyfication refers to a shift in the economics of the theatre. The new focus of economic value is not the production of a play and 'bums on seats', but the creation of an entertainment precinct and spectacle that draws in the audience to participate in much more extensive consumer relationships. Critiques of this Disneyfication of theatre arose in the USA in the 1990s. This chapter reflects on concerns about Disneyfication against the backdrop of contemporary Australian theatre. In exploring the Australian experience, we discuss structural impediments to global Disneyfication. However, we also expose the limits of copyright law in supporting the aspirations of theatre companies and theatre practitioners today.

2 The Disneyfication of US theatre

Over the past twenty years, there has been considerable controversy, particularly in US theatre literature,[1] that stems from the dynamics related

* We would like to thank and acknowledge a number of professionals who agreed to be interviewed to help us explore the contemporary Australian theatre landscape, including: Anthony Blair (Camerons' Management), Jo Dyer (Sydney Theatre Company), Angela Keefe (formerly Australian Writers' Guild), John Montgomery (formerly Events NSW), Jacqueline Elaine (Australian Writers' Guild) and Tom Wright (formerly Sydney Theatre Company). Thanks also to Amy Kapczynski, Yale Law School.

[1] See, e.g., S. Nelson, 'Broadway and the Beast: Disney Comes to Times Square' (1995) 39 *Drama Review* 71; J. Bell, 'Disney's Times Square: The New American Community Theatre' (1998) 42 *Drama Review* 26; M. Sussman, 'New York's Facelift' (1998) 42 *Drama Review* 34; E. L. Wollman, 'The Economic Development of the "New"

to the Disneyfication of New York's Times Square in the early 1990s, when the Disney Corporation took over theatre spaces and began rejuvenating the theatre district. This transformation was more than a New York City sanctioned theatre development. It was an urban renewal project. Rather than being about producing plays for theatregoers, it was about creating a safe and secure entertainment experience for consumers, supporting Disney's vertical integration into theatre spectacles as they had done so successfully with their television, film, theme park and merchandising interests in the past.

The central focus of Disney's integration into the theatrical community of New York was the restoration of the New Amsterdam Theatre on 42nd Street – the ninety-year-old 'Art Nouveau symbol of the street's halcyon days'.[2] The deal the City afforded to Disney, not offered to 'old-line' Broadway powers including the Shuberts and the Nederlanders, caused the greatest consternation in the community.[3] The arrangement rekindled long-standing anxieties over earlier special government deals afforded to the Disney Corporation, originating with the establishment of the first Florida theme park at Reedy Creek in the 1960s.[4] Disney spent approximately US$8 million of its own money renovating the theatre, with the State of New York and the City lending another US$21 million at 3 per cent interest in return for 2 per cent of the gross ticket receipts.[5] The leases provided Disney with exclusive use of the theatre for forty-nine years, which Mayor Giuliani described at the time as the vehicle to 'jump start' the Times Square redevelopment.[6]

Apart from the favourable leasing arrangements, Disney demanded the social transformation of Times Square.[7] For over a century, Times Square and the surrounding theatre precinct was arguably New York's most important entertainment district, with its cluster of theatres, bars

Times Square and its Impact on the Broadway Musical' (2002) 20 *American Music* 445; M. Wickstrom, 'Commodities, Mimesis, and *The Lion King*: Retail Theater of the 1990s' (1999) 51 *Theatre Journal* 285; S. Bennett, 'Theatre/Tourism' (2006) 57 *Theatre Journal* 407; F. Roost, 'Synergy City: How Times Square and Celebration are Integrated into Disney's Marketing Cycle', in M. Budd and M. Kirsch (eds), *Rethinking Disney: Private Control, Public Dimensions* (Middletown, CT: Wesleyan University Press, 2005).

2 Nelson, 'Broadway and the Beast', 72. 3 *Ibid.*

4 This included exemption from planning laws, taxes and allowing Disney to operate its own 'public' utilities including fire, policing, telecommunications and power. See C. Hiaasen, *Team Rodent: How Disney Devours the World* (New York: Random House, 1998), pp. 25–37; A. Bryman, *The Disneyization of Society* (London: Sage Publications, 2004), pp. 138–40.

5 Nelson, 'Broadway and the Beast', 72.

6 See Wickstrom, 'Commodities, Mimesis, and *The Lion King*'; Wollman, 'The Economic Development of the "New" Times Square and its Impact on the Broadway Musical'.

7 See Nelson, 'Broadway and the Beast'; Bell, 'Disney's Times Square'; Sussman, 'New York's Facelift'; Roost, 'Synergy City'.

and restaurants. By the 1970s, the district was also the hub of prostitution and other vices. With the introduction of television in the second half of the century, and the suburbanization of the City's middle class, live performances were replaced by movies, many of which were pornographic. Real estate redevelopment in the 1980s collapsed. Robert Styne, an architect previously associated with Disney projects, was asked to redevelop the precinct with several broad transformation objectives in mind including the restoration of the 42nd Street theatres, the creation of an entertainment district and the resurrection of buildings in Times Square. The corporatization of public space continued to develop after the New Amsterdam was rebuilt, with other conglomerates soon moving into the area.[8]

Commentators critical of the transformation that has taken place over the past twenty years often refer to the sanitization of the city as a homogenization of the space, pointing to a new and safely controlled environment that has emerged as a consequence of the arrival of corporations like Disney.[9] Homogenization has also been seen as a strategic public policy initiative. This initiative includes regulation of the adult entertainment industry by banning the concentration of adult entertainment stores in the area and the development of a business improvement district (BID) – a not-for-profit entity of local businesses that hire security guards to police the area and cleanse the streets of the unwanted.

In turn, it has been argued that as this process of homogenization takes place Disney begins to create an 'imagined' community by way of cultural anaesthesia concerning the theatre history of the precinct.[10] The company selectively highlights aspects of New York's exciting and diversified past, generating nostalgia for the halcyon days of the 1920s theatre district and the entrepreneurial spirit of the pioneering producers of Broadway.[11] There is an appeal to this dangerous, exciting, entrepreneurial world, but it is represented within the confines of this new homogenized, controlled and surveilled commercial space. It exemplifies what Mark Sussman refers to as 'safe excess', 'the "static festival", when the city begins to feel like an animated film set or the "New York" experience at the theme

[8] See Roost, 'Synergy City'. [9] See, e.g., Sussman, 'New York's Facelift'.

[10] *Ibid.*, p. 39; S. Zukin, *Landscapes of Power: From Detroit to Disney World* (Berkeley, CA: University of California Press, 1993), p. 22; Wollman, 'The Economic Development of the "New" Times Square', citing A. Feldman, 'From Desert Storm to Rodney King: On Cultural Anaesthesia' in C. N. Seremetakis, *The Senses Still: Perception and Memory as Material Culture in Modernity* (Boulder, CO: Westview Press, 1994).

[11] C. Boyer, 'Cities for Sale', in M. Sorkin (ed.), *Variations on a Theme Park: The New American City and the End of Public Space* (New York: Farrar, Straus and Giroux, 1992), p. 199.

park'.[12] This critical transformation creates a hyper-real world, exhibiting well-worn Disney archetypes of the American dream and conservative family values.[13] This is an imaginary modern cityscape, devoid of human detritus.

Audience research shows that Disney culture is associated with distinctly Americanized *and* more universal or global values.[14] With the Disney recreation of Times Square comes the transformation of the people visiting this space – no longer local audiences for discrete shows, but global consumers who come to experience the precinct.[15] An 'architecture of merchandising'[16] is reinforced by Disney through a strategy of synergy – changing the experience to one of seeing a play to one of buying into the franchise world.[17] This Disney concept, used for many years and now applied to its theatrical practice, is the notion of selling a particular product and integrating it into its broader web of properties and commercial opportunities.[18]

One of Disney's most successful theatrical synergistic strategies has involved *The Lion King*:

> Synergy allows a company to sell itself along with any product it hawks. The Broadway version of *The Lion King*, for example, can be mentioned in any Disney film, advertised on any Disney radio station, or mentioned on any one of Disney's television programs. In 1999 the musical was central to the plot of an episode of the now-defunct ABC series *Sports Night*, in which an overworked character is given free tickets to a matinee performance of the show; she reluctantly attends and is miraculously rejuvenated by the power of the production. In keeping with the application of synergy to all products, Disney musicals now help to advertise one another. As in the film version, the Broadway version of *The Lion King* features overt references to *Beauty and the Beast*, which is conveniently playing a few blocks north.
>
> The application of business synergy to a Broadway production helps explain why so many properties are currently making their way to Broadway after having become known worldwide as popular films.[19]

12 Sussman, 'New York's Facelift', 37.

13 J. Wasko, *Understanding Disney* (Cambridge: Polity Press, 2001), pp. 116–22.

14 J. Wasko, M. Phillips and E. R. Meehan, *Dazzled By Disney? The Global Disney Audiences Project* (Leicester University Press, 2001), pp. 338–40.

15 Wickstrom, 'Commodities, Mimesis, and *The Lion King*', citing J. Holusha, 'Exploiting the Fame of Times Square,' *New York Times*, 29 October 1997, p. 10; D. Martin, 'Its Greeks Bearing Glitz, Disney Parades a Hero,' *New York Times*, 15 June 1997, p. 27; Bennett, 'Theatre/Tourism'; Wollman, 'The Economic Development of the "New" Times Square', 450.

16 Wasko, *Understanding Disney*, p. 159.

17 Wickstrom, 'Commodities, Mimesis, and *The Lion King*'; Roost, 'Synergy City', pp. 263–6.

18 Wollman, 'The Economic Development of the "New" Times Square', 449.

19 *Ibid.*, pp. 449–50.

3 Space/control/influence on theatre relations

The strain these productions place on New York theatre real estate inevitably has implications for the not-for-profit sector. Tim Sanford of Playwrights Horizons suggests Disney affects what he calls 'the ecology' of the wider theatre community in a more nebulous way by cocooning their artists, 'supporting projects from the ground up until they are ready for full productions'.[20] This role has always belonged to the not-for-profit theatre community, but without the strings that Disney attaches. Disney creates an environment where there are incredible resources at the artist's disposal, but the artist is locked into long-term contracts essentially to produce variations of the same work over and over again – a 'Golden Treadmill'[21] that ultimately stifles creativity and reproduces cultural homogeneity.

The Disney theatrical model prioritizes producer control over ownership of theatrical property, as the studio's interest is in maintaining control of the content and its extended commercial potential. This model seems irreconcilable with the conventional theatrical mandate that, through copyright, gives the playwright ultimate control of the work.

Disney's model is a mega-musical model that displaces the priority of the playwright. This comes about not only because Disney has substantial resources at its disposal that place the corporation in a position of substantial bargaining power with all creators, but also because, unlike traditional Broadway producers who still have to negotiate with playwrights (Dramatists Guild of America/Producer League negotiations), Disney usually 'owns the idea' and does not have to rely on traditional capitalization activities. This is a radical restructuring of the way that producers have traditionally approached their work and leads to greater control over all aspects of the production and all associated intellectual property rights.

In a 2006 interview, veteran Broadway producer Jim Freydberg outlined traditional 'big differences' between the film and theatre industries:

> In the film industry, when you buy a property, you actually own the property. The author doesn't want it anymore. In our industry, you don't have an asset, you actually own the right to continue to produce the show, and you don't even earn a certain amount of money from the author's future, unless you produce at a certain amount of time . . . We don't have a real asset like film. When a show closes, that's the end of it . . . it's not your ownership, it's the author's . . . remember there's no asset here.[22]

[20] See S. Gold, 'The Disney Difference' (1997) 14 *The American Theatre* 14.
[21] *Ibid.*
[22] J. M. Cooper *et al.*, 'Money Makes the World Go Round: The Economics of Commercial Theatre' (2006) 29 *Columbia Journal of Law and the Arts* 423, 439.

We suggest the 'traditional' theatre model Freydberg describes does not neatly apply to a company like Disney – the intellectual property of the theatre is entirely their asset, as it is in film. The writer and other artists take on the roles of employees rather than independent contractors. Even where a writer will have rights with respect to the dramatic work adaptation, they will usually conform to the contractual assignment demands of the corporation/producer who has a superior bargaining position.

Disney's ability to assert control and reshape ownership arrangements has emerged in a number of very real and practical ways. For example, Disney engages in a novel pay-as-you-go arrangement for artistic collaborators. As Gold outlines in relation to director Julie Taymor, the standard Disney deal, modelled on the film industry, is 'for a series of steps' in the creation process rather than a deal based on the 'completed show itself'. Gold comments:

> This 'pay as you go' method of engaging artists, used also by Livent [a now defunct dodgy prototype of Disney], is generating both controversy and envy in the theatre. On the one hand, it allows the creative team to earn money during the often long haul between a project's inception and its opening night. On the other hand, artists give up a fair amount of their profit participation down the track.[23]

A second way in which ownership arrangements have been reshaped is arguably the most lucrative revenue stream in the life of a theatrical production: stock and amateur productions. In the USA alone, 100,000 high school and 9,000 community theatres perform musicals each year and high schools pay a licence fee of up to US$1,000 for a production.[24] It has long been held in the theatre community that 'you can make a killing but not a living out of Broadway'. It is the subsidiary revenue streams that support creators and can make theatrical 'flops' into financial successes over the longer term.[25]

Disney and Dreamworks have developed new novel agreements with their writers that acknowledge the profitable revenue streams that come from stock and amateur productions of their properties.[26] In a historic

23 Gold, 'The Disney Difference'.

24 R. Hofler, 'Life After Death on Broadway: Fast "Flops" Earn Big Bucks in the Sticks', *Variety*, 23 November 2009, pp. 1, 42.

25 The stage adaptation of *The Wedding Singer* was panned by critics on Broadway and ran for under 300 performances in 2006. However, *The Wedding Singer* production has more than paid its way in stock and amateur productions with up to sixty or seventy being planned around the country at any one time over the past three years: *ibid.*, p. 42.

26 It has been claimed that Dreamworks has attempted to distinguish itself as a darker satirical response to the Disney brand. See generally J. Brater *et al.*, '"Let Our Freak

2005 agreement between *Shrek* producers Dreamworks and the creatives, which was based on a similar earlier agreement forged by Disney for their production of the *Little Mermaid*, the creatives were allowed to 'copyright their material' even though that work was based on a Dreamworks movie.[27] This was a substantial win for the writer on first appearance. However, in exchange, Dreamworks bargained to keep a much greater, and more lucrative, piece of the theatre pie by participation in the show's royalty streams at the end of the standard agreement period.[28] This is completely new territory for theatrical agreements and we suggest is a significant concession by authors.

A third important way in which Disney has reshaped ownership relationships in theatre is its refusal to join the American League of Theatres and Producers (the bargaining unit between producers and the major unions and guilds, including the Dramatists Guild). Disney has decided to negotiate directly with its creatives, rather than participate actively in the Guild system. As suggested above, one cannot understand dramatic authorship in the USA without appreciating the delicate, frustrating, complex negotiations over most of the twentieth century and beyond between the League and the Dramatists Guild. These battles were fought over minimum-wage agreements and whether these agreements breached anti-trust law. Decades of struggle and litigation resulted in a compromised agreement between the Guild and the League to comply with minimum-wage terms as long as the production contracts could be characterized as 'recommended rather than mandatory'. However, the Guild to this very day continues to discipline members, including expulsion for a mandatory period, 'who sign a contract that does not substantially comply with the Guild's minimum terms'.[29] In substance, the Guild has functioned as a union, which is exempt from antitrust law. Disney upsets this balance and can do so because they are able to provide creatives with incredible resources and long-term security, with the rub being that the creative forgoes its independent contract status and control over creative output. The lure of the golden treadmill cannot be underestimated – long-term well-paid job security assures that the Guild has a limited role to play in contract negotiations.

In these examples, we see the evolution of an employer/employee relationship in theatre that appears to be far removed from the observations

Flags Fly": *Shrek the Musical* and the Branding of Diversity' (2010) 62 *Theatre Journal* 151.

27 *Ibid.*, p. 165.

28 *Ibid.*, pp. 164–5, citing Hofler, 'Life After Death on Broadway'.

29 J. Litman, 'The Invention of Common Law Play Right' (2010) 25 *Berkeley Technology Law Journal* 1381, n. 257.

of Jim Freydberg and far removed from the traditional author function imagined by copyright.

4 What work does copyright do here?

Disneyfication means a shift in the experience of theatre and the use of public space; a shift in the very idea of what theatre is. There is an associated transformation in aspirations, content and the character of entertainment consumption, and arguably in the possibilities for creativity associated with mainstream theatre. However, it is areas of law largely disinterested in questions of creativity – urban planning policy, tourism strategies and local employment rules – that set the conditions for the profitability of this kind of theatre, rather than copyright. Through contract, the conventional copyright priority awarded to the individual playwright author and the dramatic work is subverted, toppled by the supremacy of capital investment and managerial labour. Without effecting any formal change to the content of dramatic copyright itself, the legal relations of theatre come to approximate that of another capital-intensive mass-produced global entertainment experience: cinema.

5 Is Disneyfication a concern in Australia?

The former President of the Dramatists Guild, John Weidman, claims that a seismic shift has occurred in the way that theatre has been made over the last fifteen years, with consequences for the American playwright and 'the future of the American Theatre and the American theatre-going public'. Weidman argues that these challenges have primarily come from two sources:

> First, from a group of producers, new to the business, and largely new to New York, and second, from directors, acting in concert through their union, the Society of Stage Directors and Choreographers.[30]

The claims relating to producers are particularly relevant because they focus on companies like Disney where the ownership of the theatrical work is the 'maker' of that work as opposed to a logo-centric playwright author. This is a shift in ownership control from playwright to producer, akin to film. Power imbalance and control are two important issues here and it has been happening for some time, according to Weidman:

[30] J. Weidman, 'Protecting the American Playwright: The Seventh Annual Media and Society Lecture' (2007) 72 *Brooklyn Law Review* 639, 641.

> Twenty-five years ago, something happened on Broadway. The musical *Cats* opened, and in certain fundamental ways, the commercial theatre was changed forever. Prior to *Cats*, a hit show ran for two, perhaps three years. A smash hit like *My Fair Lady*, might run for five or six. *Cats* ran for eighteen years. And even more significantly, the London production, which had been replicated on Broadway, was then replicated in dozens of other Broadway-like productions around the world.[31]

Australia was one of those markets, with *Cats* touring major cities in 1985 and again in 2009.

The cultural and political concern to consider, in an Australian context, is whether there is any indication that the Disneyfication of theatre is occurring, changing the cultural experience of not-for-profits or subsidized theatre and reducing creators' rights by turning independent contractors with copyrights into employees with nothing but reduced labour conditions.

There are major and important points of distinction to note initially. Though Disneyfication is often described in the literature as culturally imperialistic, there has been no repetition of the Amsterdam Theatre experience in Australia. There is no Disney precinct and, outside of the Disney-inspired Gold Coast theme park Dreamworld, attempts to recreate 'American-style' entertainment experiences, such as Sydney's Sega World, have failed miserably. With cheaper international airfares and a strong Australian dollar the Australian middle class can experience an 'authentic' Disney theme park overseas.

Australian commercial theatre is largely dominated by franchises, including many Disney productions. In recent years, the highest grossing shows have included *Wicked*, *Mary Poppins*, *Jersey Boys*, *Annie* and *The Producers*. However, even with well-known Australian actors performing in lead roles, these are perceived as 'global' rather than as culturally Australian works. 'Australian theatre' remains culturally structured around the not-for-profit sector.

Australian theatre production is supported by a complex amalgamation of box office receipts, private sponsorship, public funding and investment. The tradition in Australian subsidized theatre is for new and original work, Australian work, adaptations that have their own integrity, and productions that also provide support for local theatre workers and satisfy audience demand, albeit largely perceived as directed towards the educated elite.

Australian theatre is built around the playwright model, supported by a well-organized writers' guild, the Australian Writers' Guild (AWG),

31 *Ibid.*, pp. 642–3.

which has broad support. The AWG is arguably in a superior position of power to the US Dramatists Guild for a number of reasons. There is no organized Guild in Australia for theatre directors or producers and therefore Australian theatre practice does not have the same history of Guild conflict that has characterized American theatre for almost a century.[32] The AWG also has a very successful history as an agitator for playwright reform over the last forty years.[33]

John Weidman argues that in the USA what one producer wants they all want, and there is some evidence to suggest that commercial contracting practices have begun to inform not-for-profit practice. Take, for example, the experience of American playwright Craig Lucas, author of the acclaimed work *Prayer for My Enemy*, which premiered off-Broadway with the not-for-profit Roundabout Theatre Company as part of its 2008–9 season. The standard originating-producer agreement, Lucas quickly discovered, required him to sign over to Roundabout no less than 40 per cent of author royalties from productions of his play for the next ten years. Lucas knew that all not-for-profit theatres earned a percentage of a playwright's future earnings. Indeed, industry-based 'subsidiary right' agreements between originating producers and playwrights have a long tradition in the not-for-profit theatre in many countries, including Australia. What startled Craig Lucas was the figure of 40 per cent, which, however standard for commercial productions in the USA, he regarded as far too high for a not-for-profit production. He took the extraordinary step of moving his play from Roundabout to Playwright Horizons, who were willing to produce it at the more standard rate of 10 per cent of future earnings.[34]

Interviews we have conducted with Australian theatre practitioners show us that there is concern over the changing expectations of the theatre-going public and some concern in the theatre community over the distribution of rights, including the rights of directors, but these concerns are not attributed to the franchise problem identified by Weidman. Commercial theatre and not-for-profit or subsidized theatre are still seen as distinct sectors, with distinct legal relations and practices. For not-for-profits, problems were more likely to be viewed as a consequence

32 The Australian Directors' Guild was established in response to changes in the Australian film industry in the 1980s. It represents film, television and digital media directors, documentary makers, animators, assistant directors and independent producers throughout Australia.

33 See G. Roncoli, 'A History of the Australian Writers' Guild' (2001), at www.awg.com.au/index.php?option=com_content?view=article?id=164?Itemid=67.

34 See B. Salter, *Copyright, Collaboration and the Future of Dramatic Authorship* (Sydney: Currency House, 2009), pp. 5–9.

of structural problems related to government and public sector policy failure in a climate of inadequate funding. Indeed, there was not perceived to be much point in discussing new, more equitable models of rights distribution in the theatre because such notions are too detached from industry realities.[35]

Our interviewees disclosed that perceived inequities and funding shortfalls were more likely to be resolved by the goodwill of the more powerful party to the negotiation such as, for example, a well-known writer willing to compromise their copyright position to avoid agitating long-term collaborative arrangements and fracturing relations within the theatre community.[36] The greater shared concerns, as gleaned from our interviews, were over profitability and sustainability of the Australian not-for-profit theatre community given competition from other entertainment sectors and the lure of more highly paid commercial theatre and overseas work opportunities for key talent.

6 Australian theatre aspirations and realities

In terms of where this leaves us, there appears to be a disarray of law in supporting the cultural aspirations of the not-for-profit Australian theatre community. A disjointed collection of policies and laws impact on theatre but none is aware of each other or co-ordinated.[37]

The Sydney Theatre Company (STC) is an interesting example of a flagship Australian theatre company that sits somewhere between the smaller not-for-profit companies that are heavily subsidized and have a highly collaborative understanding of their work in terms of ownership structures and the larger, producer-centric, commercial theatre companies that borrow from the practices of companies like Disney. The STC blends communal, global, political and commercial objectives and its

[35] Such as collaborative models where non-writer and writer collaborators enter into agreements as 'designers of special significance' sharing economic and artistic ownership over the work. The point being that the notion of the author is irrelevant for theatre-making. See generally *ibid.*

[36] See also M. Rimmer, 'Heretic: Copyright Law and Dramatic Works' (2002) 2 *Queensland University of Technology Law and Justice Journal* 131 (referring to the generous offers made by established playwrights including Nick Enright in Australia and Tony Kushner in the USA).

[37] For example, there is limited to no co-ordination between state and Commonwealth Arts bodies that fund original works and intellectual property laws aimed to protect original works funded by these bodies. There has also been limited co-ordination in the development of moral rights. Customary moral rights conventions were an established feature of Australian Writers' Guild theatre agreements before the introduction of moral rights legislation into Australian law. However, limited consideration was given to the rights of theatrical practitioners when the moral rights amendments were debated.

practices, in many respects, are governed by the amalgamation of disjointed laws and policies previously referred to, few of which pertain to intellectual property law. The highly publicized Greening Project,[38] involving a long-term commitment, not only to better environmental practices at the STC but also within the wider arts community, might be implicitly playing a role in a greater philosophical shift the company is undergoing towards collaborative theatre-making. In an interview with co-Artistic Directors and CEOs Cate Blanchett and Andrew Upton and General Manager Patrick McIntyre, the three were asked how they found working in a team, and whether the management structure was to remain:

> Upton said his and Blanchett's joint appointment reflected a generational shift . . . 'I wouldn't be surprised if, as the generations shift, there are more teams and more collaboration: that might be a hallmark of this generation. We do say a lot that we want to program productions, not plays, and what that's saying is that you want to foster and employ teams rather than individuals, although individuals might rise out of those teams . . . We don't believe it is a company to be run by an auteur'.[39]

There appears to be acceptance here that contemporary theatre companies are expected to do much more than simply put on plays. Signature companies, like the STC, are held out as the flag-bearers of national cultural identity. Productions are primarily for local consumption but there may also be significant touring of blockbuster shows, including abroad. Success overseas is well reported in the Australian press and a source of national pride. Profile is projected internationally and international star performers and directors are also brought in. There is a global theatrical network and theatre is a global business.

Dependent on private patronage and sponsorship for their programmes, theatre companies are also facilitators of corporate branding. As patron of the STC, Giorgio Armani is said to have provided the largest ever financial gift to an Australian theatre company.[40] The STC's current principal sponsor is Audi, with the developer Lend Lease and Suncorp Insurance as other major sponsors. The STC assists in generating a more sophisticated image, localized goodwill and domestic connection

[38] See NSW Public Works, 'Greening the Wharf', at http://publicworks.nsw.gov.au/updates/greening-wharf; see also Sydney Theatre Company, 'Greening the Wharf', at http://greeningthewharf.com.

[39] A. Malley, 'Sydney Theatre Company's Great Revival', *In the Black* (online), 1 March 2011, at http://itbdigital.com/people/2011/03/01/sydney-theatre-companys-great-revival.

[40] 'Giorgio Armani Welcomed as Sydney Theatre Company Patron', *Australian Stage* (online), 11 October 2007, at http://australianstage.com.au/20071010752/news/sydney/giorgio-armani-welcomed-as-sydney-theatre-company-patron.html.

for corporations associated with them. Theatre companies are themselves expected to be good corporate citizens. The STC's 'Greening the Wharf' is part of this profiling.

More traditionally, Australian theatre companies play an important role in building up and renewing artistic communities and nurturing individual talents.[41] In turn, their programmes are relied upon to build cities, communities and cultural precincts. This helps make urban locales lively and more attractive to locals and tourists. This activity provides a source of direct employment and also employment opportunities more indirectly through growing the businesses that grow up around the patronage of the theatre district. However, the burden of contributing to 'destination theatre' poses a significant challenge for not-for-profit organizations. Interviewees expressed frustration at the inability of impacting on planning problems affecting urban renewal of the theatre precinct. Given the seasonality and limited hours of operation of the STC, there are significant challenges for surrounding businesses in maintaining profitable customer bases without support from Disney-style architectures of merchandising. When traditional theatre precinct businesses – bars, cafés, restaurants, bookshops – fail, the theatre community is directly impacted by the loss of amenity, with potential implications for box office receipts. However, providing support for the extended theatre precinct is far from the traditional not-for-profit theatre's responsibility.

To put it another way, contemporary theatres are at the centre of a web of complex cultural and economic relations that they facilitate. This is not a new thing. Historically, theatre has always had a public function in bringing people together and building communities and shared identities. However, it is not clear whether lawmakers and policy-makers fully appreciate the range of activity and functions provided by theatre so as to provide suitable support for them.

Copyright presumes that the primary activity and economic entity at the heart of theatre activity is the literary property, that is, the dramatic work or the screenplay. Subsidiary rights of performers and directors that arise from the collaborative nature of theatre productions may potentially supplement core copyrights. Moral rights may also supplement economic rights, though it is hard to identify the relevance of these in practice.[42] The idea that the core activity of contemporary theatre companies is

[41] A role also supported by major publicly funded drama schools like the National Institute of Dramatic Art (NIDA), Victorian College of the Arts (VCA) and the Western Australian Academy of Performing Arts (WAAPA).

[42] Our interviewees noted that attribution and integrity issues were already part of contractual negotiations over billing and standard agreements over payment for rewrites, well before the introduction of the Copyright Amendment (Moral Rights) Act 2000 (Cth).

the production of plays, the work of playwrights and 'playwrights plus' in a copyright sense is as simplistic as it is misleading. Recourse to the usual justificatory theory that copyright is a body of law that provides 'incentives' to dramatists or theatre producers seems both absurd and embarrassing to dwell upon. Copyright's presumptions about theatre make copyright practically irrelevant to supporting the main business and cultural activity of the theatre. Legally, this void is filled by contracts for all sorts of services and properties.

However, as a matter of public policy, the presumption is that theatres primarily engage in public performances of plays. Policy initiatives are primarily limited to playwriting development programmes, fellowships and related training of talent associated with the staging of productions. By default, rather than by design, copyright law is taken to support theatre because it creates the exclusive right to own and perform plays, but, in reality, this private economic foundation requires extensive supplementation by various sorts of arts grants, infrastructure support and other more ad hoc sources of support.

The practical irrelevance of copyright may be little mourned in the theatre. The answer is also not to suggest copyright needs a bigger role to play. Rather, the point of this inquiry is to consider the nature of the legal and policy vacuum in supporting the work of theatres that is created by the presumption that the primary economic venture and entity is the production of plays.

7 The Australian policy vacuum

Disneyfication of our culture can occur without a Disney precinct and without any real oversight by law. Alan Bryman notes that:

> more and more aspects of our society are exhibiting features that are associated with Disney theme parks. The idea of Disneyization springs from a conviction that there are changes to our social world that the Disney theme park exemplifies. Disneyization thus becomes a lens through which the nature of modern society can be viewed, as well as a way of thinking about issues to do with consumption and globalization.[43]

While Disney is not the 'cause' of pressures on Australian contemporary theatre, there are some shared features of the 'entertainment economy' of a Disneyfied 42nd Street and the STC, at least in terms of enlarged expectations about the entertainment experience and the amenity of the theatre precinct. It is unrealistic to expect that not-for-profit theatre would be

[43] Bryman, *The Disneyization of Society*, p. vii.

immune from or exempt from the forces that are exemplified by our consumer society and present in commercial theatre today.

Disney is well-placed to manage larger commercial expectations because of the special powers and conditions granted to them over public space by relevant government authorities. 'Australian' commercial theatre is also supported by an array of public monies, including ready access to key bureaucrats and financial support from state agencies that assist with the logistics and marketing of mega-musicals. *Wicked the Musical*, *Jersey Boys*, *Dr Zhivago: A New Musical*, *Mary Poppins: A Musical* and *Legally Blonde – The Musical* are listed as key events recently supported by Events NSW (now Destination NSW).[44] Facilitating the touring of major West End and Broadway productions to Australia has become a core tourism activity of the state.

However, a key difference between commercial theatre and not-for-profits is that the former involves associating performance with particular fantasy narratives that link imagination and memory with private consumption and ubiquitous character merchandise. Contemporary Australian theatre retains a more traditional 'public' obligation in exploring ideas of place and identity. Our concern here is whether contemporary theatre is getting its fair share of attention and support in carrying out this public role. The combination of having a flagship role while being reliant on a mix of public and assorted private funding complicates policy formation. In Australia, supporting cultural activity is primarily a Federal 'public' concern, whereas growing the tourism and events sector and supporting the profitability of the theatre precinct fits squarely within state jurisdiction. There is little co-ordination of the two roles or even recognition that these activities and interests may be related.

8 Conclusion

How the law can support 'quality' theatre has been of long-standing concern. Eighteenth-century patents awarded to the major metropolitan theatres at Drury Lane and Covent Garden, which gave them the exclusive right to perform 'legitimate drama' in the city of London, were justified as an initiative to preserve the dignity of the national drama, as well as a response to perceived public order problems associated with unruly and disreputable performances.[45] The Dramatic Literary Property

44 Events NSW, *Corporate Report 2009/10* (2010), at http://corporatereport.realviewdigital.com/?iid=45755.

45 E. L. Bulwer, 'Parliamentary Debates on Drama and Dramatic Literature (31 May 1832)', p. 242, in L. Bently and M. Kretschmer (eds), *Primary Sources on Copyright (1450–1900)* (London: Arts & Humanities Research Council); www.copyrighthistory.org.

Act 1833 (UK), which first recognized the performance rights of playwrights, also arose, at least in part, from concern for the limitations and quality of theatre productions that had then emerged from these monopolies:

> The evil of the existing system was pretty abundantly evinced by the striking decline of the modern drama, and he [Bulwer Lytton] was quite sure that the result of the proposed change in the existing system would be, that greater talents and a higher order of genius would be enlisted in the service of the stage, and that the dramatic literature of the country would once more regain that exalted position from which it had been degraded by the want of the necessary encouragement and protection.[46]

Objectors to the new copyright legislation noted that it did not follow that granting rights to playwrights would lead to higher standards of theatre, with one critic arguing that 'theatre only brought together a set of unfortunate outcasts, who had no other means of existence'.[47] The 1833 legislation faced considerable problems in practice. Though a Dramatic Authors' Society was established to collect licence fees for its members, to sponsor publication of dramatic works and to identify copyright infringements, this did not reverse the depression affecting the theatre market. There were few improvements in the financial position of playwrights until profit-sharing models emerged in the 1860s.[48]

Creating the right structural conditions for quality theatre has always been a lot more complicated than simply creating a performance right for playwrights. Theatre is a unique cultural form because, in commercial and not-for-profit versions alike, it is site responsive. Theatre is about connecting people to a cultural experience that speaks to a history and location. Accordingly, laws and public policies have needed to consider theatre not just as a text-based art form but also in terms of public space – supporting the development of particular kinds of community experience: imaginary and real spaces for thinking about our culture, our identity and ourselves.

Through hard work and well-targeted development strategies, Australian contemporary theatres will continue to survive with their assortment of funding sources and support. But more is needed than simply funds. At a policy level we need to be more attentive to thinking about

46 E. L. Bulwer, 'Parliamentary Debates on the Dramatic Literary Property Act (12 March 1833)', pp. 560–1, in Bently and Kretschmer, *Primary Sources on Copyright (1450–1900)*.

47 B. Rotch, 'Parliamentary Debates on the Dramatic Literary Property Act (24 July 1833)', p. 1220, in Bently and Kretschmer, *Primary Sources on Copyright (1450–1900)*.

48 See R. Deazley, 'Commentary on Dramatic Literary Property Act 1833', in Bently and Kretschmer, *Primary Sources on Copyright (1450–1900)*; I. Alexander, *Copyright Law and the Public Interest in the Nineteenth Century* (Oxford: Hart Publishing, 2011), pp. 85–8.

how to support the surviving public functions and traditions of theatre.[49] If we fail to address these considerations, all we might be left with is a Disneyfied cultural experience brought about through neglect, oversight or accident rather than by design. Is the real cost of Disneyfication that we now find it hard to identify and articulate public roles that are not inflected with private, commercial considerations? If so, this has, at least potentially, quite serious implications for how we think about nationhood, community and the self, beyond our identities as bearers of corporate designs.

[49] This problem is now being publicly debated in Australia: see J. Meyrick, *The Retreat of Our National Drama* (Sydney: Currency House, 2014); W. Enoch, *Take Me to Your Leader: The Dilemma of Cultural Leadership* (Sydney: Currency House, 2014).

7 Instituting copyright

Reconciling copyright law and industry practice in the Australian film and television sector

*Kathy Bowrey and Michael Handler**

1 Introduction: the law/practice conundrum

When considering how rights are created and income streams generated in practice in the Australian film and television industry, legal scholarship invariably views these issues through the lens of formal copyright law. This approach involves asking well-established questions such as whether copyright subsists in particular types of subject matter being created and traded, who owns that copyright, and the scope of the resultant rights. When looked at in this way, it would seem that there are significant uncertainties as to the extent to which some cultural products are in fact legally protected, or who (if anyone) can be said to own the rights to them. For example, it is accepted that under Australian law something described at such a high level of abstraction as a 'television format' is not recognized as a species of copyright 'work' or 'subject matter'. Even though aspects of television formats might constitute literary or dramatic works and receive copyright protection on that basis,[1] a format per se is not something that is capable of being owned, assigned, licensed or

* We would particularly like to thank our interviewees who kindly made themselves available to talk to us about their work and the role of copyright in Australian cultural production. They have asked to remain anonymous and in attributing quotes and statements to them in this chapter we have not identified them. Our thanks also go to José Bellido, Catherine Bond and Brent Salter for discussing their ideas with us, and to the participants at the Fifth Annual International Society for the History and Theory of Intellectual Property (ISHTIP) Workshop, 'Cultural Economy and Intellectual Property', Université Panthéon-Assas (Paris 2), 26–28 June 2013, in particular, Tanya Aplin, Peter Decherney, Dev Gangjee and Jessica Silbey, for their comments and feedback on an earlier version of this chapter.

[1] See, e.g., *Nine Films & Television Pty Ltd* v. *Ninox Television Ltd* (2005) 67 IPR 46 (suggesting, by focusing only on the question of whether there was infringement, that copyright subsisted in the scenario or script of each recorded episode of a reality renovation show as a dramatic work), and see Copyright Act 1968 (Cth), s. 32 on the requirements for copyright to subsist in literary and dramatic works.

infringed under copyright law.[2] In a related manner, under Australian law the right to make an 'adaptation' of a literary or dramatic work is narrowly defined[3] and the boundaries of the scope of the right to make a 'reproduction' of a substantial part of such a work are unclear.[4] This means that it cannot be said with any degree of certainty that Australian copyright law protects 'characters' or gives copyright owners the right to make sequels, spin-offs or similar variations of their content.[5]

These copyright limitations are likely to be entirely familiar to legal scholars and students of copyright law, and similar uncertainties affect many jurisdictions. What is equally well-known is that there is a significant disjuncture between the formal law and how, in practice, cultural subject matter is in fact managed and income streams are generated. It is common knowledge that there is a long-standing industry practice of buying and selling rights to television formats, with the annual global trade in format rights valued at over 3 billion euros.[6] Although what is traded in each case will invariably encompass some intellectual property[7]

[2] The key case in the British Commonwealth remains *Green* v. *Broadcasting Corp of New Zealand* [1989] RPC 700 (copyright did not subsist in elements of a variety show format as a dramatic work).

[3] See Copyright Act 1968 (Cth), s. 31(1)(a)(vi) on the adaptation right for literary and dramatic works and s. 10(1) on the definition of 'adaptation', which is relevantly limited to making: in relation to a literary work in a non-dramatic form, a version of the work in a dramatic form; in relation to a literary work in a dramatic form, a version of the work in a non-dramatic form; and in relation to literary works generally, a translation of the work or a version of the work in which a story or action is conveyed solely or principally by means of pictures. On the British history of the 'translation' right, see, e.g., C. Seville, *The Internationalisation of Copyright Law: Books, Buccaneers and the Black Flag in the Nineteenth Century* (Cambridge University Press, 2006), ch. 3. For a recent analysis of the US derivative work right, and its expansion since the Copyright Act 1976 (US), see P. Samuelson, 'The Quest for a Sound Conception of Copyright's Derivative Work Right' (2013) 101 *Georgetown Law Journal* 1505.

[4] Compare, e.g., *Zeccola* v. *Universal City Studios Inc.* (1982) 46 ALR 189 (copyright in novel and screenplay of *Jaws* infringed by an Italian film that contained similar events, incidents and characters, but with different dialogue) with *Telstra Corporation Ltd* v. *Royal & Sun Alliance Insurance Australia Ltd* (2003) 57 IPR 453 (no copyright infringement in using a character and key catchphrases from Telstra's well-known Goggomobil television advertisement in a later advertisement for car insurance).

[5] See generally A. McGee and G. Scanlan, 'Copyright in Character' [2003] *Journal of Business Law* 470; J. McCutcheon, 'Copyright Protection for Fictional Literary Characters' (2006) 67 *Intellectual Property Forum* 14; I. Eagles, 'Copyright and the Sequel: What Happens Next?', in F. Macmillan (ed.), *New Directions in Copyright Law*, vol. 6 (Cheltenham: Edward Elgar, 2007).

[6] The Format Recognition and Protection Association, *The FRAPA Report 2009: TV Formats to the World* (FRAPA, 2009), p. 8 ('The production volume generated by traded formats has grown . . . to approximately €9.3 bn for the years 2006–2008').

[7] For example, confidential information, trade marks and assorted copyright works such as scenarios, musical works, artistic works, etc.

and production consultancy services,[8] it is clear that in the absence of overarching copyright protection for the format there is little, in strict legal terms, to prevent a competitor from copying or adapting a successful format without paying licence fees. In addition, 'derivative' or 'ancillary' rights to literary and dramatic works, defined broadly so as to encompass spin-offs, sequels and merchandising rights, are in practice routinely assigned and licensed by owners of copyright in films and dramatic works, notwithstanding that these concepts are unknown to Australian copyright law. A noteworthy example is contained in the current Terms of Trade issued by Screen Australia (the Australian government funding body for film and television production), which provide that:

> In the case of all recoupable production funding of documentary, TV drama and feature films, where the right to make a Sequel, Spin-off or Remake (including a program based on the format of the original program) is optioned or acquired . . . If the Sequel, Spin-off or Remake is to be produced by the original producer . . . Screen Australia requires the right to receive a fee in the production budget of each and every Sequel, Spin-off or Remake.[9]

Similarly, in Screen Australia's standard Production Investment Agreement for Television Drama Production Investments, the producer is required to warrant that it 'owns, or has the exclusive right to obtain . . . the Underlying Rights' in the film and script, defined to include 'Ancillary rights' such as the right to make books developed from any 'Sequel, Spin-off or Remake' and the right to use 'any fictional characters and fictional situations in the Script and/or the Film, including in any game or application'.[10] The significance of these clauses and their predecessors in earlier agreements has, to the best of our knowledge, never been the subject of litigation in Australia.

All of the above raises serious questions as to how Australian copyright law in fact supports industry practice when there are apparent, major legal uncertainties surrounding the capacity of the law to protect valuable entertainment formats, concepts and characters.

In addressing this disjuncture between law and industry practice, a number of approaches tend to be taken in Australian and international

[8] See generally A. Moran with J. Malbon, *Understanding the Global TV Format* (Bristol: Intellect Books, 2005), ch. 2.

[9] Screen Australia, *Terms of Trade* (17 February 2014), cl. 6.2(a) at www.screenaustralia.gov.au/getmedia/c416ee05-b071-438c-b689-33837801db7c/Terms_of_Trade.pdf.

[10] Screen Australia, *Core Conditions to PIA for Television Drama Production Investments with a Special Purpose Vehicle, Model E2.1* (July 2013), cl. 2.2.4 and cl. 1 definitions, at https://www.screenaustralia.gov.au/getmedia/e3355ff5-3eac-4663-a7a6-de4c6b22ae91/CC_TVdramaInvest_over1m_SPV.pdf.

scholarship. One approach, which encapsulates a good deal of the legal scholarship on the topic, is to focus on the perceived deficiencies of copyright law in leaving certain content unprotected, and to query whether these gaps in protection justify law reform. This approach proceeds on the basis that, irrespective of the way in which the film and television industry in fact operates, the legal foundations of the trade are vulnerable. It then asks whether the economic significance of the trade leads to the conclusion that the law should 'keep up' with industry practice by expanding concepts such as copyright subsistence, ownership and rights.[11] Although it is rarely articulated in this way, this approach assumes, in the value it places on potential legislative reform,[12] that the formal status and content of copyright law is of major, even driving, importance to the ordering and viability of the trade in cultural goods such as formats, spin-offs, etc.

Another, quite different, approach, which can be seen in more interdisciplinary scholarship on the subject, takes as its starting point that the existence of a flourishing trade in formats, derivative rights, etc. demonstrates that the absence of precision in copyright law is ultimately of little practical relevance in this sphere. Thus, rather than focusing on remedying gaps or deficiencies in the formal law, this scholarship focuses more on the cultural economy of the format trade. In particular, it focuses on the agreements struck between the relevant industry participants and the associated enforcement codes and mechanisms that exist to ensure the viability of the commercial trade in cultural products in the absence of clear property rights allocated by copyright law.[13] Here, the assumption

[11] See, e.g., the flurry of writing after *Green* v. *Broadcasting Corp of New Zealand* [1989] RPC 700: R. McD. Bridge and S. Lane, 'The Protection of Formats Under English Law: Part I' [1990] *Entertainment Law Review* 96; P. S. Smith, 'Format Rights: Opportunity Knocks' [1991] *Entertainment Law Review* 63 (responding to C. Miskin and T. R. Martino, 'Format Rights: The Price is Not Right' [1991] *Entertainment Law Review* 31); S. Lane, 'Format Rights in Television Shows: Law and Legislative Process' (1992) 13 *Statute Law Review* 24; D. Rose, 'Format Rights: A Never-ending Drama (or Not)' [1999] *Entertainment Law Review* 170; G. W. G. Karnell, 'Copyright to Sequels – With Special Regard to Television Show Formats' (2000) 31 *International Review of Intellectual Property and Competition Law* 886. The approach is still taken in more recent scholarship, e.g., J. E. Bergman, 'No More Format Disputes: Are Reality Television Formats the Proper Subject of Federal Copyright Protection?' (2011) 4 *Pepperdine Journal of Business, Entrepreneurship and the Law* 243; N. E. Gottlieb, 'Free to Air? Legal Protection for TV Program Formats' (2011) 51 *IDEA* 211 (especially pt. 3).

[12] It is important to note that such reform has not been forthcoming, despite the lobbying efforts of such organizations as FRAPA. On proposals in the United Kingdom in the mid-1990s to amend the Copyright, Designs and Patents Act 1988 (UK) to provide for explicit protection for formats, see Karnell, 'Copyright to Sequels', 901–3; P. Kamina, *Film Copyright in the European Union* (Cambridge University Press, 2002), pp. 81–2.

[13] See, e.g., M. Kretschmer, S. Singh and J. Wardle, 'The Exploitation of Television Formats', ESRC Digital Resource, Bournemouth University (2009), at http://tvformats.

tends to be that these agreements are constructed around industry-based understandings of what content is valuable, who should own that content and how it can be exploited. From an Australian perspective, this might be said to explain how contracts between Australian participants routinely refer to extra-legal concepts such as 'formats', 'spin-off' rights and 'ancillary' rights. Such language might be said to reflect US legal terminology that has infiltrated foreign contracts, or a more general international legal practice in the industry, which Australian stakeholders have internalized with a view to potential participation in global markets.

Both types of scholarship have their merits, and the latter is particularly useful in showing that claims made by those within the industry (often format producers) as to the vulnerability of their trade and the need for enhanced protection are often little more than strategies to drive up the price that needs to be paid by franchisees.[14] However, both perspectives share a common problem in how they construct law and the relationship between law and industry. Both approaches construct copyright as an independent and autonomous domain. Copyright either sits apart from industry or it is largely irrelevant to it. The central point of difference is whether and how copyright should aspire to do more, through a closer mirroring of perceived dominant industry views. But, in both views, copyright is perceived to have little actual practical resonance, *in the here and now*.

The presumption that copyright is 'merely' jurisprudence, possibly pregnant with the capacity to do more practical work in the Australian film and television sector, is worrying. This is because it situates those currently engaged in legal practice and/or providing advice to creators and producers in an especially curious space. Assuming these advisers are not simply engaged in sophistry, how do they understand their role? What is the foundation for their advice? How, as a practical legal matter, do they manage the uncertainties and tensions created by copyright law in this area? And, above all, what role do these parties believe copyright law actually plays in creating and sustaining a viable film and television sector?

bournemouth.ac.uk. On the importance of trade fairs and enforcement codes, see generally A. Moran and M. Keane, *Television Across Asia* (London: Routledge, 2004).

14 For a striking example, see the comment by David Lyle, Chairman of the Format Recognition and Protection Association, that the assumed security of the format trade is 'largely illusory. It is as tangible as the emperor's new clothes', in T. Colwell and D. Price, *Rights of Passage: British Television in the Global Market, A Report by the TV Research Partnership* (United Kingdom Trade and Investment, 2005), p. 40, quoted in L. Logan, 'The Emperor's New Clothes? The Way Forward: TV Format Protection under Unfair Competition Law in the United States, United Kingdom and France: Part 1' [2009] *Entertainment Law Review* 37, 37.

In seeking better to understand these dynamics we undertook empirical work over the course of 2011 and 2012. Our interest was especially focused on the production of original Australian content. This priority reflects a somewhat nationalistic presumption that Australian law, even in a global marketplace, should serve the economic and cultural interests of Australian creators, producers and consumers. An additional rider was our view that, to the extent that copyright serves a cultural function, it is desirable that it supports cultural production that is responsive to and reflective of the place in which it is made.[15] This led us to focus on the segment of the entertainment industry primarily engaged in supporting the creation of original Australian local film and television content, much of which is, in fact, also traded internationally.[16] Our empirical work consisted of interviews of legal personnel at key agencies in the Australian entertainment industry. These included Australian public broadcasters (the Australian Broadcasting Corporation (ABC) and the Special Broadcasting Service (SBS), both of which buy foreign formats and are involved in the production and distribution of local, franchised content, and both of which are subject to legislative charters that require them to provide services that have cultural goals);[17] the Australian government funding body for film and television production (Screen Australia); peak bodies representing the interests of film and television producers (the Screen Producers Association of Australia (SPAA)), screenwriters (the Australian Writers' Guild (AWG)) and screen directors (the Australian Directors Guild (ADG)); and talent agents.[18]

In section 2, 'The interviews and the industry', we disclose our detailed findings. Our discussions with stakeholders were open-ended and focused on two main areas. First, we discussed the process of negotiating contractual terms and the effects of adopting legal terminology of uncertain meaning, especially around format rights. As agreements sighted were confidential, this material is discussed only in general terms. Nonetheless, our discussions helped shed light on the complex role

[15] A view that is reflected at government policy level: see Australian Government, *Creative Australia: National Cultural Policy* (2013), p. 83, at http://creativeaustralia.arts.gov.au/assets/Creative-Australia-PDF-20130417.pdf (acknowledging 'the role that Australian copyright plays as the primary legal framework supporting the creative economy').

[16] Screen Australia regularly produces statistics pertaining to audio-visual markets, including figures on balance of trade, imports and exports of cinema, television and audio royalties. The organization also compiles relevant international comparisons. See Screen Australia, *Australia & the World*, at www.screenaustralia.gov.au/research/australia_andtheworld.aspx.

[17] See, respectively, Australian Broadcasting Corporation Act 1983 (Cth) s. 6(1)–(3); Special Broadcasting Service Act 1991 (Cth) s. 6(1)–(3).

[18] See n. 19, and accompanying text, for further details of our interviews and methodology.

played by format rights in the Australian industry. Secondly, we discussed the broader industry logics and priorities behind industry negotiations. Unexpectedly, this proved to be a much more productive and interesting avenue of inquiry, raising important but difficult questions about the role of copyright law in supporting cultural trade. It became apparent over the course of our interviews that the stakeholders had a considerably different conception of the role that copyright law plays in the Australian industry compared with the views that tend to be put forward in scholarship on the topic. It became clear that the sort of rights ownership questions in which copyright law is traditionally interested (who owns the rights; what entitlements do copyright owners get; what are the limits to those rights, etc.) are far less important to those in the industry than a much larger, overarching issue: how best to support the production of Australian content and to find ways of generating income streams to pay for the labour of all those involved in the making of Australian film and television programmes.

Our research reveals that copyright ownership, as provided for by formal law, is of relatively little direct productive use in mobilizing capital or labour in this sector. That work has to be done by the interaction of copyright law with a range of other institutions. As we will show, investment and other subsidies are channelled to the creative sector via public bodies. Media regulations set quotas that guarantee the production of certain quantities of 'Australian' film and television content. Industry labour agreements, negotiated by guilds and embodied in standard industry contracts (which, on occasion, are registered with the government's competition regulator), provide a key mechanism for managing and working around apparent limitations of copyright ownership. We suggest that these guilds and quasi-public institutions provide an alternative and supplementary mechanism for ordering the copyright trade, and that we need to understand and value the work of these other institutions and agents in order to understand why there is a gap between how copyright jurisprudence understands rights ownership and how rights are created and income streams generated in practice in Australian film and television. More broadly, this work brings the labour question back into copyright focus, not as an issue of ownership, but as a day-to-day practical issue of managing social relations and cultural expectations. Thus, in section 3, 'Instituting copyright', we argue that scholarly understandings of the role that copyright law plays in creating a viable cultural sector need to be rethought and, in particular, closer attention needs to be paid to the relationship between copyright law and other cultural institutions.

By way of conclusion, in section 4, we argue that the way copyright is commonly being constructed in legal inquiries creates an oversimplified, somewhat misleading picture of the role played by law and the significance of property rights in the culture industries. By not fully accounting for the role of other institutions and laws that support cultural production, the existing approaches tend either to overestimate or underestimate the relevance and role of copyright law in the Australian film and television industry, and do not paint a full picture of the role of the law in helping create a sustainable industry.

2 The interviews and the industry

Our interviewees fell within two distinct classes. Some were lawyers engaged in commissioning content, acquiring rights to content (including rights to make local versions of successful programming originating overseas) and negotiating sales and distribution agreements. Legal issues were often identified with reference to rights relating to production, transmission and retail. Standard contracts and variations thereof were generally identified with reference to distinctive kinds of programming, such as drama, documentary or factual, children's programming, and sport. Merchandise and tie-in products were related to all kinds of programmes. Other interviewees were not involved in commercial transactions involving film and television content but rather provided policy and legal advice to commercial parties and/or to creatives engaged as small sub-contractors, especially around employment issues and recommended contractual terms.[19]

2.1 Explaining format rights

As outlined in the Introduction, one issue in which we were particularly interested related to industry understandings of the effects of adopting uncertain legal terminology in commercial transactions, particularly in relation to format rights. Lawyers from the broadcasting organizations painted a complex picture of how format rights are understood and managed in practice. Much depended on the roles that these advisers were playing with their organizations; that is, whether they were involved

[19] A total of fourteen separate interviews were conducted in 2011 and 2012, with a total of twenty interviewees, from twelve institutions (what might appear to be a small sample size is simply the result of the very small size of the Australian industry). Each interview lasted between sixty and ninety minutes. Each interview was semi-structured: they involved the researchers asking a number of set questions, as well as lengthy, free-flowing discussion based on the interviewees' responses. All interviews were recorded and transcribed. We undertook to keep the identity of the interviewees confidential, and consequently all quotes and statements have been attributed to interviewees by the letters A–T in this chapter, determined by the chronology of the interviews.

in commissioning content from third-party producers, or whether they were involved in negotiations over the acquisition of rights and the sale of content. In the former case, the lawyers, unsurprisingly, would correctly restate Australian law: 'if we are asked to advise on format rights, there aren't any!'[20] However, in the latter case, the position as regards format rights became 'yes, we must have those to sell!'[21] In explaining the first response, there was recognition that, as copyright lawyers advising on rights clearance and on the making of new content, it was important to allow for the freedom to develop ideas, and that strong rights might impede the capacity to develop and sell new programmes.[22] In commissioning content the lawyers recognized that 'the industry . . . is a bower-bird and picks from all over the world.[23] That's the reality and so to try and lock up those rights would be [a problem]'.[24] At the same time, it was noted that third-party producers often had high expectations in regard to protecting their creative ideas and often felt morally entitled to control the global copying of successful formats.[25] This meant that format rights were put forward in negotiations between producers and broadcasters as valuable commodities, for which broadcasters would routinely need to pay to acquire.

In seeking to unpack the above, seemingly contradictory, understandings of format rights, there were three different logics that we saw at play. The first logic was strategic and related to the reasons broadcasters would pay to acquire rights in content from overseas. The second logic related to production of new and original content, where perceptions of allowing 'reaping without sowing' by rival networks and producers created an interest in securing returns from use of formats as a form of commercialization and distribution of programmes. The third logic related to the utility of a perceived need to transact with overseas producers over format rights so as to allow for the original commissioner to broker 'access to talent'.

In terms of the first logic, namely the strategy of Australian broadcasters paying fees to overseas production houses for television formats when there was, in strict legal terms, no need to do so, one explanation that was presented was the need to take away the aggravation of a

[20] Interviewee C. [21] Interviewee C. [22] Interviewee C.

[23] It is worth emphasizing the subtlety of the 'bower-bird' metaphor, which is often used to describe both a collecting obsession and appropriation for competitive advantage. The bower-bird is an Australian species of bird that is known for placing a selection of brightly coloured objects to decorate a nest as part of courtship display. The objects are also commonly stolen from the rival nests of birds competing for a mate: I. Lovette, 'Stealing from the Neighbours' (2008) 22(2) *BirdScope*, at www.birds.cornell.edu/Publications/Birdscope/Spring2008/bowerbirds_lovette.html.

[24] Interviewee C. [25] Interviewee B.

potential claim.[26] Paying for rights to such formats was seen to make the potential for later litigation or production delays less likely. It helped facilitate timely access to overseas broadcasting content and related merchandise (especially where that content had demonstrated success in overseas markets) and helped keep local production, inspired by original formats developed elsewhere, on track to meet broadcast deadlines.[27] Here, commercial logic takes priority over legal technicalities.

It was noted that some overseas producers insisted on negotiating rights 'on their terms', completely uninterested in acknowledging any significant jurisdictional differences that might affect contractual enforcement. We were referred to examples where the overseas producer was pedantic in insisting that the 'integrity' of the format be maintained, allowing for little variation or adaption thought to make the programme more appealing to local audiences.[28] In such cases the will to control could extend to dictating legal terms to the extent that even neutral translation of key legal terms into the relevant equivalent Australian provisions, undertaken simply in order to give those terms efficacy under Australian copyright and broadcasting law, was rejected.[29] This phenomenon suggests that in some cases the trade in format rights can be explained with reference to law operating on more of a symbolic level. 'Rights' were perceived almost exclusively in terms of producers wielding cultural and economic power across the globe.[30] Format rights are just one instance of a larger drive to dictate the terms that serve to establish a particular kind of business reputation. For Australian broadcasters, this means that if they want to do business with a successful party (such as a producer or production company) in a global marketplace, they have to engage on their terms, even when, from another perspective, the behaviour of the parties may appear commercially illogical and legally irrational. This kind of 'take it or leave it' attitude is commonly thought of as a characteristic of monopolistic corporate actors. In our interviews it was largely identified in terms of the particular personalities of certain individuals or companies who, due to recent overseas success, had something to sell to one of a small number of broadcasters operating in the Australian market.[31] The problem had less to do with the size of the player and more to do with the perceived demand for their content in a crowded global market due to their proven standing as an entity capable of assembling significant audiences through provision of programming that was 'fresh' to audiences.

In terms of the second logic, the 'reaping without sowing' concern was explained in these terms by one public broadcaster:

[26] Interviewee C. [27] Interviewee C. [28] Interviewee A.
[29] Interviewee A. [30] Interviewee A. [31] Interviewee A.

> So we were investing a lot of time and money into programs that might run for several series [which would] then go and jump off into the world of the commercial sphere and [we] would have no return from that. So I think that, yes, we have a role to foster that independent sector, but we also have an obligation to get a return on our investment as best we can.[32]

The perceived need to seek return on concept development was recognized as a relatively recent cultural shift. If, after initial success, the programme 'would then go over to [a commercial network] . . . and the public broadcaster would get no return, I think there is a concern that this is not a good use of taxpayer dollars.'[33] In a climate of politicization over funding of public broadcasters, when commercial broadcast revenues are down, public broadcasters are fighting to maintain existing funding.[34] They face a struggle to continue with the traditional roles expected of a public broadcaster while also managing technological convergence and learning to innovate with new methods of distribution.[35] In this environment there was a need to be seen to be commercially responsible in the use of public money. On the other hand, it was also noted that when a successful programme 'goes to commercial we have done our job well. We have come up with a new idea, fostered something that wasn't there before and then that producer has gone off and commercialised it'.[36]

A third logic related to the use of a format right to leverage other personal connections. One interviewee suggested that when they were selling original local formats overseas the 'key hook' was not really the intellectual property in the form of the production bible, the documents, the music, etc.; it was the broadcaster being able to facilitate access to the

[32] Interviewee C. [33] Interviewee C.

[34] See N. Miragliotta and W. Errington, 'The Rise and Fall and Rise Again of Public Broadcasting? The Case of the Australian Broadcasting Corporation' (2012) 71 *Australian Journal of Public Administration* 55, 58 (noting that the $2.1 billion increase to the ABC's base funding over three years announced in 2009 would 'not restore the broadcaster's funding base to mid-1980 levels, even though its cost pressures are significantly greater . . . The ABC will have to continue to deliver increased services across a range of platforms, and do so despite increased costs of maintenance'. See also Australian Broadcasting Corporation, *Annual Report 2012*, p. 16, at http://about.abc.net.au/wp-content/uploads/2012/10/ABC-AR-2012-combined-web-revised-17-Oct.pdf (noting the ABC's real funding in 2010–11 to be $93.9 million lower than in 1990–1).

[35] See generally Australian Broadcasting Corporation, Submission to Department of Broadband, Communications and the Digital Economy, Australian Government, *Convergence Review Interim Report* (February 2012), at http://about.abc.net.au/wp-content/uploads/2012/06/ABCSubmissionConvergenceReviewInterimReportFeb2012.pdf.

[36] Interviewee C. Similarly, interviewee A told us: 'There is a general acceptance that public broadcasters have an important role in developing talent and we know that we can't . . . always retain rights . . . I think that's why as a broadcaster it's hard to continue on with certain program series because they get bigger.'

home-grown *talent* (in the form of personal recommendations of particular people) that had been involved in originating the programme in the first instance.[37] We were told that overseas producers did not necessarily have an interest in closely replicating the original Australian programme, when, in all likelihood, broadcast rights to the original programme could be obtained if there were thought to be an audience for the content. But they might well have an interest in seeking assistance from certain individuals in fine-tuning remakes of programmes. Access to the original talent was described as assisting the overseas producer 'adding value' to the remake.[38] The original talent was seen as able to assist in conveying the underlying dynamics behind the development of the original idea and the reasons for paths not taken, as well as having new ideas about improving the format and scripts.[39]

Under Australian law, the original talent would, in all likelihood, be free to roam. However, the broadcaster sometimes played an ongoing role in supporting and advising them. There was a perceived mutual advantage in the broadcaster being able to provide legal advice to the original producer, as well as in the producer maintaining an ongoing connection and good commercial relations with the local broadcaster, while exploring broader opportunities overseas. The notion of a format right allowed for conversations that in reality were less about the right to reproduce, to adapt or maintain the integrity of the programme concept, and more about getting reliable information about who could advise on how to modify and adapt that format without destroying its broader consumer appeal.

In summary, there were multiple reasons given for the use of format rights in the film and television industry. However, it is telling that none of our interviewees expressed concern about the current state of the law and its uncertainties in this area. To return to a point we made in the Introduction, to suggest that law reform, in the form of statutory recognition of 'format' as a category of copyright subject matter, is needed oversimplifies the matrix of factors at play here. Enhancing the power of the purported format rights owner in order to reduce legal uncertainty hardly seems necessary. Legality in relation to format rights did not appear to be a remotely significant factor that routinely affected commercial negotiations. Indeed, enhancing the rights of the format owner would seem to us to have negative consequences to the extent that it

[37] Interviewee B. [38] Interviewee B.

[39] In this sense, our research corresponds with the findings of Moran as to the importance of production consultancy services in the franchising of formats: see Moran with Malbon, *Understanding the Global TV Format*.

might impact on the flexibility need by Australian public broadcasters to manage their many and competing priorities. In this regard our empirical research supports the research undertaken by Martin Kretschmer, Sukhpreet Singh and Jon Wardle, which was focused more on the commercial television sector.[40]

While interviewees did not express concern over the state of copyright law concerning format rights, the fragile state of the Australian production industry and poor pay and conditions for many engaged in it was a recurring hot topic of conversation. Copyright was a part of these conversations too, but not discussed in the terms to which copyright scholars are accustomed. Our discussions of these issues with our interviewees generated far more interesting and unexpected information as to the role that copyright actually plays in sustaining the Australian film and television sector.

2.2 *The role of copyright in sustaining a viable industry*

As we noted in the Introduction, when looked at through the lens of formal copyright law, the challenges faced by the film and television industry seem to take on a particular form. Apparent 'gaps' in protection and uncertainties in the operation of certain copyright principles loom large. In looking at the industry from this perspective, what tends to be assumed is that copyright is worth considering because it plays the dominant role in ordering the trade in film and television production. That is, there is an underlying assumption that, notwithstanding such gaps and uncertainties in the law, copyright is what provides incentives for the creation of new works and other subject matter and the generation of royalty streams to be allocated amongst participants in the industry, which in turn provide a spur for further cultural creativity.

What is rarely considered, however, is what other factors we need to account for in explaining how the Australian industry operates, and how these intersect with copyright law. Copyright is quite clearly not the only body of law that is relevant to understanding film and television markets. Copyright, through the award of certain kinds of exclusive property rights, turns creative content into commodity or product, and exclusive rights conferred over the distribution of works and other subject matter assist in creating audiences as a further commodity.[41] But what role does copyright actually play in incentivizing such cultural production,

[40] Kretschmer, Singh and Wardle, 'The Exploitation of Television Formats'.

[41] That is, copyright's exclusive rights facilitate the assembling of audiences for discrete markets – at first instance, for film through the box office; later, for television programmes through broadcasting – and in targeting particular demographics these audiences can be onsold to advertisers.

particularly given that Australian copyright law is uninterested in promoting particular forms of cultural expression,[42] does not privilege works or other subject matter made or published in Australia[43] and makes little distinction between imported and domestic content in terms of the rights afforded to owners?[44] And to what extent does copyright generate revenue streams that are distributed amongst those within the sector to sustain the material conditions for film and television production?

What became clear from our interviews is that understanding the role of copyright in the sector requires an appreciation of two key factors. The first is the *regulatory* interest that the Australian government has taken in the cultural content that is produced and made available to Australian audiences. Public policy is not effected through copyright, but policies effected through other laws have implications for understandings of copyright within the jurisdiction and for global entertainment markets. The second factor is that of *labour*. Specifically, it is that the labour contracts currently being used in the industry are designed to create a chain of entitlements that facilitate not merely the creation of copyright works and other subject matter but also payments back to many of the contributors to such products, even if these parties are not authors or copyright owners. These factors are rarely addressed in copyright scholarship.

2.2.1 Australian film and television production

From the earliest days of the Australian film industry concerns were raised about the ability of local film-makers to achieve financial stability.

> The most common cry of producers, from the 1920s to the 1960s, was that the grip of powerful foreign production companies over the Australian distribution and exhibition trade was stifling the local industry by making Australian screens inaccessible to Australian filmmakers... Pressures on governments to protect film producers began as early as 1912 when filmmakers pleaded for a tariff barrier against imported films to protect them from excessive foreign competition.[45]

42 That is, the law looks only to whether the creative output can be classified as a 'work' or 'subject matter other than a work', rather than imposing any requirements of cultural value.

43 By virtue of the breadth of the Copyright (International Protection) Regulations 1969 (Cth), and their intersection with the copyright subsistence provisions in ss. 32 and 89–92 of the Copyright Act 1968 (Cth), works or subject matter made or first published in most countries of the world will be afforded protection under Australian law.

44 With only rare exceptions (such as the fact that under Australian law the right to cause a sound recording to be heard in public is not afforded in respect of certain recordings from a number of foreign countries: Copyright (International Protection) Regulations 1969 (Cth), reg. 6).

45 A. Pike, 'The Past: Boom or Bust', in S. Murray (ed.), *The New Australian Cinema* (Melbourne: Cinema Papers, 1980), pp. 11–12.

Australian film and television production and the markets for new releases are now affected by the provision of substantial public funding. This is made available through Screen Australia and state film funding bodies, and through the commissioning role of public broadcasters. Film production is also indirectly influenced through provision of investment and tax incentives. Tax incentives include a producer off-set, location off-sets, and post-, digital and visual effects production offsets.[46] There are also treaties to support film and television co-productions with Canada, China, Germany, Ireland, Israel, Italy, Singapore, South Africa and the United Kingdom, and MOUs with France and New Zealand.[47] It is important to note that the Australian market is not seen as necessarily the primary market or the only relevant market for subsidized productions, with one of our interviewees noting:

> I think it is definitely seen as a global market. We participate in all the major festivals . . . but obviously the client we service is the Australian industry. Not just in terms of marketing the particular films but in terms of attracting foreign investment.[48]

Foreign investment is targeted to bring large-scale commercial productions to Australia to support employment and growth of the local film and television industry. While the number of local feature films produced has remained steady for the past two decades, the role of foreign investment is steadily increasing. However, this is largely due to a small number of high-budget feature films, where the film-maker or star is internationally known and makes films both in Australia and overseas.[49]

Compliance with policies can be effected through the contractual agreement between the producer and the public funding body. However, Screen Australia bolsters its contractual right by retaining a 1 per cent copyright interest in the resulting film and through giving notice to third parties of their interest by requiring a copyright notice be attached to films.

> [Screen Australia] gives the producer in their production investment agreements the right that they hold . . . in the script, underlying the film itself . . . and once the film is made they'll give the producer the right to go and market the film – on certain terms. And if that right is breached . . . they'll call the rights back in . . . It is a bargaining chip.[50]

[46] See Australian Government, Department of Regional Australia, Local Government, Arts and Sport, *Australian Screen Production Incentive*, at http://arts.gov.au/film-tv/australian-screen-production-incentive.

[47] See Screen Australia, *Co-Pro Program*, at www.screenaustralia.gov.au/coproductions.

[48] Interviewee H.

[49] See Screen Australia, *Production Industry: Drama*, at www.screenaustralia.gov.au/research/statistics/drama.aspx.

[50] Interviewee H.

then they have the ability to say . . . 'no you can't give it away' to someone who is never going to let it see the light of day.[51]

It does give . . . a power of veto in certain circumstances if they need to provide it . . . After [a] seven-year reversion period they still maintain that 1 per cent to keep track of where the films go and end up . . . [F]rom a research perspective, they have a large research division that tracks the exploitation of films.[52]

It was acknowledged that a 1 per cent interest may not provide sufficient leverage if a party is determined to act in bad faith.[53] However, Screen Australia also has an unusually powerful position in being able to affect the reputation and ongoing opportunities of those employed in the industry, at least in Australia. The significance of this is discussed further below, and can only be understood in the context of the various media regulations affecting television broadcasting in Australia.

In relation to Australian commercial television broadcasting markets, commentator Nick Herd notes:

The fact that the Commonwealth had the constitutional power to enact copyright laws, in accordance with Australia's adherence to international covenants on intellectual property, meant that there was a pre-existing understanding as to what was being traded. However, in other areas the Government attempted to control aspects of both the audience-commodity and product-supply markets through regulatory interventions.[54]

Licence conditions of commercial broadcasters directly affect what is produced. All commercial free-to-air broadcasters are required to broadcast a minimum of 55 per cent Australian content between the hours of 6 a.m. and midnight on their core or primary commercial television broadcasting service.[55] This requirement is designed to 'promote the role of commercial television broadcasting services in developing and reflecting a sense of Australian identity, character and cultural diversity by supporting the community's continued access to television programs produced under Australian creative control'.[56] There are also minimum yearly hours mandated for the screening by commercial broadcasters of

[51] Interviewee I. [52] Interviewee H. [53] Interviewee H.

[54] N. Herd, *Networking: Commercial Television in Australia* (Sydney: Currency House, 2012), p. 84.

[55] Broadcasting Services Act 1992 (Cth) s. 121G(1) and (4), as introduced by the Broadcasting Legislation Amendment (Convergence Review and Other Measures) Act 2013 (Cth), sch. 1 item 5, which commenced on 31 March 2013. Before this date, the requirement had been contained exclusively in the Broadcasting Services (Australian Content) Standard 2005 (Cth), s. 9 (made under under s. 122(1) of the Broadcasting Services Act 1992 (Cth)). On content quotas, see generally T. Flew, 'Images of Nation: Economic and Cultural Aspects of Australian Content Regulations for Commercial Television', in J. Craik, J. Bailey and A. Moran (eds), *Public Voices, Private Interests: Australia's Media Policy* (Sydney: Allen & Unwin, 1995).

[56] Broadcasting Services (Australian Content) Standard 2005 (Cth), s. 4.

children's television[57] and local drama content,[58] as well as Australian programmes generally on secondary channels.[59] Regulations affect when and how certain programming can be screened and, for children's television, what can be advertised in those time slots, in turn affecting advertising revenues that can be generated from assembling these audiences. Definitions of 'Australian program' affect who can be engaged to produce content that meets the local content quota by setting minimum levels of employment of Australians and New Zealanders as producer, director, writer and cast and in production and post-production.[60] These broadcasting laws and regulations exist because of perceived market failures.[61] The regulations provide additional incentives to meet specific quota and content requirements for Australian audiences. Compliance with media and broadcasting regulations is overseen by the Australian Communications and Media Authority (ACMA).

Because of the way these regulations affect operations in the global market, for some kinds of programming on free-to-air channels there is often little expectation of profit. Children's television provides an excellent example of this. In a recent ACMA report into the state of children's television production in Australia it was noted that for television drama that met the relevant Children's Television Standard (CTS) investment was shared equally between the Australian government, Australian industry and foreign investors, but that it was becoming increasingly difficult to finance:

> Producers generally are adamant that CTS quotas underpin their business. Drama producers believe that without a quota system there would be no C drama programs[62] produced in this country for commercial networks . . . Network executives view the quota as a community obligation.[63]

[57] *Ibid.*, ss. 12–15. [58] *Ibid.*, ss. 10–11.

[59] Broadcasting Services Act 1992 (Cth), s. 121G(2), with every hour of first release Australian drama counting for two hours in meeting this quota: s. 121G(3).

[60] *Ibid.*, s. 121G(6) and Broadcasting Services (Australian Content) Standard 2005 (Cth), s. 7.

[61] It is easier to account for the financial implications than the perceived cultural benefits of these regulations. If the mandated 55 per cent minimum Australian content requirement were to be abandoned a recent report indicates a likely fall in Australian content broadcast to 43 per cent, and a fall in investment in producing Australian content of 28 per cent, with different impacts for different production sectors. See Pricewaterhouse Coopers, *How Do Content Requirements Impact Australian Productions? Convergence Review Research Report* (May 2011), at www.archive.dbcde.gov.au/__data/assets/pdf_file/0010/148825/PwC-How_do_content_requirements_impact_Australian_productions.pdf.

[62] That is, programmes classified as 'C' by ACMA that meet the requirements currently set out in CTS 17 of the Children's Television Standard 2009 (Cth).

[63] ACMA, *Children's Television Production Project* (April 2007), p. 7, at www.acma.gov.au/webwr/_assets/main/lib310132/childrens_tv_production_project.pdf.

Budgets for all children's drama and non-drama were very small. In a climate where international licensing fees were diminishing due to competition and, in particular, perceptions of 'dumping' of product from dedicated US children's cable channels, local programming made to comply with CTS obligations was considered 'too Australian' to have wide international appeal. Further, as production was focused on meeting minimum licence requirements, networks often only made short-term, series-by-series commitments and invested relatively little in promotion of these programmes. A short-run series of thirteen or twenty-six episodes was taken to lack the brand recognition necessary to build a potentially lucrative merchandise tie-in revenue stream.[64] By way of comparison, in-house produced pre-school (or 'P') programming has to compete with overseas product that may be available for no or a very low licence fee because overseas producers derive returns from merchandising, DVD sales and live concerts.[65]

Combined, the regulatory initiatives designed to support Australian film and television production significantly disrupt and distort the operation of copyright markets. Copyright underpins all the works produced, but it is far less relevant in creating production incentives in the Australian market. An overarching and a priori concern is raising the finance required to make the film or television programme in the first place, and to make the necessary mix of programming to meet regulatory requirements and commercial expectations. This challenge, of course, involves paying the many people who make all these products, and such parties are far more numerous than those that are deemed to be deserving of the grant of copyright protection. This raises questions about the relationship between copyright and the labour markets that sustain Australian cultural production.

2.2.2 *Underlying labour markets*

Our interviewees consistently noted the leadership role played by Screen Australia in setting industry standard terms and conditions of employment for film and television work, affecting both commercial and publicly funded productions. As one interviewee observed,

> Screen Australia has a much bigger role in the industry here than the UK Film Council . . . If you compare Ofcom[66] to ACMA, you have Ofcom that has a lot of weight, and threw it around . . . whereas the UK Film Council just invested in stuff but didn't set the agenda . . . Where I find, here, projects don't happen

[64] *Ibid.*, p. 18. [65] *Ibid.*, p. 20.
[66] That is, the independent regulator of the UK communications industries.

unless Screen Australia invests in them . . . [Screen Australia has] a really big role, even just in the contracting process . . . here, everyone looks to Screen Australia [, which] has the primary document everyone feeds into. It is just a very different role to the agencies in the other various markets.[67]

The role of Screen Australia in setting standards goes beyond their role in establishing terms and conditions as a party to film funding and investment agreements with producers. All our interviewees noted that they set the tone for the trade and this includes adhering to broader industrial expectations around pay and conditions for many others involved in the productions. Screen Australia indirectly supports the industrial awards negotiated and rates set by unions such as the Media, Arts and Entertainment Alliance and guild bodies such as the Australian Writers' Guild. This role was considered particularly important in an industry that would otherwise be open to exploitation, with a workforce predominantly made up of independent subcontractors working in creative, production and post-production roles, with relatively unstable work, often working long hours under difficult conditions and engaged on short-term contracts.[68]

Technicalities as to whose efforts warranted a grant of copyright under the Copyright Act were frequently overlooked due to the higher priority of ensuring the correct people were kept on board and got paid. So, for example, there were common 'work-arounds' for directors who are not awarded full ownership rights in their films under Australian law:[69]

There's an interesting thing happening at the moment because of our copyright issues . . . [Highly successful directors get] credited as a producer, and part of that reason is because of the control of the copyright issues.[70]

[H]istorically, a lot of the films . . . in the [nineteen] eighties were with – you know – if you like, 'auteur' directors, particularly feature film[s]. And they often didn't take credits of producer . . . [T]hey may have been a writer or a co-writer . . . but, [for example,] Peter Weir: in that whole era, you won't find his name . . . credited as a scriptwriter. I think you will, more and more, now, in his works.[71]

67 Interviewee I.

68 See generally D. Throsby, *The Economics of Cultural Policy* (Cambridge University Press, 2010), pp. 80–2. For an organizational management perspective, see M. L. Jones, G. K. Kriflik and M. Zanko, 'Understanding Worker Motivation in the Australian Film Industry', paper presented at the Australian and New Zealand Academy of Management Conference, Canberra, 2005 at http://ro.uow.edu.au/commpapers/48/.

69 To explain, s. 98(6) of Copyright Act 1968 (Cth) affords only non-employee directors of non-commissioned films the right to receive remuneration, and only when their films that are broadcast over free-to-air television are retransmitted by subscription television broadcasters. See generally M. Handler, 'Continuing Problems with Film Copyright', in F. Macmillan (ed.), *New Directions in Copyright Law*, vol. 6 (Cheltenham: Edward Elgar, 2007).

70 Interviewee S. 71 Interviewee T.

Auteur directors and scriptwriters can spend years progressing a project to get it to the stage that it is possible to apply for funding support and, then, once funding is on board, to develop it to get it on screen. Depending on the subject matter, at all stages this may involve ongoing collaborations with many other creative workers whose ephemeral contributions are incapable of giving rise to copyright. Accordingly, in copyright terms, much of this labour is invisible and may as well be unremunerated. However, the Australian Writers' Guild and Australian Directors Guild set payment rates for many of these non-copyright contributions that can be charged once funding for the project has been secured.[72] Likewise, under Australian legislation, only the scriptwriter and producer have a relevant copyright interest in the underlying dramatic work and film, respectively.[73] However, creative use of attribution of 'co-writer' and 'co-producer' titles can work to remedy copyright's blindness to the merits of respective claims by contributing parties who might not fit the law's definition of 'author' or 'producer'.[74] In any case, there is some degree of fluidity as to what contributions are perceived to be relevant to which role, and in how individuals perform these.[75] Thus, contractual agreements as to attribution can lead to significant reallocations of both copyright revenue to key parties involved in the production and degrees of artistic control, contrary to what is imagined as possible when viewed from a doctrinal perspective of copyright law's taxonomy of rights and ownership provisions.

Actors, who have only limited performers' rights under Australian copyright law,[76] are also beneficiaries of revenues generated by copyright through relevant industry agreements. For example, in television there are fees for repeats and residuals paid to actors related to those uses. These rates are based on a percentage of sales and other kinds of exploitation of copyright in ancillary markets.[77] Interviewees agreed that these agreements now pose a major problem in the industry:

72 Interviewee T.

73 Subject to the very limited rights for directors, outlined in n. 68, above.

74 This dynamic is discussed further in L. Bently and L. Biron, 'The author strikes back: mutating authorship in the expanded universe', in this collection.

75 Where matters appear to be more controversial is where the roles of non-drama directors are blurred with those of drama directors, for example, for awards purposes: see, e.g., G. Hardie, 'Directors Slam Academy's Race', *Sydney Morning Herald* (online), 6 December 2012, at www.smh.com.au/entertainment/tv-and-radio/directors-slam-academys-race-20121206–2ax8h.html.

76 These include rights to prevent unauthorized recording of live performances, and various moral rights of performership. See generally Copyright Act 1968 (Cth), pts. XIA and IX respectively. But see Beijing Treaty on Audiovisual Performances, opened for signature 24 June 2012, 51 ILM 1214 (not yet in force).

77 See Media, Entertainment and Arts Alliance, *Actors Television Programs Agreement, 2008*, at www.alliance.org.au/award-summaries/view-document/actor-s-television-programs-agreement.

> There were loads of historical rights at the broadcaster I was working at and basically they got to the point that there is no way we can exploit this going forward because there is no way we can possibly get all the releases . . . we just don't know what we've got and what we're going to do with it.[78]

Also,

> we have a particular problem, the repeats and residuals agreements that we have are actually too expensive now in terms of clearing rights by comparison with what the market is paying. So that's why you are not seeing 'Water Rats' and [other] old Australian TV series [on Australian television] because they are too expensive to clear the [actor residual] rights.[79]

Labour agreements with actors piggyback on copyright royalties that are generated downstream and over time. These agreements create copyright-related payments to performers that, in formal copyright terms, have no direct interest in the copyright needing consideration. Difficulties in clearing actor residuals were reported to us as a much larger problem affecting the film and television industry than problems with 'orphan works'.[80] While copyright scholarship and the current reform agenda in countries like Australia may currently be preoccupied with the latter issue,[81] any reform to permit more-efficient exploitation of historical rights will most likely fail if these provisions as they affect further film and television exploitation are drafted in ignorance of implications for underlying labour agreements with non-copyright owners.

A striking feature of our interviews is that in an age of declining union power, in an industry dominated by independent contractors, and where, through government supported places for relevant professional degrees there is an ongoing and bountiful supply of skilled labour coming through film, television and acting schools, it is clear that union or guild labour agreements still hold much sway. This historical power base is no longer well supported by Australian industrial law, which views collective bargaining with suspicion.[82] Organizations such as Screen Australia indirectly facilitate an ongoing union and guild influence, but this was not

[78] Interviewee I. [79] Interviewee G. [80] Interviewees B, C, F, G.

[81] See, in Australia, Australian Law Reform Commission, *Copyright and the Digital Economy*, Report 122 (November 2013), ch. 13, at www.alrc.gov.au/publications/copyright-and-digital-economy-report-122; D. Brennan and M. Fraser, *The Use of Subject Matter with Missing Owners – Australian Copyright Policy Options* (August 2011), at http://web.archive.org/web/20120322162439/http://www.law.uts.edu.au/comslaw/Researchreports/MissingOwnersDiscussionPaperAugust11.pdf.

[82] Australian industrial law has been subject to an extraordinary amount of legal change in the last decade. See generally A. Forsyth and A. Stewart, *Fair Work: The New Workplace Laws and the Work Choices Legacy* (Sydney: Federation Press, 2009); R. Owens, J. Riley and J. Murray, *The Law of Work*, 2nd edn (Melbourne: Oxford University Press, 2011).

identified to us as the only or even the main reason for ongoing reliance on collective bargaining around standard terms. While we were privy to some disagreement about whether guilds serving creatives should be 'dominated' by unionists who are not actually themselves experienced writers, directors or producers, collective bargaining was often referred to as a preferable way of managing relations than relying on employment law and contract alone. While labour law will always continue to regulate some aspects of the sector, it was felt to be not necessarily sympathetic to all of the artistic and economic issues involved. Individual entitlement-based employment law is largely insensitive to problems of obtaining funding for projects in the first place, to the short-term nature of the employment in the film and television industry and to the broader questions of industry sustainability that flow from this. There are significant problems of proper accounting for production costs that usually need to be paid before royalties for exploitation of copyright can be counted. Predicting, and accounting for, revenue from exploitation of copyright through sales and distribution is problematic. Standard industry agreements are attractive because they provide some greater certainty and financial stability for all involved in what can be an unstable trade based on exploitation of copyright and, in particular, since these agreements can facilitate minimum pay and conditions for a much larger number of contributors than those covered by awards.

There is some formal institutional recognition of the need for standard labour terms. This can be seen from a recent application to the Australian Competition and Consumer Commission (ACCC) by the AWG seeking authorization to bargain collectively and not be caught by prohibitions on cartel conduct.[83] SPAA and Screen Australia were parties to the application. The AWG membership draws from writers employed in film and television in Australia:

> Writers are almost always independent contractors, not employees, and therefore unable by law to unionize, or to collectively bargain without ACCC authorization. [The AWG's] industrial status is that of a professional association, not [one comprised of] unionized employees. So what AWG has done over the years is negotiate with SPAA to establish some recommended minimum rates/conditions and model contracts. Negotiated agreements exist for children's television, television series and serials, television mini-series and telemovies, [and] there are also recommended agreements for feature film, theatre and other forms of writing.[84]

[83] See Australian Writers' Guild Ltd, Authorisation A91274 (2011), at http://transition.accc.gov.au/content/index.phtml/itemId/1006639.
[84] Interviewee R.

The application to the ACCC was brought on the ground that most screenwriters are freelancers and not entitled to minimum rates of pay that would apply to employees of production houses. Services rendered were described as project-specific and time-specific, where the writer would often be unable to secure work unless they were attached to a producer able to attract public funding for the project. It was argued that this situation placed writers in an unfair bargaining position respective to producers 'who control the flow of money'.[85] Frequent changes in taxation law applying in the industry and to Australian content policies were cited in the application to the ACCC as creating additional definitional uncertainties affecting funding. This, it was alleged, 'makes it difficult for Screen Australia, producers and the individual writers themselves, to have any certainty themselves around what constitutes "fair and reasonable" conduct by public funding recipients in relation to writers'.[86] AWG writers compete against one another for work and AWG benchmarks are not mandatory. AWG members are not obliged to adhere to the benchmarks, but most do.[87]

The public benefit of allowing for the establishment of model terms of trade was stated as providing:

- guidance for Screen Australia as to what constitutes 'fair and reasonable' conduct when public-funded recipients engage writers to inform Screen Australia terms of trade;
- improvements in the level of input writers have in contractual negotiations;
- efficiencies that arise from the establishment of an industry benchmark;
- reduced transactions costs for both writers and producers;
- improvements in information flow between writers in different geographic locations; and
- for the continued quality of Australian content.[88]

In authorizing the AWG collectively to negotiate model agreements that can be used by current and future members, the ACCC noted that collective bargaining was likely to

[85] Australian Writers' Guild, Application A91274, Form B, 'Agreements Affecting Competition or Incorporating Related Cartel Provisions: Application for Authorisation', Submission in Support, 6 September 2011, p. 8, at http://transition.accc.gov.au/content/index.phtml/itemId/1006639/display/application.

[86] *Ibid.*, p. 10.

[87] We were referred to examples in theatre where parties took less than their standard entitlement. However, this was done in order to assist productions going ahead, and, in one case, a prominent writer took a cut so that other contributors to the performance would be able to be paid at a modestly acceptable rate: interviewee Q.

[88] Australian Writers' Guild, Application A91274, Form B, 'Agreements Affecting Competition or Incorporating Related Cartel Provisions: Application for Authorisation', Submission in Support, pp. 13–15.

> provide AWG members with a greater opportunity to have effective input into the terms and conditions of their engagement contracts. This improved input provides a mechanism through which AWG members may be able to negotiate more efficient outcomes when compared to a situation where they individually negotiate contracts or accept terms from producers on a take it or leave it basis.[89]

The ACCC authorization permits the establishment of benchmark fees for a range of contributions by writers that copyright law would not necessarily recognize as requiring payment, such as for story conferencing, brainstorming sessions and providing original concepts. Fees overall are set with reference to the different royalty rates that apply for particular genres. A standard inclusion is the disclaimer that 'Nothing in this clause shall prevent the Producer from acquiring from the Writer the full copyright of the original concept at any time prior to or during the production'.[90]

Within the industry there is some disagreement about whether the ACCC authorization is particularly significant. It does not actually change industry practice. It simply permits existing agreements to continue without risk of falling foul of the Competition and Consumer Act 2010 (Cth). Further, from a strict doctrinal perspective, terms of trade that allow for 'copyright-like' payments for a range of services are arguably irrelevant to understanding copyright as a body of law. In an Australian context, lawyers drafting film and television contracts that include, as a standard term, rights to concepts or formats could be taken to be merely implementing relevant industrial agreements rather than attempting to alter the legal rights conferred by copyright law. The disclaimer referred to above could certainly be interpreted in this way. That is, the clause confirms that while a model agreement creates certain entitlements for writers providing a range of services it does not affect the operation of copyright law.

However, this interpretation ignores the reality that implicit in these 'labour' agreements is the idea that the original concept can in fact be owned in copyright. Further, the reason the producer needs to own all 'rights' related to the original concept is in order to manage the distributions of payments to the very large number and different kinds of

89 Australian Competition and Consumer Commission, Determination, 'Application by the Australian Writers' Guild in Respect of Collective Bargaining of Model Terms of Engagement on Behalf of Current and Future Members with the Screen Producers Association of Australia', Authorisation Number A91274, Public Register Number C2011/771, 25 January 2012, at http://transition.accc.gov.au/content/index.phtml/itemId/1006639/display/acccDecision.

90 Australian Writers' Guild, Application A91274, Attachment 1 – Television Model Terms of Engagement, cl. 4.2, at http://transition.accc.gov.au/content/index.phtml/itemId/1006639/display/application.

contributors involved in the project, regardless of whether or not a particular contribution also gives rise to a copyright interest. We think there is a need to consider these arrangements as involving more than a question of the interface between copyright and labour law. This is because the clauses are actively performing much of the role that copyright claims to do, serving as the lynchpin of the economic opportunities created by and through law for a wide range of contributors to projects.[91]

In our view, the formal legal distinction made between creation of property and provision of labour services as a contractor has little traction in practice. What is being secured through these legal practices is not 'trickle-down' revenue to subsidiary exclusive rights holders but basic entitlements as negotiated between the relevant industrial actors and public funding bodies, as required to sustain the material conditions of film and television production.

This conclusion draws inspiration from the seminal work of Bernard Edelman, *Ownership of the Image*.[92] This book traces changes in the interpretation of labour associated with photography and film-making in the early twentieth century. Edelman argues that there was a change in the interpretation of the significance of the labour of photographers that accompanied the commercial development of cinema, allowing them to move from the status of mechanical worker into the creative class. This recharacterization justified the creation of new image rights to the benefit of capital. The film-maker/producer, through contract, automatically owned the product of the efforts of the cinematographer, but they needed a claim to 'creative' labour to lay the foundation for a new kind of ownership of the image.[93]

Following Edelman, our work also suggests that film copyright is integrally related to the establishment of an extended chain of labour relations. However, at least in Australia today, this is not a one-way transaction where all benefits accrue to the producer who 'owns' the image rights. The labour contracts currently being used (and as supported by collective bargaining, standard contracts and public money) create a chain of entitlements that facilitate creation of the copyright work *and* payments back to some of these contributors from copyright royalties.

[91] This is not only overlooked in legal scholarship, but also by cultural economists. For example, in *The Economics of Cultural Policy*, Throsby considers labour relations and the role of copyright in chapters 5 and 13 in complete isolation from one another.

[92] B. Edelman, *Ownership of the Image: Elements of a Marxist Theory of Law* (London: Routledge, 1979).

[93] For a critique of Edelman's theory, see K. Bowrey, '"The World Daguerreotyped – What a Spectacle!" Copyright Law, Photography and the Economic Mission of Empire', in B. Sherman and L. Wiseman (eds), *Copyright and the Challenge of the New* (Alphen aan den Rijn: Kluwer Law International, 2012).

We believe that, in this context, film copyright is less about establishing exclusive private rights to specific kinds of works that, in a Marxist sense, allow for extraction of surpluses from labourers, and more about using contract, labour and copyright in combination to support and sustain extended creative communities that, we were told, would otherwise find it hard to exist.

To put it another way, in the Australian film and television industry, and as deployed through standard institutionalized practices, royalties serve as far more than 'just deserts' for making particular kinds of 'creative' works or other subject matter. What copyright facilitates is the collective management of a wide range of labour relations, with a view to bringing an 'original concept' of perceived cultural value to 'completion', so it can be consumed by assembled audiences and begin to generate revenues in many and varied ways. The primary form of consumption for first-release film and television products is well established, but terms of trade are not restricted to revenues generated by broadcast or screening rights. There is anticipation of the possibility of spin-offs, tie-ins and merchandising rights as a standard term, even though in many cases there will be no market for these kinds of derivative or ancillary products. This possibility is anticipated at the outset, because what needs accounting for is not simply all the revenues derived from sales of discrete products and their associated copyright royalties but all the commercial opportunities directly and indirectly generated by the original production, up and downstream. In this sense, royalties generated are pooled assets that enable a much larger and fluid network of creative and productive relations with benefits shared (not necessarily equally or fairly)[94] amongst members of the relevant creative communities.

3 Instituting copyright

In an important discussion of the concept of property in the 1990s, Alain Pottage noted

> that property theory offers only a simple ontology of persons and things. This limitation might be traced to the deeply entrenched assumptions that property presupposes some naturalistic form of 'scarcity' . . . The idea of scarcity is informed by the common sense representation of 'society' as a set of interactions taking place between individuals inhabiting a determinate area of linear social space.[95]

[94] There are, of course, long-standing disagreements between writers, directors, producers and performers about appropriate recognition of the importance of their respective roles. See, e.g., ABC Radio National, 'Moral Rights', *Law Report*, 17 April 2001, at www.abc.net.au/radionational/programs/lawreport/moral-rights/3479646.

[95] A. Pottage, 'Instituting Property' (1998) 18 *Oxford Journal of Legal Studies* 331, 337.

He added further that property theory 'has lost touch with the practical, social, meaning of ownership', and notes that, in relation to large-scale enterprise centred on the corporation, 'ownership is a problem rather than a pre-proposition'.[96]

Copyright scholarship adopts the standard common law property ontology in the assignation of its owners and objects. Copyright law is taken, through the significance attributed to 'the author' (or 'the maker') to demarcate individual owners of discrete limited exclusive rights to particular intangible objects that would not exist 'but for' the incentive of the monopoly. However, as we have shown, in practice the designated rights fail to mobilize all the necessary labour and capital essential for the creation of Australian film and television products. A much wider network of productive relations is required to generate cultural commodities capable of exploitation. In the Australian film and television industry, public institutions and labour guilds are required to step into that breach. They, individually and collectively, through the adoption of standard terms of trade, administer key mechanisms that help manage the 'problems of ownership' and facilitate the pursuit of profit.

Further, the pursuit of profit has a more complex relationship with time and space than that envisaged in conventional copyright discourse. Scholarship conventionally imagines a simplistic vector from origination to exploitation to end-user, where the legal object (in the form of the copyright work or other subject matter) retains its ontological identity as a form of property through time. However, as is well understood in industry, notwithstanding the deployment of marketing and media strategies, audience and critical reception of creative work is unpredictable.[97] Further, 'success' is not fixed to the original 'window' for the product. Audience appeal, measured in box office returns and ratings, creates the impetus to revisit the significance of the 'original concept' because a 'good' audience reception generates the possibility of more and new audiences, and more and new ways of consuming different versions of the 'same' product, made in the original format (as prequels, sequels, spin-offs, new series) and as entirely new and different kinds of tie-in merchandise.[98] As success is unpredictable, there is always uncertainty and instability in defining what is 'the hook', the point of emotional connection or the essential identity of the original work, at first instance.

[96] *Ibid.*, p. 338.

[97] See generally K. Bowrey, 'The Manufacture of Authentic Buzz and the Legal Relations of *Masterchef*', in D. Hunter *et al.* (eds), *Amateur Media: Social, Cultural and Legal Perspectives* (London: Routledge, 2012).

[98] It is thus no surprise that many television formats also found extended product franchises.

The logic of commodification of film and television product drives us towards adopting vague and indeterminate boundaries around the originating legal object so that the owner can 'capture' an economic potential that will fluctuate for a wide range of reasons (many of which may be entirely beyond the owner's control), over time. The recourse to contractual clauses assigning ownership of 'original concepts' currently reflects the commercial logic of copyright law by allowing potential value to be captured as opportunities rise and fall. For this reason, simplistic and doctrinally focused explanations of the 'relevant' legal rights created by fixed copyright works only further mystifies the complexity of social and economic relations in play.

The case that copyright is not merely law but is institutionalized through industry practice that adopts, as common sense, the need for ownership of 'concepts', raises significant questions about how we should construct the relevant economy in reviewing the purpose and efficacy of copyright laws and the appropriate copyright 'balance' more generally. It has become fashionable to produce economic data on the copyright industries. This often involves myopically looking at the economics of copyright through the lens of the respective interests of 'owners' and 'users'.[99] Economists for different lobbies produce rival accounts of the value of the sector, and costs and benefits of copyright to owners, technology makers and users.[100] In constructing the key issues as if copyright alone were the central incentive for production, and that the size and health of the production sector depends primarily on owner initiative supported by strong copyright, *absent any habitual acknowledgement of the key support provided by government through a wide range of other laws and quasi-public institutions*, many economic analyses, both pro and anti strong owner rights, are creating a highly misleading simulation.

4 Conclusion

In our view, contracts create purported legal rights to own formats, spin-offs and ancillary rights that copyright law says cannot be owned because of a need to manage the extended chain of labour relations that

[99] For example, see the terms of reference of the Australian Law Reform Commission's inquiry into *Copyright and the Digital Economy*, 29 June 2012, at www.alrc.gov.au/inquiries/copyright/terms-reference.

[100] See, e.g., Copyright Agency Ltd, Submission No. 766 to Australian Law Reform Commission, *Copyright and the Digital Economy*, Discussion Paper 79 (May 2013), attachment 2 (March 2011), at www.alrc.gov.au/sites/default/files/subs/766._org__attachment_2_2011_pwc_final_report.pdf, and attachment 3 (March 2012), at www.alrc.gov.au/sites/default/files/subs/766._org_attachment_3_an_economic_analysis_of_education_exceptions_in_copyright_-_pwc_final_report.pdf.

underlie the creation of value associated with the production and exploitation of copyright. There is a need for considerable flexibility in defining the relevant material relations and associated legal objects that underpin production of value and impact on the creation of commercial opportunities that manifest downstream. Further, with Australian cultural production there is also an intermingling of cultural and economic agendas that adds an additional layer of complexity and mix of incentives.

Copyright law does not operate in isolation. Copyright owners do not negotiate over the value of copyright fees and royalties separate from consideration of other factors and revenues gained from other sources that contribute to the financial viability of the enterprise. Attempts to map copyright as if it were an autonomous domain ignore the key interaction between copyright and other laws that support Australian cultural production.

The Australian Law Reform Commission, in its *Copyright and the Digital Economy* inquiry, noted an increasing reference to and reliance on 'economic evidence' by stakeholders about the copyright industries, and a concern that any reform of Australian law be 'evidence-based'. However, much available evidence was judged to be unreliable, self-serving or inadequate.[101] In evaluating industry economics there is a danger of treating copyright law as intrinsically valuable, divorced from real engagement with addressing this body of law's purported social purpose and the value of strong links with other key areas of cultural and economic policy. Copyright discourse today habitually strips the cultural agendas out of the consideration of creation of cultural production, assuming those are catered for by 'neighbouring' areas of media law and broadcasting regulation which are not of direct relevance to copyright in practice. In doing so, what is created in copyright is a barren discourse based upon free market fantasies about the economics of the cultural industries and of copyright. What is required instead – and what this chapter is intended to contribute towards – is an enrichment of copyright discourse by a refocus of attention on the interaction between copyright and other related laws and policies designed to serve the interests of all those engaged in Australian cultural production.

For much of copyright's history it has been difficult to trace the development to this body of law without reference to the roles of guilds and key institutional players. However, scholarly interest in guilds and other institutions has largely been directed towards tracing the wins and losses of competing classes of 'owners' and their ability to influence specific law

[101] Australian Law Reform Commission, *Copyright in the Digital Economy*, Report 122, pp. 74–9.

reform enactments.[102] There has been insufficient attention to the role of institutions as managers of 'problems of ownership' and as brokers of the labour relations that underpin copyright productions. It is provocative to focus legal discussion in copyright on the wider network of social relations between people built through laws and contracts, rather than on the formal rights of persons to things. However, we strongly believe that the conventional copyright inquiry is too simplistic. The full matrix of social relations that copyright sets in train needs accounting for, including the way interests are collectively managed and maintained through law and interested institutions. This research hopes to bring the labour question back into copyright focus, not as an issue of ownership but as a bread-and-butter practical issue, and in so doing help work towards building a better understanding of how copyright works in practice.

[102] See, e.g., J. Feather, *Publishing, Piracy and Politics: An Historical Study of Copyright in Britain* (London: Mansell, 1994); M. Rose, *Authors and Owners: The Invention of Copyright* (Cambridge, MA: Harvard University Press, 1995); I. Alexander, '"Neither Bolt nor Chain, Iron Safe nor Private Watchman, Can Prevent the Theft of Words": The Birth of the Performing Right in Britain', in R. Deazley, M. Kretschmer and L. Bently (eds), *Privilege and Property: Essays on the History of Copyright* (Cambridge: OpenBook Publishers, 2010).

8 Flamenco music in copyright historiography

*José Bellido**

1 Introduction

This chapter explores the status of flamenco music in the historiography of Spanish and international copyright. The appearance of flamenco at the 1887 annual conference of the *Association Littéraire et Artistique Internationale* (*ALAI*), held in Madrid,[1] only a year after the signing of the Berne Convention for the Protection of Literary and Artistic Works, caused considerable political and cultural scandal. Flamenco music, a Spanish art form with a long tradition, challenged the new international copyright norms emerging in the late nineteenth and early twentieth centuries. The chapter explains why flamenco initially seemed so challenging to copyright. Further, it explores how and why key institutions, especially the Spanish Collecting Society of Authors (*Sociedad de Autores Españoles* (SAE))[2] and Madrid's Royal Conservatory of Music, successfully brought the administration of professional flamenco musicians into the nascent copyright regime. A historical study of flamenco's place within the copyright regime unsettles some existing ideas about the nature of copyright. In fact, the trajectory of flamenco demonstrates why it is important to consider copyright law from the perspective of legal institutions and professional agents, each of which sought to refashion copyright's domain to suit their cultural agendas and aspirations. The 1887 conference, too, reminds us of the contingency of copyright's history. More specifically, the story of flamenco draws attention away from

* I would like to thank Kathy Bowrey, José Manuel Gamboa, Michael Handler, Enrique Martín Garea, Carmen García-Matos and David Lobenstine for many helpful discussions. Thanks as well to Elena Magallanes and Marí-Luz González Peña for facilitating access to archival materials.

[1] A more detailed exploration of the event and the discussions about the incorporation of Latin America in international copyright is found in J. Bellido, 'Copyright in Latin America: Experiences of the Making (1880–1910)', PhD thesis, University of London (2009), ch. 3.

[2] The name and the corporate structure of the society varied greatly during the twentieth century until it became known as the *Sociedad General de Autores y Editores* (SGAE) in 1939. I have kept the first acronym (SAE) but highlighted the changes in the chapter.

an easy fixation: that copyright is primarily about the private rights of authors to particular kinds of works. Flamenco instead enables us to focus on what is arguably a far more significant power – that which copyright organizations vest in managers and bureaucrats, allowing them to map the movement of people, control social settings and public spaces, and in turn transform the nature of our shared cultural experience.

2 A scandalous meeting

The Madrid *ALAI* conference was much anticipated. A few years earlier, the Association had to cancel a meeting there because of plague spreading across the country.[3] Now there was an opportune moment to travel to that picturesque country to spread the good news: *ALAI* was eager to capitalize on the success of the international copyright agreement completed just a few months earlier,[4] and some prominent figures in the incipient field of international copyright 'doctrine' decided to cross the Pyrenees to participate in the conference.[5] Academic exchanges were peppered with social entertainment, demonstrating the relational matrix that existed between a very particular type of casual social engagement and the development of international copyright doctrine. Entertainment, however, had its limits. Some members worried about inviting jurists to embrace the underworlds of flamenco music and dance. Those fears were soon confirmed. As one cartoon depicted, it was a terrible surprise to see these reputed scholars veering from the high road of copyright debate to low amusements such as bullfights and flamenco parties (Fig. 8.1).[6]

Spaniards seemed embarrassed to witness these foreigners, experts in copyright, actively involved in 'the clapping of the women surrounding the dancers'.[7] Newspapers described 'dancers in tight dresses with lavish sparkling flounces' and criticized the organizers for inviting learned copyright scholars to listen to 'lascivious and monotonous music from the guitar played by the skilled fingers of someone versed in that popular art

[3] 'Bulletin', Conference of the *Association Littéraire et Artistique Internationale* (Madrid), 1887; see also Archivo diplomático y consular de España, 30 September 1887, p. 2235.

[4] For a comprehensive history, see S. Ricketson and J. Ginsburg, *International Copyright and Neighbouring Rights: The Berne Convention and Beyond*, 2nd edn (Oxford University Press, 2006).

[5] José del Castillo y Soriano, letter to Jules Lermina, 30 July 1887, Archivo de la Asociación de Escritores y Artistas (AAEA).

[6] 'Resultados Prácticos del Congreso Literario', *El Cabecilla* (Madrid), 22 October 1887, p. 2.

[7] J. O. Munilla, 'Madrid', *El Imparcial*, 17 October 1887, p. 1.

Figure 8.1 The magazine *El Cabecilla* (1887) with the caption: 'Practical results of the *ALAI* Literary Conference: reception, dinner, bullfight and flamenco'
Courtesy of Biblioteca Nacional de España

coming from Cadiz'.[8] Flamenco was not the only controversial subject matter of the conference. Tensions emerged about the future of international copyright itself,[9] as did anxieties about the role of these 'foreign' experts in dealing with politically sensitive topics such as the right of translation.[10] Spain, too, remained troubled by her place in international copyright. Tensions that had become apparent at the Berne Convention a year earlier continued. Spain was seeking to maintain regional influence in Latin America at a time when the USA was not a signatory to Berne.[11] The conference also drew particular attention to questions about the role of Spanish-speaking countries in the emerging international copyright regime.[12] It brought to the fore cultural tensions that a fragile international copyright network, and Spain in particular, would need to manage if the promise of an international regime was to bear economic fruit.[13]

3 Flamenco as a work of authorship

Flamenco did not sit comfortably amongst traditional works of copyright. It depended on oral tradition. The expression of flamenco itself was inseparable from the people and the place of its making. A romanticized description can be found in Irving Brown's *Nights and Days of the Gypsy Trail* (1922):

> The aspect of the hall was no less sinister than that of the people who were dancing in couples, or drinking at little tables. The women were majas, and the men looked as though they might have been cutthroats. 'I thought I might find

8 See above; F. Martín, 'Otras Consideraciones Sobre el Titulado Congreso Literario', *El Siglo, Diario Político* (5 and 7 November 1887).

9 'These congresses [are] extremely controversial because they deal with the manner in which the international discourse is grounded': Martín, 'Otras Consideraciones Sobre el Titulado Congreso Literario', p. 1; 'We do not agree with all the statements made by Manuel Fernández Martín but most of his appreciations are accurate', *El Fígaro. Periódico Liberal Conservador*, 17 November 1887, p. 1.

10 The right of translation was the key debate in international copyright by the end of the nineteenth century. See, e.g., L. Bently 'Copyright and Translations in the English Speaking World' (1993) 12 *Translatio: FIT Newsletter* 491; C. Seville, *The Internationalisation of Copyright Law: Books, Buccaneers and the Black Flag in the Nineteenth Century* (Cambridge University Press, 2006), ch. 3; and E. H. Wirtén, 'A Diplomatic Salto Mortale: Translation Trouble in Berne, 1884–1886' (2011) 14 *Book History* 88.

11 J. Bellido, 'Colonial Copyright Extensions: Spain at the Berne Convention (1883–1899)' (2010) 58 *Journal of the Copyright Society of the USA* 243.

12 F. Martín, *Signos del Tiempo: Congreso Literario-Artístico-Internacional de 1887* (Madrid: J. A. García, 1887).

13 J. Bellido, 'Latin American and Spanish Copyright Relations (1880–1904)' (2009) 12 *Journal of World Intellectual Property* 1.

some of our people here, and organize a little entertainment, a juergacita; my Gypsy guide offered by way of explanation. The place reminded me of the café cantante in Seville.'[14]

Flamenco was supposedly conceived as a collective expression of popular culture. It was said to be a kind of musical genre of the region of Andalusia.[15] The music, seemingly by definition, was improvisational and informal. *Juergas* ('happenings') were arranged in a peculiar, spontaneous way that required audience participation. Flamenco's shifting and ephemeral nature stymied the usual identificatory gestures of copyright: there were no written works, no identifiable authors. It was certainly not 'high culture', and it was even difficult to determine what music might be performed in advance.[16] 'Folklore', not copyright, was the distinction used to classify these kinds of popular expressions. Nevertheless, although the SAE was initially dismissive, soon after the *ALAI* conference in Madrid it was fielding inquiries about the copyright status of flamenco. The SAE was constituted in 1888 to collect copyright revenue for literary, dramatic and musical works, including theatrical performances of copyrighted works.[17] Soon thereafter the SAE distributed copyright representatives throughout the majority of Spain's provinces and abroad, and starting in 1910 the Society produced atlases to facilitate copyright collection from music venues in Spain, and with the ambition of including Latin American venues (Fig. 8.2).

As agents visited music halls and other theatrical venues in order to collect royalties, they soon realized that flamenco should also come under the SAE's regulatory purview. However, the Society's atlas was of little help in gathering information about flamenco happenings.[18] Flamenco did not produce a paper trace – there were no programmes, playbills or *bordereaux*, no evidence that would enable the Society to function in its usual task of collecting copyright.[19] In describing the features

[14] See I. Brown, *Nights and Days of the Gypsy Trail: Through Andalusia and on Other Mediterranean Shores* (New York: Harper & Row, 1922), pp. 53–4.

[15] An excellent musicological study of flamenco and copyright is given by P. Manuel, 'Composition, Authorship, and Ownership in Flamenco, Past and Present' (2010) 54 *Ethnomusicology* 106.

[16] 'A los Autores de Flamenco' (1934) 24 *El Derecho de Autor* 231.

[17] See generally S. Delgado, *Mi Teatro* (Madrid: Hijos M. G. Hernández, 1904); and L. G. Iberni, 'La Constitución de la Sociedad de Autores' (2001) 8–9 *Cuadernos de Música Iberoamericana* 227.

[18] See, e.g., *Boletín de la Sociedad de Autores Españoles* (Madrid), October 1927, p. 9, n. 159 (demanding a list of establishments).

[19] On the importance of *bordereaux*, see J. Bellido, 'Copyright at a Distance: From Action to Management (1880–1910)', paper presented at First Annual International Society for the History and Theory of Intellectual Property conference, 'The Construction of Immateriality, Practices of Appropriation and the Genealogy of Intellectual Property',

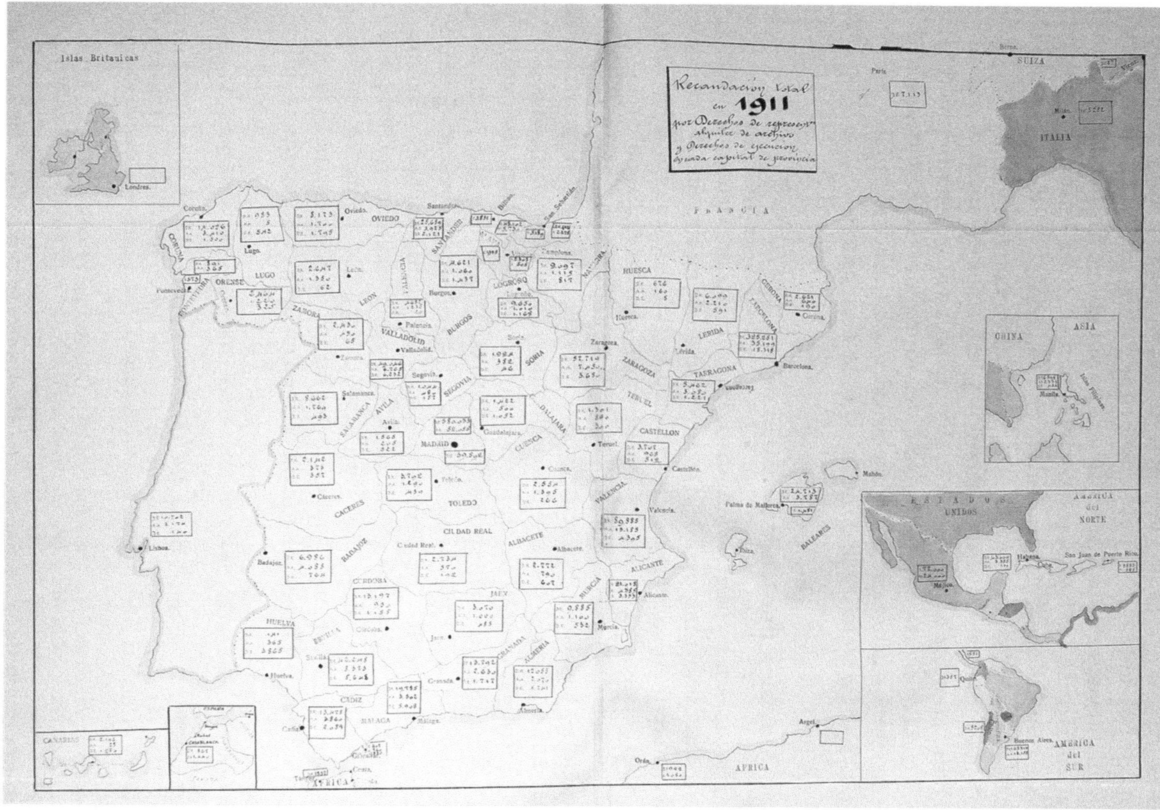

Figure 8.2 1911 Atlas produced by the Spanish Collecting Society of Authors (1910)
Courtesy of *Sociedad General de Autores y Editores* (SGAE) – Luis Camacho/archivo SGAE

of flamenco venues, Alfonso Sánchez highlights their opposition to the norm; indeed, many of these places developed extraordinary subterfuges precisely designed to avoid copyright royalties.[20] The Society frequently complained of companies of *aficionados* advertising these entertainments in ephemeral ways or on displays that were not visible from outside, such as chalkboards.[21] Rather than specify a flamenco performance, events were announced using generic titles such as 'vals', 'cante' or 'polka' in order to evade copyright regulation.[22] Both in theory and in practice, the spatial and temporal features of flamenco performances formed a significant blind spot for copyright. The difficulties encountered by the SAE as they tried to figure out the possibilities for royalty collection revealed flamenco performances as more like private showings than public performances. So how were these difficulties to be overcome?

4 Mapping flamenco performances

Locating the exact places where these impromptu performances would happen was almost impossible. However, identifying the specific type of venue where these entertainments tended to flourish was feasible. This kind of music tended to pop up in one particular type of establishment, known as *café cantantes*.[23] Copyright representatives were given special instructions, legislative extracts, even a pocket-sized book of copyright rules in order better to traverse the difficulties of this kind of venue.[24] The *café cantante* was defined as a nightclub in which the show and the performance were included in the price of the drinks. This pricing structure, not surprisingly, created additional problems for collecting royalties – there was no reliable vector for levying fees such as seating capacity. For this and many other reasons the SAE would struggle to regulate *café cantantes* until sometime around 1930. But after about 1924 flamenco entered into a new theatrical stage, known in the history of Spanish music as flamenco 'opera'.[25] This development created an opportunity for new allies

Università Bocconi, Milan, 26–27 June 2009. See also 'Programas' (1932) 2 *El Derecho de Autor* 58.

20 A. Sánchez, 'Café Cantante', *Diario ABC* (Madrid), 18 January 1955, p. 37.

21 'Circular', *Boletín de la Sociedad de Autores Españoles* (Madrid), October 1911, p. 1, n. 105; 'Los Actores Aficionados y Los Profesionales', *Boletín de la Sociedad de Autores Españoles* (Madrid), September–October 1928, p. 6, n. 168.

22 'Sección de Variedades', *La Propiedad Intelectual* (Madrid), February 1923, p. 25, n. 104.

23 J. L. Ortiz Nuevo, *Las Mil y una Historias de Pericón de Cádiz* (Madrid: Sílex Signos, 1990) p. 243.

24 'Instrucciones de Uso Frecuente Para los Representantes de la SGAE' (1932) 2 *El Derecho de Autor* 61.

25 J. M. Gamboa and M. Espín, *Luis Maravilla 'Por Derecho'* (Seville: Fundación Machado y Área de Cultura del Ayuntamiento de Sevilla, 1990), pp. 24–5; J. M. Gamboa, *Una Historia del Flamenco* (Madrid: Espasa Calpe, 2005), pp. 213–19.

to join in regulating flamenco. First, and as an 'urgent and practical solution', the SAE requested that Spain's copyright registry monitor receipts from these more easily categorized theatrical flamenco performances.[26] Secondly, the SAE sought assistance from Carlos Hernández 'Vedrines', the well-known flamenco *impresario* from Madrid. Through a contractual arrangement, the SAE gained access to a reliable calendar and a list of venues, the regularity of which they had previously been unable to establish. At a stroke, they were able to monitor times, routes and programme details better than they ever had, and thus had a better chance of capturing possible copyright revenues arising from that hybrid mixture of theatre and flamenco.[27] Thirdly, the SAE relaxed its own attitude and its membership rules that had led to the exclusion of flamenco artists as authors for four decades.

The SAE had originally been dismissive of the rights of flamenco artists even though there was an interest in flamenco venues from at least the beginning of the twentieth century. For instance, the bulletin of the Society developed a farcical Q&A section in which it published ironic comments made to enquiries about the possibility of protecting flamenco's music styles. Not surprisingly, these questions always came from the very centre of flamenco's geography, Andalusia.[28] However, despite this derisive treatment, some flamenco artists remained interested in recognition as members of the Society and as authors of works that could be subject to copyright.[29] As part of expanding its copyright empire, the SAE began to accept flamenco members in 1933,[30] initially without resolving their precise categorization within the Society. The Society, as a co-ordinating institution, had many practical attractions to offer to flamenco artists. It provided opportunity, a pension and health care.[31] It also opened the door to a network of agents, artists and other musicians. Undoubtedly, the bureaucracy of the Spanish copyright regime, for all of its burdens, also helped to professionalize flamenco within the entertainment industry. One consequence of the increased ambition of the SAE was that the organization gradually came to take on some of the regulatory functions previously carried out by the state.[32] For instance, registration forms, reciprocity agreements between the SAE and foreign collecting societies

[26] 'A Los Autores de Flamenco' (1934) 24 *El Derecho de Autor* 231.

[27] 'Las Tarifas de Ópera Flamenca' (1934) 25 *El Derecho de Autor* 237.

[28] See, e.g., 'Consultas', *La Propiedad Intelectual* (Madrid), February 1923, pp. 7–8, n. 106 (answering a query from Seville about flamenco's style 'polo'); 'Consultas', *La Propiedad Intelectual* (Madrid), May 1923, p. 7, n. 107 (answering a query from Xerez about 'redondillas').

[29] J. M. Gamboa, *Perico el del Lunar: Un Flamenco de Antología* (Cordoba: Ediciones de la Posada, 2001), p. 153.

[30] Gamboa and Espín, *Luis Maravilla 'Por Derecho'*, p. 55.

[31] Gamboa, *Perico el del Lunar*, p. 153.

[32] See Bellido, 'Copyright at a Distance'.

and diplomatic tactics were eventually absorbed by the Society's institutional umbrella.[33] This was more than a mere administrative change. In assigning these legal and political roles to a corporation, the Spanish government transformed, and arguably privatized, the management of disputes about distinctions between authors and their entitlements. To give one small example: political controversies concerning copyright were common between Catalan and Spanish authors and between Latin American countries and Spain.[34] In the nineteenth century, those issues came within the purview of the country's parliament.[35] But by 1928 some of these controversies also began to be managed by and consulted with the SAE.[36] Thus, as the SAE expanded its reach, tensions surrounding authorial status were internalized and rarely came to public judgement. This arrangement was also opportune for resolving conflicts concerning the status of flamenco 'authors'.

5 Flamenco within the SAE

As early as 1851, the French *Société des Auteurs Compositeurs et Éditeurs de Musique* (SACEM) recognized a differentiation between *petit droit* and other rights in copyright. The SAE followed suit, forging a distinction between 'high literature' authors and other authors who were embraced by the catch-all label of 'variety'.[37] The variety department consisted of pretty much anything from humorists to ventriloquists to *coupletists*,[38] with the SAE bureaucrats administering a vast array of works from comic sketches to vaudeville pieces.[39] The chaotic messiness of the variety department facilitated the inclusion of flamenco, but also exacerbated existing tensions and rivalries. Many members – from poets to classical musicians to dramatists – looked down upon the 'illiterate newcomers' entering into the variety department. The attempted integration of

[33] E. Endériz, *Guerra de Autores* (Madrid: Polonio & Margelí, 1935), p. 18 (reciprocity).

[34] Bellido, 'Latin American and Spanish Copyright Relations'.

[35] M. Vergara, *Legislación de la Propiedad Literaria en España* (Madrid: Librería de Moya y Plaza, 1864), p. 114.

[36] Endériz, *Guerra de Autores*, pp. 64–5. The constitution of a permanent committee to study bilateral copyright conventions facilitated and triggered this interest. Two members of the society were appointed by the ministry of state to form part of this committee. See *Gaceta de Madrid* (Madrid), 27 June 1928.

[37] 'A Los Representantes', *Boletín de la Sociedad de Autores Españoles* (Madrid), January–February 1929, p. 2, n. 170; Endériz, *Guerra de Autores*, p. 19.

[38] A historical overview of variety shows is given in J. Blas Vega, *La Canción Española* (Madrid: Taller El Bucaro, 1996), p. 37. A reference to the combination is in Endériz, *Guerra de Autores*, p. 5.

[39] 'Repertorio de Humoristas, Intermediarios, Maquetistas y Ventrílocuos', *Boletín de la Sociedad de Autores Españoles* (Madrid), October 1929, p. 13, n. 176.

'high' and 'low' artists in the one society became a sensitive internal affair. However, to the SAE, which was attempting to procure copyright income from a broad spectrum of artists, the new inclusion made perfect sense. The most successful and profitable works often emerged from the variety department,[40] and soon the department became the most salient feature of the SAE.[41]

An internal battle between different groups of authors dominated the Society for the first half of the twentieth century.[42] In seeking to manage authorship disputes, it exposed tensions in the SAE's mandate. There was a conflict between copyright as something that was individually owned versus something collectively administered. To manage the combative environment, on 28 January 1929, the SAE divided its departments into distinct sections: variety, mechanical, and theatrical.[43] However, this strategy meant the beginning of the end for the SAE's traditional corporate structure. The change did not necessarily lead to a resolution of conflict. Rather, the problem simply re-emerged in other ways. Nothing better demonstrates the tension between members of the Society than the book written by a past president of the variety section, Ezequiel Endériz (1889–1951), entitled *War of Authors*. Endériz describes how new politics of authorship resurfaced after the 1929 division that were frequently tied to the changes in the by-laws and structures of participation within the Society.[44] Eventually, the difficulties between the variety, the mechanical and the theatrical sections became so unsustainable that the Society collapsed. The irony is that because of the nature of the entertainment industry these combative parties were nevertheless forced to work together in everyday life. The dysfunction was so great that just three years later, in 1932, the SAE replaced its organizational structure with a federation of societies.[45] The new system allowed for the variety society,

[40] 'Los intereses de la SGAE en Sudamérica', *Boletín de la Sociedad de Autores Españoles* (Madrid), March 1955, p. 5 ('Es muy satisfactorio para nosotros consignar que el repertorio español folklórico y de Pequeño Derecho es el más solicitado allá').

[41] C. Alonso, 'Cultura Popular y Propiedad Intelectual: La Sociedad de Autores Españoles y el Pequeño Derecho (1899–1924)', in C. Alonso, C. J. Gutiérrez and J. Suárez-Pajares (eds), *Delantera de Paraíso: Estudios en Homenaje a Luis G. Iberni* (Madrid: ICCMU, 2008), p. 390.

[42] See, e.g., 'Copia taquigráfica de la Junta General Extraordinaria celebrada por la sociedad de autores el día 25 de octubre de 1929 bajo la presidencia de don Serafín Álvarez Quintero', *Boletín de la Sociedad de Autores Españoles* (Madrid), April–May 1931, pp. 39–73, n. 170.

[43] 'Aviso Importantísimo', *Boletín de la Sociedad de Autores Españoles* (Madrid), January–February 1929, p. 1, n. 170.

[44] Endériz, *Guerra de Autores*, p. 9.

[45] J. de Arozamena, *La Sociedad General de Autores de España* (Madrid: SGAE, 1961), pp. 21–3; Endériz, *Guerra de Autores*, p. 32.

the lyrical society and the theatrical society to come under a single frame of reference while maintaining the particular idiosyncrasies of the different genres.[46] By locating the societies within the same headquarters, it helped them achieve international recognition.[47] The structure was further amended in 1941 and became a general society with sections and departments.[48] Perhaps reflecting the heightened civil disruption of the Spanish Civil War, the more protracted confrontations between the representatives of high art and the always more vulgarized popular culture were once again, to some extent, handled by the federal government.[49]

6 Folklore and the public domain

The distinction drawn between high culture and popular culture (a usually derisive designation that encompassed both traditional music and folklore) was used for a very specific and strategic political purpose after the Spanish Civil War. Works of popular culture were considered to be in the public domain. Therefore, in registering what might be classified as a work of popular culture, an individual risked being accused of registering in their own name a work that was in the public domain. This was an extremely serious and potentially embarrassing allegation, not least because it was a difficult claim for the accused to address. When such an allegation was made, the federally structured society opened up a case and conducted an internal investigation. If an author was found to have registered public domain works under his or her name – in other words, to have claimed credit for creating what was in fact a work that already existed in popular or traditional culture – he or she was sanctioned internally by not being distributed royalties and by being given reduced participatory rights at the Society. However, the distinction between copyright and public domain was itself contingent, not surprisingly, and there is no doubt that allegations were levelled at members for instrumental reasons. Further, the Society had a conflict of interest. Revenues drawn from public domain works, pending works and orphan works contributed a fund that served to finance other activities carried out by the Society rather

[46] 'Razón y Programa' (1932) 1 *El Derecho de Autor* 1.

[47] 'Ingreso de Nuestra Sociedad en el Cartel Internacional de Pequeño Derecho' (1934) 20 *Derecho de Autor* 146.

[48] See generally Arozamena, *La Sociedad General de Autores de España*, pp. 26–7.

[49] Gamboa and Espín, *Luis Maravilla 'Por Derecho'*, p. 54 ('no nos pagaban derechos de autor por las composiciones de música flamenca. Me decían en la Sociedad de Autores. – Eso es popular –').

than going to a particular author. It is no surprise that 'folklore' and 'traditional music' were cursed words within the Society because the reference could leave a member without any royalties.

7 'Professional' flamenco authors

At first, the Society developed stringent processes to make it more difficult for flamenco artists to register with the Society. While the Society did not formally assess the quality of the works that were forwarded for registration through what was called a declaration form, it was curiously obsessed with the professional capability of those who wanted to be administered by its collective apparatus. If a flamenco artist wished to become a member, he or she faced bureaucratic hurdles established by the Society in the form of 'entry requirements' that were different from those required, for example, of a classically trained composer or a dramatist. The application process was complex and tacit rules supplemented explicit requirements. Flamenco practitioners had to prove their 'professional' musical abilities. However, no matter how tough the exam requirements were, astute artists developed stratagems to succeed. Some bypassed the exam altogether and entered the Society through a back door as joint authors.[50] The creation of the high threshold for qualification for flamenco authors actually produced an impetus to collaborate. Certain flamenco artists paid or collaborated with 'literate' musicians just in order to gain recognition. Indeed, the years between 1930 and the 1950s – prior to flamenco's growing acceptance – witnessed a proliferation of collaborative projects between flamenco artists and other musicians.[51] Others hired impersonators to take the exam on their behalf. Still other flamenco candidates tried more flexible and less risky tactics that were adapted to the moment and to the circumstances of the forthcoming exam. For instance, following a rumour that there was a greater chance to get into the Society if one wrote a song's lyrics in addition to the music, some flamenco artists began writing lyrics as well.[52] The Society, in turn, became particularly suspicious of applicants who claimed to be both the author and performer of a work. Indeed, there was a presumption that an author did not usually perform his or her composition. It is curious to note that in order to avoid being singled out, and therefore to avoid an initial mistrust of their submissions, some flamenco artists exchanged compositions before declaring ownership of their works at the

[50] Gamboa, *Perico el del Lunar*, p. 153. [51] *Ibid.*
[52] *Ibid.*; Gamboa and Espín, *Luis Maravilla 'Por Derecho'*, p. 55.

SAE. As one famous flamenco guitarist recalled: 'in order to avoid problems, he registered my works whereas I registered his music. However, at the end of the day, each of us interpreted his [own] music'.[53]

As stratagems to overcome obstacles succeeded, the Society took increasing measures to curb 'cheating'. In order to control the quality of the exams and in an attempt to uncover dubious practices, not only did the presentation of identity cards and two passport-sized photographs become mandatory,[54] but the examiners were often also selected from the staff at the music conservatory to block any creative inadequacy.[55] Similarly, exam dates and venues for candidates to show their talents were also carefully scheduled. Despite the fact that exams could be taken in the provinces, they were not corrected there but sent back to the major capitals of Madrid, Barcelona and Valencia. Another counter-measure to limit the success of undesirable candidates was to investigate those who sided with flamenco artists. That is, collaboration itself came under suspicion.[56] At least one well-known, literate musician who also loved flamenco – Genaro Monreal (1894–1974)[57] – was investigated and eventually suspended for facilitating membership entries.[58] SAE bureaucrats also discussed the creation of specialized 'courts of honour':[59] internal tribunals constituted to determine and solve the various problems that could arise from flamenco music.

8 Instituting folklore

Rather than tackling the more difficult issue – reconciling the copyright status of flamenco and other works with folkloric roots – the Society

[53] Gamboa, *Perico el del Lunar*, p. 153; Gamboa, *Una Historia del Flamenco*, p. 139.

[54] Notes on the exam instructions can be read at Sociedad General de Autores Españoles, *Actas de la Comisión Permanente* (Madrid), 10 September 1965, pp. 35–7, and the photo requirement in Sociedad General de Autores Españoles, *Actas de la Comisión Permanente* (Madrid), 14 February 1966, pp. 35–7; Archivo de la Sociedad General de Autores Españoles (ASGAE).

[55] Until 1964, one of the examiners was Victorino Echevarría (Professor of Harmony at the Conservatory). See Sociedad General de Autores Españoles, *Memoria Que Presenta el Consejo de Administración de la Sociedad General de Autores a la Junta General Ordinaria* (Madrid), 21 December 1965, p. 42; ASGAE.

[56] Particularly interesting are the discussions about collaboration and copyright apportionment at the society and the possibility that they were hiding strategies of royalty collections: Sociedad General de Autores Españoles, *Actas de la Comisión Permanente* (Madrid), 24 June 1966, p. 92; ASGAE.

[57] Collaborations between Monreal and flamenco guitarist Perico el del Lunar are listed in Gamboa, *Perico el del Lunar*, p. 154.

[58] Endériz, *Guerra de Autores*, pp. 60–2.

[59] Sociedad General de Autores Españoles, *Junta General Extraordinaria de la Sociedad de Autores* (Madrid), 19 December 1964, p. 17; ASGAE.

initially took the simpler path of placing 'administrative' obstacles in front of flamenco artists. As mentioned above, as a general position, the Society tried to avoid interventions and aesthetic judgements that would determine which flamenco songs were considered folklore and therefore in the public domain, and which could be subject to copyright and hence submitted to its collective administrative enterprise. However, when faced with a particular allegation the Society was forced to take a stance in that particular case.

The Society was not the only party with an interest in arbitrating this kind of dispute. Madrid's Royal Conservatory of Music, the main place where music was studied in Spain,[60] had a strong interest in discussions of musical roots and genres, and in musicology disputes. The conservatory, since even before the SAE was founded, had also been involved in lobbying with trade unions concerning the regulation of the music profession.[61] Throughout the first half of the twentieth century the SAE was dominated by composers and lyricists who had been trained at the conservatory.[62] There was no better example of the connection between the SAE and the conservatory than José Forns (1898–1952), a composer who simultaneously held a chair in the conservatory and a high-profile job at the Society.[63] Forns was a well-known musical copyright expert[64] and was no doubt well versed in the complexities of authorship and originality in music. He took a leading role in the emerging discussions of copyright in cinematographic films,[65] including campaigning for and

[60] F. Sopeña, *Historia Crítica del Conservatorio de Madrid* (Madrid: Ministerio de Educación y Ciencia, Dirección General de Bellas Artes, 1967).

[61] Real Conservatorio de Música, *Actas del Claustro de Profesores* (Madrid), 5 May 1966, pp. 87–9 (discussions about encroachments on their professional domain); Real Conservatorio de Música, *Actas del Claustro de Profesores* (18 June 1965), pp. 79–80 (meeting about the possibility of regulating music professionals with a membership card issued by the conservatory and the trade union); Archivo Real Conservatorio de Madrid (ARCM).

[62] For instance, members of the society included Victorino Echevarría (Professor of Harmony) and José Forns (Professor of Composition): see 'José Forns' and 'Victorino Echevarría', Expedientes del personal, ARCM.

[63] J. Subirá, 'Necrología: José Forns Quadras', *Boletín de la Real Academia de Bellas Artes de San Fernando* (Madrid), 1952, p. 395, n. 4; J. Gómez, 'La Enseñanza de Composición en el Conservatorio Madrileño y su Profesorado', *Boletín de la Real Academia de Bellas Artes de San Fernando* (Madrid), 1959, pp. 29–58, 31 and 48.

[64] Examples of his work on copyright law are the following essays: J. Forns, *El Derecho de Autor de los Artistas* (Madrid: Real Academia de Bellas Artes de San Fernando, 1945); J. Forns, 'El "Copyright" Americano y la Protección de las Obras Españolas: Nuevo Régimen de Registro' (1950) 402 *Revista de Derecho Privado*; J. Forns, 'Nuevo Concepto Jurídico de la Edición', *Revista Critica de Derecho Inmobiliario* (Madrid), 1950, pp. 391–7, n. 265; J. Forns, 'Sobre una Definición Lógica del Concepto de Publicación en Derecho de Autor' (1951) 408 *Revista de Derecho Privado* 304.

[65] Endériz, *Guerra de Autores*, p. 89.

finally creating a society specializing in cinema.[66] It is curious that Forns did not make explicit his views on musical copyright, folklore or flamenco throughout his career at the Society, despite the problems they were generating for the SAE as a whole.[67] He explained that he knew more might have been expected of him in this regard given his expertise, but he had 'sacrificed' himself in order to deal with more practical and urgent issues.[68] Forns' timid positioning pointed to the difficulty of resolving the issues around flamenco, especially without support from other quarters.

In the 1950s, a shift occurred in the values ascribed to the words folklore and flamenco that interested a variety of organizations. The Royal Conservatory of Music appointed a chair in folklore who provided a learned gloss to flamenco as popular music. The growing commercial and critical success of flamenco and various iterations of folklore, especially those iterations produced as sound recordings, also provided flamenco with a more 'serious' profile. Some of the first flamenco and folk LPs were anthologies accompanied by essays from noted academics such as Tomás Andrade de Silva (1913–2003), Roberto Pla (1915–2004) and Manuel García Matos (1912–1974). In this sense, it is worth noting that Andrade de Silva was a pianist and certainly not an authority on flamenco music; the value of his authorship was undoubtedly derived from his professorship at the conservatory.[69] Around the same time, an institute for the study of flamenco and folklore was created.[70] Music labels such as Hispavox also contributed to the promotion of flamenco with excellent recordings, international prizes and memorable anthologies.[71]

66 'Nuevo Académico Numerario', *La Vanguardia* (Barcelona), 10 November 1944, p. 1; Subirá, 'Necrología: José Forns Quadras', p. 398.

67 Implicit were his views if one reads some of his copyright essays. For example, he wrote that 'Por muy seductora que resulte la teoría de una completa igualdad entre todos los seres humanos, solo a una selecta minoría ha concedido Dios el privilegio de dirigirla la conciencia de sus semejantes para proporcionarles el valioso tesoro de sus pensamientos con el goce estético de las creaciones de su genio': J. Forns 'Derecho de Propiedad Intelectual en sus Relaciones con el Interés Público y la Cultura' (1951) 4 *Anuario de Derecho Civil* 985, 987.

68 On this excuse, J. Forns and C. del Campo, 'El Derecho de Autor de los Artistas' (Madrid: Real Academia de Bellas Artes de San Fernando, 1945).

69 See, for instance, the booklet in the LPs: T. A. de Silva, *Antología del Cante Flamenco: Anthologie du Chant Flamenco: Anthology of Cante Flamenco* (Madrid: Hispavox, 1958). See also 'Andrade de Silva', Expedientes del personal, ARCM.

70 Gamboa, *Una Historia del Flamenco*, pp. 166–7 (La cátedra de flamencología de Jerez).

71 See 'Hispavox, Nueva Productora Fonográfica al Servicio de las Obras Maestras en España' (1956) 25 *Ritmo*, pp. 24–5, n. 277; and also 'Con los Realizadores del Disco Europeo, Roberto Pla, Director Artístico de Hispavox' (1958) 28 *Ritmo*, n. 292, pp. 20–1. It is also worth to mention here the historical importance of the record label *Nuevos Medios* for the commercial success of flamenco. Founded in the early 1980s,

Further, in 1959, UNESCO embarked on the larger task of reappraising the status of folklore and flamenco.[72] This international development had many specific, local ramifications across Spain, namely new commissions, recordings and funding opportunities.[73] The institutional attention brought a new respectability to flamenco and folklore. However, it did not provide the Society with a practical solution to the problem of how to catalogue and reorganize its repertoire, how to classify new submissions and what to do with the large number of flamenco works that had already been registered, many of which had been classified as 'popular music'.[74] Copyright scholars highlighted that for this reason registration could not grant any property rights on music with folkloric roots.[75]

In order to rationalize the catalogue, and particularly to redress the overlaps between popular and traditional music, a special department, the new information management division, was created in November 1963.[76] It is ironic that an eminent Spanish folklorist, Manuel García Matos,[77] who was not a lawyer, was hired for the department in the hopes of bringing order to copyright.[78] Matos would simultaneously teach music at the conservatory and provide expert advice at the copyright society, including advising on how to differentiate flamenco from folklore.[79]

one of the revolutionary approaches of the label was to develop, distribute and mix 'flamenco' with other genres such as 'pop'.

72 UN Educational, Scientific and Cultural Organisation, Liaison of International Organisations in the Field of Arts and Letters: Accomplishments of the International Music Council, Paris, 15 November 1959 (3CLAL/4(b), UNESCO, 1959). See also generally L. H. C. de Azevedo, 'UNESCO Activities Related to Folklore' (1961) 4 *The Folklore and Folk Music Archivist* 2.

73 An example is the folk collection (17 LPs), *Magna Antología de Folklore Musical de España* (Madrid: Hispavox, 1979), no. 7999762.

74 Sociedad General de Autores Españoles, *Memoria Que Presenta el Consejo de Administración de la Sociedad General de Autores a la Junta General Ordinaria* (Madrid), 21 December 1967, p. 53; ASGAE.

75 S. Radaelli, *Los Derechos Intelectuales y el Folklore* (Madrid, 1953) as extracted in *Boletín de la Propiedad Intelectual* (Madrid), December 1953, pp. 1–8.

76 Sociedad General de Autores Españoles, 'El Consejo Aprueba por Unanimidad la Creación Dentro de la Sección Musical, del Nuevo Negociado de Información, Documentación e Identificación', in *Actas del Consejo de Administración* (Madrid), 15 December 1963, pp. 145–6; ASGAE.

77 J. Subirá, 'Un Insigne Folklorista Español: Manuel García Matos' (1945) 126 *Revista de Ideas Estéticas* 137. Federico Sopeña (1917–91) described him not only as 'a great folklorist but *the* folklorist, someone entirely unique', in F. Sopeña, *Historia Crítica del Conservatorio de Madrid* (Madrid: Ministerio de Educación y Ciencia, 1967), p. 185.

78 'En diciembre de 1964 la Junta Directiva de la Sección Musical de la Sociedad General de Autores de España acuerda nombrarlo Asesor de la misma para la revisión de fichajes que contengan temas musicales de carácter popular o folklórico no identificados', M. Querol, 'Manuel García Matos (1912–74): In Memoriam', *Magna Antología del Folklore Musical de España* (Madrid: Hispavox, 1978), p. 3.

79 Gamboa, *Una Historia del Flamenco*, p. 108 ('El estudio de nuestro género artístico saldrá beneficiado por el auge de los estudios etnográficos y musicológicos, que en

9 From field work to copyright

In contrast to his predecessor José Forns, García Matos linked the internal infrastructural demands of the Society to his musicological investigations. He did not prioritize his professional career at the Society over his creative ambitions.[80] Neither was he particularly interested in copyright law. However, Matos had the rare ability to harmonize the apparently contradictory positions created by perceived conflicts between copyright and folklore. It is no coincidence that the paper forms and collecting devices he used in his field work – conducted to gather information about songs – looked like the declaration forms used at the SAE. Eventually, the mapping exercises developed by folklorists such as García Matos resembled and then merged with the atlas that the SAE had produced for the last several decades (Fig. 8.3).

As a researcher, Matos had spent almost three decades developing a plethora of techniques for collecting Spanish music and dances.[81] With a recording machine always on hand, he travelled around Spain in an attempt to convert popular music, folklore[82] and flamenco alike into an object of study.[83] He was skilled in media transformations: from music to description to notation,[84] from song to record and from the field to the recording studio. In doing so, he created a personal archive of recordings of more than 10,000 songs.[85] At the same time that the SAE struggled

los cincuenta alcanzar un techo, aunque luego más adelante haya acuerdo en sacar al flamenco del marco folclórico').

80 V. G. Macías, 'Gerifaltes Extremeños: El Eminente Folklorista Manuel García Matos' (1984) 48 *Revista de Folklore* 211, 212.

81 Gamboa, *Una Historia del Flamenco*, p. 108; see also generally I. J. Katz, 'The Traditional Folk Music of Spain: Explorations and Perspectives' (1974) 6 *Yearbook of the International Folk Music Council* 64.

82 The anthology of Spanish folklore constituted a series of LPs published by Hispavox under the auspices of UNESCO. See 'Estadística de la Antología del Folklore Musical de España', *Antología del Folkore Musical de España* (Madrid: Hispavox, 1960), no. HH 10107/8/9/10.

83 M. Schneider and J. R. Figueras (eds), *Cancionero Musical de la Provincia de Madrid: Materiales Recogidos por Manuel García Matos*, vol. 1 (Barcelona and Madrid: Consejo Superior de Investigaciones Científicas, 1951); M. Schneider and J. R. Figueras (eds), *Cancionero Musical de la Provincia de Madrid: Materiales Recogidos por Manuel García Matos*, vol. 2 (Barcelona: Consejo Superior de Investigaciones Científicas, 1952); J. Tomás and J. R. Figueras (eds), *Cancionero Musical de la Provincia de Madrid: Materiales Recogidos por Manuel García Matos*, vol. 3 (Barcelona: Consejo Superior de Investigaciones Científicas, 1960); J. Crivillé i Bargalló (ed.), *Cancionero Popular de la Provincia de Cáceres: Materiales Recogidos por Manuel García Matos* (Barcelona: Consejo Superior de Investigaciones Científicas, 1982).

84 See, e.g., L. A., 'Danzas Populares de España. Castilla la Nueva. Vol. I by Manuel García Matos' (1960) 12 *Journal of the International Folk Music Council* 101, 101–2.

85 C. G. Matos, 'García Matos y la Música Flamenco', *La Caña* (Madrid), 1993, p. 22. Some of these recordings were unique, as highlighted in Gamboa, *Una Historia del*

Figure 8.3 Map of the folkloric missions in which García Matos participated
Courtesy of CSIC (Madrid) – Luis Calvo. See L. Calvo i Calvo, 'La Etnomusicología en el Instituto Español de Musicología' (1989) 44 *Anuario Musical* 167, 177

to find flamenco nightclubs, he had already visited those clubs – from Zambra in Madrid to Tablao El Guajiro in Seville – and recorded the improvised performances within.[86] Matos took a programmatic and careful interest in comparing and differentiating between genres often accused of being ill-defined.[87] He both experimented with and analysed the range of different tasks involved in this kind of music – for instance, writing *and* producing, writing *for* producing and producing *for* writing. While writing about the originality and distinctiveness of flamenco's music in relation to folklore, he also served as an artistic producer of records with flamenco's *cantaores* and guitarists.[88] Matos believed that studying the musical or literary document was key to hearing (or seeing) the similarities and differences between genres.[89] His obsession with documentary evidence served as an antidote to the era's excesses of theory.[90] His forensic practices allowed him not only to distinguish between different musical works but also to demonstrate those differences in legal forums.[91] Over more than a decade at the Society, he provided a mechanism for crediting flamenco authorship and attributing ownership to what otherwise might be dismissed as folkloric works. Most consequential was his role on *Una Historia del Cante Flamenco*, an LP released in 1958 (Fig. 8.4).

10 The impact of new technologies

García Matos was hired by the Society after a recommendation from Enrique Martín Garea, the founder of Hispavox, the most successful Spanish music recording and publishing house.[92] By the 1960s, just

Flamenco, p. 458 ('El polo natural y el de Tobalo los dejó registrados en 1947, para el archivo personal del profesor Manuel García Matos, Pepe el de la Matrona').

86 Interview with Carmen García Matos (Madrid, May 2011).

87 See M. G. Matos, 'Introducción a la Investigación de los Orígenes del Cante Flamenco', *Actas de la Reunión Internacional de Estudios Sobre los Orígenes del Flamenco* (Madrid), 1969, pp. 33–46.

88 See e.g., M. G. Matos, 'Bosquejo Histórico del Cante Flamenco para la Obra una Historia del Cante Flamenco' (Madrid: Hispavox, 1958).

89 Interestingly, when Matos was presenting a paper at a conference, he often used musical and literary documents to point out the similarities and differences to the audience. See Matos, 'Introducción a la Investigación de los Orígenes del Cante Flamenco', p. 42 ('Se hicieron oír en la reunión en que se leyó este trabajo, cosa que hízose igualmente con los ejemplos musicales que a estos van a seguir').

90 R. Pelinski *et al.*, *Presencia del Pasado en un Cancionero Castellonense: Un Reestudio Etnomusicológico* (Castellon: Universitat Jaume I, 1997) p. 32; Macías, 'Gerifaltes Extremeños', 211; M. G. Matos, *Lírica Popular de Extremadura: Documentos Inéditos* (Madrid: Unión Musical Española, 1944).

91 Pepe Rey humorously recreated the experience of a copyright case related to plagiarism in popular music in which García Matos appeared as an expert witness; see P. Rey, 'Musicología Forense' (1987) 8 *Musica Antiqua* 17.

92 Interview with E. M. Garea (Madrid, June 2011).

Figure 8.4 *Una Historia del Cante Flamenco* (Hispavox)
This was one of the first collaborative enterprises amongst a flamenco artist (Manolo Caracol), a musical publisher and member of the SAE (Martín Garea), and a musicologist (García Matos), who was commissioned to write a documentary gloss to the LP
Courtesy of University College London, Learning and Media Services

as flamenco and folklore alike grew in their acceptance through the release and commercialization of records,[93] membership in the Society also changed.[94] Music publishers became members of the SAE in

[93] de Silva, *Antología del Cante Flamenco*; A. Mairena, *Antología del Cante Flamenco y Cante Gitano* (Madrid: Columbia, 1965); I. Román, *La Verdad del Cante* (Madrid: Zafiro, 1966).

[94] The internal affairs and management were modified with the enactment of the new articles of association (RD 1163/1963, 16 May 1963, Por el que se Aprueban los Estatutos de la Sociedad General de Autores de España. BOE [128], 29 May 1963, pp. 8765–72).

1963 and contributed to the management of the Society.[95] A new structure attempted to co-ordinate the interests of authors, music publishers and producers. It also incorporated different industry alliances that were afterwards translated into musical projects.[96] Such shifts show the transformation in copyright administration that comes with evolving technologies and related new commercial opportunities.[97] The impact was felt not just in Spain but also around the world.[98] Historically, the sound recording was appreciated in copyright law not only as a new (reproductive) medium[99] but also as a technological shift that gave rise to a second tier of copyright: so-called 'neighbouring' rights. The technology also led to increased tensions surrounding musical arrangements. Musical arrangements were particularly problematic in the SAE not only, as we have seen, owing to the possibility of infringing a pre-existing copyright. Such entries could also generate double-registrations. For instance, even the vice-president Moreno Torroba (1891–1982) was subjected to an investigation as to whether he had registered compositions that his son had also registered.[100] Especially now that music publishers were SAE members, a variety of internal rules were elaborated to clarify musical arrangements, particularly in the increasingly common case in which the arranger was also the music publisher.[101]

The changes to the SAE membership structure that came about in the 1960s increased the visibility and identification of popular artists. This

[95] The board of directors of the musical section at the society was formed as follows: nine composers, seven writers, two musical publishers; see the discussions in Sociedad General de Autores Españoles, *Junta General Extraordinaria de la Sociedad de Autores* (Madrid), 8 April 1963, pp. 16–29; ASGAE.

[96] It is no surprise then that companies such as Hispavox or Zafiro became members of SGAE. See I. Román, *Crónicas de la Copla* (Madrid: Fundación Autor, 2006), pp. 265–75.

[97] In an interesting overview, Antonio Delgado Porras provides an account of the institutional response to technological changes without paying attention to the internal membership struggles. See A. Delgado, 'Cien Años Tras la Protección Efectiva del Derecho de Autor: Historia de las Herramientas Legales de la SGAE (Segunda Parte)' (2000) 2 *Revista Trimestral de doctrina, legislación y Jurisprudencia* 7.

[98] K. K. Shelemay, 'Recording Technology, the Record Industry and Ethnomusicological Scholarship', in B. Nettl and P. V. Bohlman (eds), *Comparative Musicology and Anthropology of Music: Essays on the History of Ethnomusicology* (University of Chicago Press, 1991), pp. 282–5.

[99] Therefore it produced a series of doctrinal outputs to domesticate and subsume under existing copyright laws. See, for instance, a legal advisor of the society of authors, Molas Valverde, rapidly writing on the topic: J. M. Valverde, 'La Reproducción Magnetofónica' (1948) 47 *Revista Jurídica de Catalunya* 635.

[100] See, e.g., Sociedad General de Autores Españoles, *Consejo de Administración* (Madrid), 25 May 1962, pp. 43–4; ASGAE.

[101] See Sociedad General de Autores Españoles, *Memoria que Presenta el Consejo de Administración de la Sociedad General de Autores a la Junta General Ordinaria* (Madrid), 18 December 1964, p. 43; ASGAE.

impacted on flamenco in two ways. First, it allowed for unprecedented recognition of flamenco artists and other 'illiterate' musicians as authors in the Society.[102] Secondly, the evidence of sound recordings increased the managerial demands of control over the repertoire. Recordings and the resulting documentary trail became an object of investigation. An example of these effects could be seen in the use of commercial catalogues of LPs as indexes to control the exploitation of Spanish works.[103] Sound recording involved a mechanism for finally legitimating flamenco within the SAE. A tiny example: the Society started recording flamenco entertainments in order accurately to survey what the musical content of those 'confusing' flamenco clubs could be.[104] However, in the early years, the act of recording a piece of live music was primarily done to document and preserve. As the distribution of record players and recordings grew, music was sold as never before. The SAE never explicitly attempted to legitimate popular forms of music such as flamenco, but that may be the most important, though unintended, consequence of this technology. By the end of the 1960s and the beginning of the 1970s, both flamenco and popular artists who were signed to a record deal were able to overcome the Society's entry requirements, the Society's derision and general institutional obstacles. Flamenco and other popular music were becoming the most commercially successful genres in the Society's entire repertoire.[105] It was only a matter of time before a credit on a sound recording became the first step to the recognition of authorship at the SAE. Indeed, starting in 1966, LPs were allowed as an indication of authorship.[106] Above all,

[102] R. Molina, 'La Antología de Hispavox', in J. L. N. García and M. Ropero (eds), *Historia del Flamenco* (Seville: Ediciones Tartessos, 1995), p. 333.

[103] Sociedad General de Autores Españoles, *Memoria que Presenta el Consejo de Administración de la Sociedad General de Autores a la Junta General Ordinaria* (Madrid), 21 December 1967, p. 53; ASGAE.

[104] 'En los locales denominados – tablaos flamencos – se hacen ya inspecciones a base de grabación total del espectáculo; en la forma en que anteriormente se hacían no era posible detallar el repertorio total por lo complicado y confuso de tales espectáculos', Sociedad General de Autores Españoles, *Memoria que presenta el Consejo de Administración de la Sociedad General de Autores a la Junta General Ordinaria* (Madrid), 21 December 1965, p. 55; ASGAE. From the 1950s, flamenco pubs were called 'tablaos' and took some of the characteristics of the predecessor (*café cantante*). A brief historical overview of this transformation is found in M. Espín, 'Tablaos Flamencos', in J. L. N. García and M. R. Núñez (eds), *Historia del Flamenco* (Seville: Ediciones Tartessos, 1996), p. 339.

[105] The final battle for recognition is narrated in A. D. Olano, 'Los jóvenes compositores españoles contra la sociedad de autores', *Diario ABC* (Madrid), 11 November 1970, pp. 161–7; and A. D. Olano, 'Los máximos contribuyentes a la SGAE siguen siendo considerados silbadores', *Diario ABC* (Madrid), 10 October 1971, pp. 122–3.

[106] Sociedad General de Autores Españoles, *Actas de la Comisión Permanente* (Madrid), 12 December 1966, p. 2; ASGAE; see also Gamboa and Espín, *Luis Maravilla 'Por Derecho'*, p. 28.

attribution in a sound recording became the best evidence of one's qualification as a professional musician.[107] Obstacles built upon distinctions such as between performance and authorship,[108] and which had stood for more than a half-century, were swept aside.

11 Conclusion

The inclusion of flamenco in the copyright regime was arguably inevitable once the mechanisms existed for new methods of commercial exploitation through sound recordings. However, the possibility of flamenco's inclusion and the structures that enabled this transition were established decades earlier. The struggles over the status of flamenco waged by, and within, the SAE following the Berne Convention, and the involvement of other interested parties, such as key personnel of the Royal Conservatory of Music, laid the groundwork that facilitated flamenco's inclusion. The SAE provided the institutional structure and the bureaucratic means to overcome the obstacles that blocked recognition of this 'lowly' art – obstacles that the SAE had for decades itself upheld. Although long considered mere folklore, or an amateur performance entirely within the public domain, flamenco found a place in the copyright regime within a few decades.

Modern copyright is more about collective administration than private rights, and the relationship between the two dimensions is one of the most neglected sites in copyright historiography. The historical experience of flamenco music demonstrates the importance of inquiring into this connection as a way better to understand the forces unleashed by copyright and the new opportunities it created for artists and for administrators, for creativity and for governance alike. More importantly, copyright management and the technologies on which it depends, such as cartography, expertise and accounting, shaped the ways in which legal categories of copyright developed. Flamenco shows how neither the presumed limitations in notions of authorship nor the need for the serial reproducibility of the copyright work were necessarily obstacles to the creation and administration of new, exclusive legal rights. It is easy to assume that copyright

[107] By the end of the 1960s, the society had had to change on more than one occasion the entry requirements. The first change referred to the proficiency exam and was made optional and not compulsory. However this option continued for less than a decade as an internal requirement to pass from provisional to permanent membership. Sociedad General de Autores Españoles, *Memoria que Presenta el Consejo de Administración de la Sociedad General de Autores a la Junta General Ordinaria* (Madrid), 21 December 1967, pp. 39, 41; ASGAE.

[108] See, e.g., R. Arnold, *Performers' Rights* (London: Sweet & Maxwell, 2008).

coalesced around certain foundational ideas that came to the fore in the late nineteenth century, such as the persona of the author and the copyright work, and that seem to limit copyright's reach and prevent the protection of folklore or genre. But flamenco demonstrates that these seemingly 'key' theoretical constructs of the law are actually loose and malleable.

Part IV

Group rights and culture

9 Arts festivals

Property, heritage or more?

*Fiona Macmillan**

1 Introduction

One of the interesting things about arts festivals is that many of the activities that occur as part and parcel of them can be mapped onto existing categories of copyright works. Indeed, so powerful is the rhetoric of these categories that there is a question about the extent to which they have constituted the very idea of 'arts' in this context – so that festivals typically identify themselves as film festivals, musical festivals, theatre festivals and so on, even if in fact empirical research reveals that almost no festival confines itself to only one form of 'artistic' output.[1] It would, therefore, be tempting (and much easier) to treat festivals as being just like any other form of distribution of copyright-protected works. Kenneth Turan, for example, argues that film festivals, at least, are an alternative form of distribution for films that have failed to find the usual commercial outlets for distribution.[2] This observation might also hold good for music festivals given that there are particular constraints on commercial distribution in both the film and music industries that, like all constraints, are likely to produce a drive for alternative means of fulfilling desire.[3] However, limiting our understanding of festivals to their being merely another means of distribution is really limiting our understanding of the nature of arts festivals and their social, political and economic significance. While it is undoubtedly true that arts festivals,

* Part of the research for this chapter was conducted while I was Visiting Professor of Law at the University of Technology Sydney. My thanks go to colleagues there for the warm welcome into their scholarly community and generous logistical support.

[1] See F. Macmillan, 'A Taxonomy of Arts Festivals: Mapping Issues in Cultural Property and Human Rights', Working Paper 2, HERA Cultivate Project (2013).

[2] K. Turan, *Sundance to Sarajevo: Film Festivals and the World They Made* (Berkeley, CA: University of California Press, 2002), pp. 7–8.

[3] See F. Macmillan, 'Copyright and Corporate Power', in R. Towse (ed.), *Copyright and the Cultural Industries* (Cheltenham: Edward Elgar, 2002); F. Macmillan, 'The Cruel ©: Copyright and Film' [2002] *European Intellectual Property Review* 483.

particularly some arts festivals, produce economic value for the entertainment industries, they also encompass a range of other values that are less easily measured but are nevertheless present. In this chapter, it is argued that arts festivals should be recognized as a form of cultural heritage. If this case can be made, then it presents us with a problem. This is that the public and communal values of arts festivals, as forms of cultural heritage, appear to be in potential conflict with the intellectual property rights that appear to be also a feature of the arts festival environment.

2 Defining 'arts festivals'

The fact that arts festivals have become, to some extent, a means of distribution of commodified cultural products suggests that they cannot be so easily conceived of as challenging the needs of the capitalist system, as it has been argued was the case for the traditional European agrarian festivals that form the historical antecedents to the current concept of the festival.[4] As with the whole of Western society they have been captured and transformed by capitalist relations. But perhaps the important point is that despite the fact that the concept of the festival – with its inherent notion of a departure and suspension from the everyday – does not serve the need for 'regular, disciplined labour and the rational accumulation of capital',[5] its form continues to flourish. In order to consider how this form relates to the private property relations of the intellectual property system and how it relates to the somewhat different considerations that pertain to the protection of cultural heritage, it is first necessary to put some flesh on the bones of the concept of the arts festival. The following discussion first considers the meaning of 'festival' and then moves on to the effect on this concept of the qualifier 'arts'.

2.1 'Festival'

In the literature, the concept of the 'festival' tends to be defined compositely in both positive and negative terms. In other words, it is defined both by what it is and by what it is not. On the positive side of this coin, the

4 C. Hill, *Society and Puritanism in Pre-Revolutionary England* (London: Secker & Warburg, 1964), pp. 146–59, 183–94 and 209, cited in R. Bauman, 'The Place of the Festival in the Worldview of Seventeenth-Century Quakers', in A. Falassi (ed.), *Time Out of Time: Essays on the Festival* (Albuquerque, NM: University of New Mexico Press, 1987), pp. 93–8.

5 Bauman, 'The Place of the Festival in the Worldview of Seventeenth-Century Quakers', p. 95.

overriding and perhaps most general characterization of the festival is that it is, in some sense, a suspension in time and space, during which life – or business – does not carry on as normal.[6] Developing this idea of the festival as a period of suspension, the festival has also been described by commentators as a space of openness, de-territorialization and exchange;[7] part of the 'public sphere';[8] a site of democratic debate and transnational identifications;[9] an 'interpretation of cosmopolitan community';[10] and, in the words of Jean Cocteau, an 'apolitical no-man's land'.[11] As all of these characterizations suggest, the idea of the festival is closely tied to the notion of being in a particular community, or being together, in a distinct place in time and space. In his description of the Cannes Film Festival, Cocteau also described the festival as 'a microcosm of how the world would be if people could have direct contacts and speak the same language'.[12] Thus, Monica Sassatelli, citing Émile Durkheim's work on festivals,[13] describes them as an 'intensification of the collective being' and, in Durkheim's words, a 'collective effervescence'.[14] Along similar lines, Alexandros Vrettos conceives of festivals as a manifestation of the human need to gather, socialize and exchange ideas.[15] Developing this line of thought, Alice O'Grady and Rebekka Kill argue that in an age of digital and social media, with their consequent personal isolation, the festival presents the chance to be with other people, and thus represents an opportunity for '[s]ociability, participation, togetherness and excitement'.[16]

[6] See (amongst many possible citations for this proposition) A. Falassi, 'Festival: Definition and Morphology', in Falassi, *Time Out of Time*.

[7] S. Nordmann, 'A History of Cultural Festivals in Europe', in J. Segal and L. Giorgi (eds), *European Arts Festivals from a Historical Perspective* (EURO-FESTIVAL Project: European Arts Festivals and Public Culture, Deliverable 2.1, WP2 Main Report, July 2009), p. 28.

[8] L. Giorgi, 'Between Tradition, Vision and Imagination: Literature(s) in Search of a Festival', in Segal and Giorgi, *European Arts Festivals from a Historical Perspective*; M. Sassatelli, 'Public Culture, Cosmopolitanism and Festivals', in M. Sassatelli (ed.), *European Public Culture and Aesthetic Cosmopolitanism* (EURO-FESTIVAL Project: European Arts Festivals and Public Culture, Deliverable 1.1, WP1 Main Report, October 2008).

[9] Sassatelli, 'Public Culture, Comospolitanism and Festivals'. [10] *Ibid.*, p. 25.

[11] Jean Cocteau, quoted in J. Segal and C. Blumauer, 'Cannes: A French International Festival', in Segal and Giorgi, *European Arts Festivals from a Historical Perspective*, p. 53.

[12] *Ibid.*

[13] É. Durkheim, *The Elementary Forms of Religious Life* (Glencoe, IL: Free Press, 1954 [1912]).

[14] Sassatelli, 'Public Culture, Cosmopolitanism and Festivals', pp. 18–19.

[15] A. Vrettos, 'About the Economic Impacts Studies of Arts Festivals' (2009) 3 *Economia della Cultura* 341.

[16] A. O'Grady and R. Kill, 'Exploring Festival Performance as a State of Encounter' (2013) 12 *Arts and Humanities in Higher Education* 268, 271.

Building on the idea of festivals as distinct[17] and sociable places in time and space are conceptions of festivals that refer to their value as social, cultural, economic or political institutions and, thus, as expressing values associated with such institutions.[18] O'Grady and Kill write about the festival as a cultural artefact,[19] while Guido Guerzoni refers to them as a way of filling 'il vuoto pneumatico della cultura televisiva'.[20] Values such as the promotion of cultural diversity,[21] internationalization[22] or alternative social identities[23] frequently form part and parcel of the festival concept. Festivals may also be understood as a form of asserting identity 'in the face of a feeling of cultural dislocation brought about by rapid structural change, social mobility and globalisation processes'.[24] Other types of cultural values pave the way for understanding the festival as a type of economic institution. For instance, festivals may play a role in legitimating new artistic forms or new genres within existing artistic forms.[25] At the same time, they function to commodify those new forms or genres.[26] Importantly, as already noted, they also offer an alternative avenue for distribution,[27] particularly in highly commodified cultural industries like the film industry, where one effect

[17] Albeit semi-permeable (Sassatelli, 'Public Culture, Comospolitanism and Festivals', p. 22) and paradoxical (A. O'Grady and R. Kill, 'Environments for Encounter and the Processes of Organizing for Interactivity and Performative Participation within the Festival Space', paper presented at the conference 'Visuals and Performativity: Researching Beyond Text', Segovia, Spain, May 2011), p. 3 (copy on file with author).

[18] See T. J. Dowd, K. Liddle and J. Nelson, 'Music Festivals as Scenes: Examples from Serious Music, Womyn's Music and SkatePunk', in A. Bennett and R. A. Peterson (eds), *Music Scenes: Local, Translocal and Virtual* (Nashville, TN: Vanderbilt University Press, 2004). See also Turan, *Sundance to Sarajevo*, who writes about three classes of festivals: festivals with business agendas, festivals with geopolitical agendas and festivals with aesthetic agendas.

[19] O'Grady and Kill, 'Exploring Festival Performance as a State of Encounter', 280.

[20] '[T]he pneumatic vacuum of television culture' (my translation): G. Guerzoni, 'L'impatto economico dei festival: un'annosa prospettiva di ricerca' (2009) 19 *Economia della Cultura* 473.

[21] J. Segal, 'Film Festivals', in Sassatelli, *European Public Culture and Aesthetic Cosmopolitanism*, pp. 115 and 117.

[22] L. Giorgi, 'Literature Festivals: Literature (Festivals) as a Subject of Sociological Inquiry in Search of Cosmopolitanism', in Sassatelli, *European Public Culture and Aesthetic Cosmopolitanism*, p. 107; L. Mazdon, 'The Cannes Film Festival as Transnational Space' (2006) 25 *Post Script* 19.

[23] M. Santoro, J. Chalcraft and P. Magaudda, 'Music Festivals: An Interdisciplinary Literature Review', in Sassatelli, *European Public Culture and Aesthetic Cosmopolitanism*, p. 83.

[24] D. Picard and M. Robinson (eds), *Festivals, Tourism and Social Change: Remaking Worlds* (Clevedon: Channel View Publications, 2006), p. 2, quoted in Sassatelli, *European Public Culture and Aesthetic Cosmopolitanism*, p. 26.

[25] Santoro, Chalcraft and Magaudda, 'Music Festivals', p. 82.

[26] *Ibid.*, p. 83, where it is argued that this observation applies, in particular, to music festivals.

[27] See Turan, *Sundance to Sarajevo*, p. 8.

of commodification has been to suppress independent production and diversity.[28]

Festivals can be distinguished from the regular programming of concerts, theatre, film and so on that occurs in concert halls, auditoriums, theatres, cinemas and other such venues on the bases that: first, these are not generally the connected elements of a single cultural event;[29] secondly, the concept of the arts festival seems to imply some degree of audience participation, which might be considered to be linked to the idea, asserted above, of the festival as a period of being in community in a physical sense;[30] thirdly, and perhaps most significantly, regularly programmed arts events might be considered to be part of the ordinary course of life precisely because they are regularly programmed in venues established for this purpose and accordingly are not occasions of suspension in time and space.

2.2 'Arts'

It seems impossible to tackle the question of how the word 'arts', as an adjectival qualification to the word 'festival', contributes to the definitional process without considering the impact of the copyright system. This is because one of the open questions pervading the relationship between copyright law and the 'arts' is that of constitution and authorization. In other words: is it some generally accepted definition of what amounts to the 'arts' that constitutes and authorizes the subject matter of copyright or, on the other hand, does copyright law constitute and authorize concepts of what are the 'arts'? In either case, it seems clear that there are recognized disciplines within the arts and, at the very least, copyright law has contributed to the compartmentalization of these disciplines.

The historical association between the subject matter of copyright and the concept of the arts is somewhat ambiguous. There seems to be some general acceptance that copyright was born out of the device of printers' privileges, most probably originating in fifteenth-century Venice[31] and then subsequently adopted with local variations in a range of other European countries.[32] Under the Venetian system, which was designed

[28] See Macmillan, 'The Cruel ©: Copyright and Film'.

[29] Falassi, 'Festival: Definition and Morphology', p. 2.

[30] O'Grady and Kill, 'Exploring Festival Performance as a State of Encounter'; O'Grady and Kill, 'Environments for Encounter and the Processes of Organizing for Interactivity and Performative Participation within the Festival Space'.

[31] See J. Stapleton, 'Art, Intellectual Property and the Knowledge Economy', PhD thesis, Goldsmiths, University of London (2002), ch. 2.

[32] See further E. Armstrong, *Before Copyright: The French Book Privilege System, 1498–1526* (Cambridge University Press, 1990).

to stimulate foreign trade rather than to engage in aesthetic debates about forms of creative output, the important distinction drawn between various possible forms of the arts was whether or not they were reproducible through the new(ish) technique of printing. Consequently, nothing in the law turned on the general distinction between, for example, written works and images. Considerations of local market stability and foreign trade value were paramount in obtaining a printing privilege.[33] In this sense, the origins of the intellectual property system lie in market regulation and not in a particular aesthetic theory. Nevertheless, there is some evidence that in framing their arguments for privileges the petitioners came to reflect the predominant discourse or paradigm of creativity, which was based in theories of rhetoric. The rhetorical paradigm of creativity, which continues to retain considerable purchase in some quarters, focused upon the labour or creativity of the artist in gathering together and arranging 'ideas' into a particular and distinctive end product.[34]

Despite the tortuous and twisting path from the Venetian system to the modern systems of copyright protection, this early history resonates through modern copyright protection of the 'arts' in a number of ways. In particular, the fact that creativity is protected under copyright law only where its product falls within one of the categories of 'copyright work' has various implications for the relationship between copyright and the creative arts, two of which might be usefully emphasized in the present context. First, to the extent that any concept holds the list of copyright protected works together, however loosely, it is one derived from the rhetorical discourse of the Renaissance period. In the hands of modern copyright law, this is reduced to a focus on the production of the discrete 'work' by a recognizable creator or creators. Secondly, while copyright recognizes that more than one of its protected subject matters can exist simultaneously in one creative work, there is no evidence that it applies to hybrid works that cross the boundaries between the different categories of protected works. In this way, copyright law and its pervasive influence on the concept of the arts tends to harden the divisions between different types of creative works.

Overall, it might be said that while at certain points in its history copyright law reacted to developments in the creative arts by drawing them

33 Stapleton, 'Art, Intellectual Property and the Knowledge Economy'.

34 Between the medieval and the Renaissance periods an important alteration had taken place in relation to the origins of the 'ideas', which resulted in an emphasis on the creator's contribution to the ensuing artistic work: *ibid.*, pp. 70–1, citing E. Panofsky, *Idea: A Concept in Art Theory* (trans. J. J. S. Peake) (London: Harper & Row, 1968), pp. 35–40 and 51; U. Eco, *Art and Beauty in the Middle Ages* (London: Yale University Press, 1986).

into its scheme of protection,[35] it seems that this scheme of protection has now become relatively rigid. One of the results of this is that there is somewhat little space for the copyright protection of innovation in form in the arts. Another important result is that it increasingly appears that copyright law defines, controls or affects the meaning of 'arts' in the broader social and cultural spheres. This very effect is evident in the way in which many arts festivals brand themselves as being literary festivals, film festivals, music festivals, theatre festivals, dance festivals and so on.

3 Arts festivals, cultural heritage and international law

The inevitability of the relationship between the arts and copyright law gives the latter an obvious presence in the arts festival environment.[36] The existence of cultural heritage rights, particularly as counterweights to copyright, seems an inherently less certain thing. This is partly because of the nebulous nature of the concept of cultural heritage rights, which in turn results in obvious difficulties in explaining its relationship to arts festivals. In an attempt to approach a solution to these difficulties, this part considers the cultural heritage credentials of arts festivals in the context of the protection of cultural heritage under international law instruments.

Despite the fact that cultural heritage is an object of protection under international law, as a concept it remains notoriously difficult to define. This chapter adopts a working definition of cultural heritage as being those things (moveable and immoveable, tangible and intangible) that a community or people considers worth handing on to the future.[37] The next task is to understand how this concept relates to legal notions of cultural heritage, which need to be understood in light of the fact that there is an obvious political element in identifying what is considered to be worth handing on to the future.[38] This element of communal choice renders the concept of cultural heritage particularly malleable and perhaps a bit slippery.

The sources of the legal concept of cultural heritage are the various international law instruments that have been generated under the auspices of UNESCO, where the politically determined, malleable and slippery concept of cultural heritage has gradually emerged from an earlier

35 L. Bently and B. Sherman, *Intellectual Property Law*, 3rd edn (Oxford University Press, 2009), pp. 33–4.

36 For a full account of which, see Macmillan, 'A Taxonomy of Arts Festivals'.

37 See J. Blake, 'On Defining the Cultural Heritage' (2000) 49 *International and Comparative Law Quarterly* 61, 68–9.

38 *Ibid.*, p. 68.

concern with cultural property.[39] In this century, the UNESCO regime's concern with tangible cultural heritage has given way to an increased focus on the intangible aspects of cultural heritage. In the festival context, where the cultural heritage aspects appear to be largely intangible,[40] the two Conventions of particular importance are the Convention on the Protection and Promotion of the Diversity of Cultural Expressions[41] and the Convention for the Safeguarding of the Intangible Cultural Heritage.[42]

According to Article 2.1 of the latter Convention, 'intangible cultural heritage' means:

> the practices, representations, expressions, knowledge, skills – as well as the instruments, objects, artefacts and cultural spaces associated therewith – that communities, groups and, in some cases, individuals recognize as part of their cultural heritage. This intangible cultural heritage, transmitted from generation to generation, is constantly recreated by communities and groups in response to their environment, their interaction with nature and their history, and provides them with a sense of identity and continuity, thus promoting respect for cultural diversity and human creativity.

Article 2.2 provides:

> The 'intangible cultural heritage', as defined in paragraph 1 above, is manifested inter alia in the following domains:
> (a) oral traditions and expressions, including language as the vehicle of the intangible cultural heritage;
> (b) performing arts;
> (c) social practices, rituals and festive events;
> (d) knowledge and practices concerning nature and the universe;
> (e) traditional craftsmanship.

In the context of this definition, there seems to be ample scope for an argument that arts festivals, or at least some arts festivals, fall within the concept of intangible cultural heritage. This is particularly the case given the strong identification that many (if not the overwhelming majority of) arts festivals have with a particular place.

The Convention on the Protection of Cultural Diversity employs the concept of cultural heritage in order to define the idea of cultural diversity with which it is concerned. Article 4.1 provides:

39 For a critique of the concept of cultural property, see *ibid.*, pp. 65–7.

40 See further Macmillan, 'A Taxonomy of Arts Festivals'.

41 Opened for signature 20 October 2005, in force 18 March 2007, 2440 UNTS 311 ('Convention on the Protection of Cultural Diversity').

42 Opened for signature 17 October 2003, in force 20 April 2006, 2368 UNTS 1 ('Convention on Intangible Cultural Heritage').

'Cultural diversity' refers to the manifold ways in which the cultures of groups and societies find expression. These expressions are passed on within and among groups and societies.

Cultural diversity is made manifest not only through the varied ways in which the cultural heritage of humanity is expressed, augmented and transmitted through the variety of cultural expressions, but also through diverse modes of artistic creation, production, dissemination, distribution and enjoyment, whatever the means and technologies used.

According to Article 4.3 of the Convention on Intangible Cultural Heritage, '"cultural expressions" are those expressions that result from the creativity of individuals, groups and societies, and that have cultural content', while Article 4.2 tells us that '"cultural content" refers to the symbolic meaning, artistic dimension and cultural values that originate from or express cultural identities'. There is, of course, some circularity in these definitions.[43] Nevertheless, it seems reasonable to suggest that arts festivals may act as a means of expressing, preserving and promoting cultural diversity. This is perhaps particularly so when festivals operate as a means of reinforcing a particular traditional culture or community identity,[44] although it would not seem to be limited to this case.

So, while it seems generally safe to assert that arts festivals have cultural heritage credentials, the more difficult problem is to try and understand exactly where they lie on an imaginary festival map and how they relate to the intellectual property rights that also seem to be an obvious part of the festival topography. Would cultural heritage be represented as the container or border on the basis that the festival, as event, is the vehicle of the cultural heritage? Such a representation might be based on the notion of the 'cultural space' provided by the festival within the meaning of Article 2.1 of the Convention on Intangible Cultural Heritage or on the reference to 'festive events' in Article 2.2(c). Or is the cultural heritage element of the festival more pervasive? Does it appear somewhere between the lines of what is already protected by copyright or other intellectual property interests? Or does it, in fact, overlap with what is already protected by intellectual property? Such a reading could easily be justified according to paragraphs (a) and (b) of Article 2.2 of the Convention on Intangible Cultural Heritage. Similarly, as already noted, many elements of festivals seem to offer expressions of the sort of cultural

43 See F. Macmillan, 'The UNESCO Convention as a New Incentive to Protect Cultural Diversity', in H. Schneider and P. van den Bossche (eds), *Protection of Cultural Diversity from a European and International Perspective* (Mortsel: Intersentia, 2008).

44 See, e.g., A. Kaeppler, 'Pacific Festivals and Ethnic Identity', in Falassi, *Time Out of Time*, pp. 162–70.

diversity with which the Convention on the Protection of Cultural Diversity is concerned. The most likely answer to all these questions is that the cultural heritage nature of festivals is evident in all these festival spaces. In other words, arts festivals are saturated by cultural heritage. It is also evidently the case that arts festivals are saturated with copyright interests, which means that some accommodation between cultural heritage and copyright needs to be reached.

4 The relationship between cultural heritage and intellectual property rights

The question of the relationship between private property rights, into which description intellectual property rights fall, and cultural heritage rights is one that has received scant attention in law. To some extent, this may be because it involves a 'category' problem. The organization of law as a discipline depends on a distinction between public and private rights, which tend to be considered in discrete categories. This way of thinking about law creates difficulties in resolving conflicts across these notional boundaries. Historically, and consistently with the requirements of capitalist relations, this has led to the legal sacralization of private property rights. In the late twentieth century, this unquestioning devotion to the sanctity of private rights and private property started to come under some pressure, not the least as a result of the rise of a strong human rights discourse. However, the power balance between the discourse of private property and that of public rights, such as human rights, always rests on a knife-edge. Cultural heritage rights, which derive their normative impact from the human rights regime, have certainly not been immune from this conflict.

In relation to the regime for the protection of tangible cultural heritage, private ownership rights have not necessarily prevailed over cultural heritage rights, but they have been given substantial recognition.[45] In the world of intangible cultural heritage, the Convention on the Protection of Cultural Diversity uncritically accepts the role of private property rights, in the form of intellectual property rights, in sustaining the type of cultural creativity that it regards as essential to the flourishing of cultural diversity.[46] A similar uncritical acceptance characterizes the Convention

[45] Convention on the Means of Prohibiting and Preventing the Illicit Import, Export and Transfer of Ownership of Cultural Property, opened for signature 14 November 1970, in force 24 April 1972, 823 UNTS 231, art. 7(b)(ii).

[46] According to its Recitals, the Convention recognizes 'the importance of intellectual property rights in sustaining those involved in cultural creativity'; see also art. 20. For a further analysis, see Macmillan, 'The UNESCO Convention as a New Incentive to Protect Cultural Diversity'.

on Intangible Cultural Heritage.[47] In contradistinction to the protection of tangible cultural heritage, the two twenty-first-century UNESCO Conventions do not seem to envisage the need for any limitation on the extensive private property rights wielded by copyright owners and other intellectual property holders. This is despite the fact that the role of cultural heritage rights must surely be to limit in some way the privatization of, or the exercise of private property rights over, the cultural heritage in question.

Based on the definitions of intangible cultural heritage described in section 3 of this chapter, it does not seem controversial to assert that there is an overlap between the subject matter of intangible cultural heritage and some intellectual property rights. The difficult issue in a case of overlap is how we should understand the relationship between the two both in reality and in law. Joseph Slaughter argues that the relationship between intellectual property and cultural property can be mapped onto global geopolitical relations, with the result that we think of the developed world as having intellectual property and the developing world as having cultural property.[48] By this, he means to suggest not a difference in the subjects of these property rights but rather a difference in their treatment:

> In the Western tradition, cultural property may be what becomes of some literary texts and their creators after copyrights run out (for example, when Proust becomes French, Goethe German, Joyce Irish, Dickens British, Melville American); but historically the distinction between cultural and intellectual property has generally (once again) been mapped onto the divide between the developing and developed world, trailing behind it a long series of old familiar orientalist oppositions: individual versus collective, personal property versus group commons, formal versus informal knowledge, and so forth. Accordingly, we in the West produce spontaneous original intellectual property; they in the rest of the world have a rich (though probably burdensome) collective legacy of cultural heritage and traditional knowledge that is, so the logic goes, part of what keeps their societies underdeveloped.[49]

As Slaughter goes on to argue, the 'power and prestige' of the formal system of property relations which governs intellectual property overwhelms the informal and 'traditional' system of cultural heritage protection.[50]

[47] See art. 3(b).

[48] This characterization might well be regarded as reinforced by the contents of the Representative List of the Intangible Cultural Heritage of Humanity, established under the Convention on Intangible Cultural Heritage, art. 16, which is overwhelmingly populated by contributions from the global south.

[49] J. R. Slaughter, 'Form and Informality: An Unliterary Look at World Literature', in R. Warhol (ed.), *The Work of Genre: Selected Essays from the English Institute* (Cambridge, MA: English Institute in Collaboration with the American Council of Learned Societies, 2011), pp. 198–9 (footnote omitted).

[50] *Ibid.*, p. 200.

Despite some rather simple formalization as a result of the requirement that intangible cultural heritage must be listed to have protection under the Convention on Intangible Cultural Heritage,[51] it seems relatively clear that intellectual property has the upper hand since it is a formalized technique of private appropriation of intangible cultural property.[52] The fact that something appears on a UNESCO list of intangible cultural heritage does not, at least in international law, give it any protection from this type of appropriation (or, indeed, from any other potentially hostile acts). The rules here all seem to be set by the intellectual property regime, which has spawned the idea of the public domain in order to explain its relationship to everything else that exists in intellectual space. When intellectual property rights are used as a technology to appropriate intangible cultural heritage or property then, so far as the intellectual property regime is concerned, what is consequently privatized is taken from the intellectual public domain. Under these circumstances, any understanding of the relationship between intellectual property and cultural property also depends on the geography and architecture of this public domain.

5 The relationship between cultural heritage and the public domain of intellectual space

The public domain has been invented by intellectual property scholars in order to attempt to explain and understand the limits on intellectual property's colonization of intellectual space. Much has been made of the intellectual public domain. It has been reified, and then valorized, as the place where community and culture are protected from 'property', meaning privately owned property, and where creativity consequently flourishes. However, while being a place of potential political significance, in the sense that it might offer a bulwark against the creeping propertization of everything, it has been so seriously under-imagined that its political potential has not been realized.[53] Even worse, some writers regard it, or the rhetoric that sustains it, as potentially damaging

[51] Convention on Intangible Cultural Heritage, arts 16 and 17.

[52] See Slaughter, 'Form and Informality'; F. Macmillan, 'The Protection of Cultural Heritage: Common Heritage of Humankind, National Cultural "Patrimony" or Private Property?' (2013) 64 *Northern Ireland Legal Quarterly* 351; M. Rendix, 'Copyright as Moral Strategy of Reclaiming the Past: The Return of the Icelandic Sagas', in H. Porsdam and T. Elholm (eds), *Dialogues on Justice: European Perspectives on Law and Humanities* (Berlin: de Gruyter, 2012).

[53] See F. Macmillan, 'Many Analogies, Some Metaphors, Little Imagination: The Public Domain in Intellectual Space' (2010) 2 *Pòlemos* 25.

to other rights.[54] The basic problem with the public domain (apart from the fact that it is an imaginary space) is that it is more or less lacking in any legal architecture. It has been imagined only as the place where there are no intellectual property rights; only as a place defined by absence. The absence of intellectual property rights in the public domain can be explained by a variety of reasons that largely depend upon the nature of intellectual property itself. Thus, intellectual property itself defines the terms of its own absence from the public domain. For example, intellectual property rights might not exist because copyright law does not protect ideas but only specific expressions of ideas; or because patent law protects only industrially applicable inventions and not discoveries. In some circumstances, it might be said that intellectual property rights exist but cannot be exercised, such as when an exception or defence arises.

While the things that intellectual property pushes out of the propertized zone are relatively well understood, much less attention has been paid to the question of what is, or should be, pulled out of the propertized zone by *other* legal rights. The effect of human rights law in carrying out this task has received some attention.[55] Overall, however, the legal architecture of the public domain is not well articulated or imagined. This is evident from the sometimes peculiar analogies, similes and metaphors that legal scholars have used to describe the relationship between the propertized domain and the public domain of intellectual space. Some of the most popular are contrasts between raw materials (public domain) and manufactured products; knowledge (public domain) and innovation; idea (public domain) and expression; nature (public domain) and culture. This last metaphor, in particular, exposes the lack of lucidity in thinking about the public domain. If culture, cultural property and cultural heritage are not privately owned rights, but rather communal or public rights,[56] then the place of culture must be in the public domain of intellectual space and not in the propertized domain.

The idea of the public domain in intellectual space is heavily dependent on principles of Roman law governing physical space. However, the metaphorical existence of modern intellectual space lacks the complexity of its antecedent in physical space. The relevant principles of Roman law recognized various dimensions of non-exclusive – but not

54 See, e.g., K. Bowrey and J. Anderson, 'The Politics of Global Information Sharing: Whose Cultural Agendas are Being Advanced?' (2009) 18 *Social and Legal Studies* 479.
55 See, e.g., Macmillan, 'Many Analogies, Some Metaphors, Little Imagination'.
56 See further Macmillan, 'A Taxonomy of Arts Festivals', sect. 7.2.3.

necessarily public – property.[57] The most extensively used of these, so far as the intellectual-property/public-domain debate is concerned, are *res communes* and *res publicae*. The former refers to things incapable by their nature of being exclusively owned, while the latter refers to things open to the public by operation of law. These seem to have translated into the modern-day debate about property in intellectual space in the specific form of the concepts of the commons and the public domain, although the two expressions are often used interchangeably. This confusion between the commons and the public domain, *res communes* and *res publicae*, has done nothing to simplify the epistemological basis of the dichotomy between intellectual property and intellectual public space.[58] More than this, it has tended to conceal the fact that, traced back to their Roman law origins, neither of these concepts seems to provide a particularly strong basis for a vibrant public or non-exclusive intellectual space in today's world.

So far as *res communes* is concerned, one might be forgiven for thinking that because of the non-rivalrous and non-wastable nature of things in intellectual space they are all incapable by their nature of being exclusively owned or appropriated. Intellectual property law has, however, put paid to that idea. To the extent that intellectual property laws continue to exclude certain parts of intellectual space from the propertized domain, it is far from clear whether their exclusion is because they are, by their legal nature, incapable of being owned, and therefore part of the commons, or because they should not be brought into the private domain of intellectual property but should be kept in the public domain. Arguably, because things in intellectual space are all incapable of ownership in the sense that things in physical space may be owned, but are all – or nearly all – quite capable of being appropriated in another way by force of law, the concept of the commons or *res communes* is a difficult one to apply to intellectual space. At least, it is difficult once we concede any concept of ownership in intellectual space, unless by referring to the commons we merely mean to be descriptive and refer to those things that have not yet been subsumed into the intellectual property regime. The concept of the *res publicae* seems to offer far greater promise. Unlike the concept of *res communes*, *res publicae* in physical space does not reject the notion of private property. According to Carol Rose, *res publicae* is always open to the possibility of

57 See C. M. Rose, 'Romans, Roads and Romantic Creators: Traditions of Public Property in the Information Age' (2003) 66 *Law and Contemporary Problems* 89.

58 See also E. H. Wirtén, 'Out of Sight and Out of Mind: On the Cultural Hegemony of Intellectual Property (Critique)' (2005) 20 *Cultural Studies* 282, 284, who suggests that it is time for 'some good old epistemological soul-searching'.

ownership 'subject to the requirements of reasonable public access'.[59] One consequence of this is that it is necessary for something or someone to defend *res publicae*.

In physical space, *res publicae* is regarded as normatively justified by the need to ensure productive synergistic interactions that would otherwise be obstructed by denying public access.[60] The irony in the application of this concept to intellectual space is that precisely because things in intellectual space are non-rivalrous and non-wastable there are not many reasons why productive synergistic interactions should not take place.[61] That is, there are not many reasons apart from intellectual property law itself. By regarding things in intellectual space as capable of appropriation and not therefore *res communes*, intellectual property law has created a system of obstructions to synergistic interactions. Then, in response to these obstructions, it has created its own mechanisms to defend *res publicae*. Perhaps this sounds slightly more ridiculous than it actually is. One of the reasons that productive synergistic interactions might not take place in unfettered intellectual space is because, in the absence of reward, appropriate investment and effort might not be made. Even accepting this argument and accepting that the most appropriate form of 'reward' is the creation of intellectual property rights,[62] it seems reasonably clear that to achieve productive synergistic interactions there needs to be a carefully calibrated balance between property rights in intellectual space and rights that preserve *res publicae*. In intellectual property law, this is generally achieved through three mechanisms: disclosure requirements, limits on duration, and exceptions to the exercise of the exclusive rights. With respect to the first two mechanisms, the provisions of the law automatically defend the *res publicae*, whereas in relation to the last, those seeking to use the exceptions must make a case. Despite the existence of these mechanisms, it would be straining credulity to suggest that the balance between property rights and rights that preserve *res publicae* in intellectual

[59] Rose, 'Romans, Roads and Romantic Creators', 99. On the attributes of *res publicae*, see pp. 96–100.

[60] *Ibid.*, pp. 96–8. [61] *Ibid.*, pp. 102–3.

[62] A point that is not universally accepted: see, e.g., J. Smiers, 'The Abolition of Copyrights: Better for Artists, Third World Countries and the Public Domain', in Towse, *Copyright and the Cultural Industries*, p. 120; M. van Schijndel and J. Smiers, 'Imagining a World Without Copyright: The Market and Temporary Protection, a Better Alternative for Artists and the Public Domain', in H. Porsdam (ed.), *Copyright and Other Fairy Tales: Hans Christian Andersen and the Commodification of Creativity* (Cheltenham: Edward Elgar, 2005); J. Smiers and M. van Schijndel, *La fine del copyright: Come creare un mercato culturale aperto a tutti* (Viterbo: Stampa Alternativa, 2010).

space is carefully calibrated. The history of intellectual property law has marked a progressive extension of the duration of intellectual property rights and the contraction of their respective exceptions and defences.

The dominance of *res communes* and *res publicae* in informing our notion of the public domain as it relates to intellectual property in intellectual space appears to be connected to its somewhat impoverished and under-imagined nature. While there is nothing inherently unusual about a lack of imagination, especially in relation to legal concepts, its absence here is a little more surprising. This is because there are two further concepts of Roman law that could be employed to flesh out the public domain in intellectual space. One of these is *res divini juris*, referring to things that cannot be owned because of their sacred or religious nature.[63] In the context of the current debate, this concept might be adapted to recognize the cultural power of the iconic. It might be possible, therefore, to conceive of concepts such as cultural property, cultural heritage and human rights as part of the iconic, or even sacred. If so, and if festivals can be regarded as carriers of such iconic or sacred legal values, then perhaps it is possible to construct an argument that festivals and their contents should be pulled out of the privatized domain and located in the public domain of intellectual space. At least one problem with this argument is that pulling festivals out of the propertized zone of intellectual space may have the effect of leaving their contents completely unprotected, so that instead of being a suspension in time and space their contents simply become a free-for-all for all time. What, rather, is needed here is some way to recognize a (limited) legal suspension that mirrors the temporal and spatial suspension of the festival. This is where another category of non-exclusive property under Roman law, *res universitatis*,[64] may be regarded as having some resonance.

In modern parlance, *res universitatis* refers to a regime that is bounded by property rights, but creates a type of limited public domain (or commons) within its boundaries. In intellectual space the utility of *res universitatis*, or the bounded commons, must be to preserve productive synergies while maintaining the incentive to produce such synergies through the exercise of rights against outsiders. This concept of the bounded creative community may prove a useful basis on which to build a suspension of the intellectual property regime that might otherwise apply in the festival context, but only within the spatial and temporal bounds of the festival itself.

[63] Rose, 'Romans, Roads and Romantic Creators', 108–10.
[64] For a description of *res universitatis*, see *ibid.*, pp. 105–8.

6 Conclusion

The arguments for regarding the festival as a rupture in legal space flow from its inherent nature as a rupture in time and space. As Alessandro Falassi notes, scholars have drawn on Durkheim's famous opposition of the sacred and profane,[65] or Victor Turner's updated distinction between 'liminal (obligatory, highly formalized) and liminoid (optional, free flowing) social events'[66] to try and explain the space of the festival.[67] Denise Lawrence, for example, conceives the festival as a state of 'ritual disorder'.[68] A similar notion of disorder in relation to festivals is also used by Roger Abrahams, who, however, contrasts it with ritual:

> While ritual underscores the harmonies and continuities in the expressive resources of a culture, emphasizing the wholeness of the world's fabric, festivals work (at least at their inception) by apparently tearing the fabric to pieces, by displaying it upside-down, inside-out, wearing it as motley rags and tatters . . . Festivals seize on open spots and playfully enclose them. Spaces are found and are invested with the meaning of the moment and the power of the occasion . . . Festivals thus draw their own boundaries for the occasion and redraw the boundaries of the host community, ironically establishing themselves in areas that, in the everyday world, have their own boundaries . . . Openness, central to our experience of festival, is temporal as well as spatial.[69]

Festivals, on this argument, fit badly within the highly institutionalized and legally regulated world of private intellectual property law.[70] As Abrahams goes on to observe:

> Festivals are ultimately community affairs. Indeed, they provide *the* occasion whereby a community may call attention to itself and, perhaps more important in our time, its willingness to display itself openly. It is the ultimate public activity, given its need for preparation and coordination of effort, and its topsy-turvyness, in which many of the basic notions of community are put to test.[71]

[65] See Durkheim, *The Elementary Forms of Religious Life*. See also M. Eliade, *The Sacred and the Profane* (New York: Harper Torchbooks, 1961).

[66] See, e.g., V. Turner, 'Liminal to Liminoid, in Play, Flow and Ritual: An Essay in Comparative Symbology', in J. C. Harris and R. J. Park (eds), *Play, Games and Sports in Cultural Contexts* (Champaign, IL: Human Kinetics Publishers, 1983).

[67] In the introductory notes to R. Abrahams, 'An American Vocabulary of Celebrations', in Falassi, *Time Out of Time*, p. 173.

[68] D. Lawrence, 'Rules of Misrule: Notes on the Doo Dah Parade in Pasadena', in Falassi, *Time Out of Time*, p. 134.

[69] Abrahams, 'An American Vocabulary of Celebrations', p. 178.

[70] This argument might also be regarded as consistent with the observation of Lawrence, 'Rules of Misrule', p. 134 that 'Institutionalizing inherently unstable socio-cultural forms, such as ritual disorder [into which category she places festivals] and spontaneity, is theoretically as well as pragmatically problematic'.

[71] Abrahams, 'An American Vocabulary of Celebrations', p. 181. See also M. Mesnil, 'Place and Time in the Carnivalesque Festival', in Falassi, *Time Out of Time*, p. 192,

What festivals thus represent is a public (in the sense of not being private), communal and bounded space of openness. This idea of the festival should be reflected in the law's treatment of the creative and synergistic reactions that occur within the rupture or suspension created by the festival space. Clearly, the concept of *res universitatis* has some potential in this respect.

An interesting question that arises in this context is the relevance of the arts festival as a cultural heritage institution. In some ways, the use of the words 'institution' is problematic because the festival is anti-institutional.[72] However, in seeking to establish the balance between intellectual property and the public domain, the identification of the arts festival as a form of cultural heritage may be useful. This is partly because it may help to give legal shape to the bounded, but open, space of the festival. In addition, as already noted, the function of cultural rights should be to defend the public domain by either resisting privatization or even actively pulling material out of the privatized domain and into the public domain. However, the version of the public domain being considered here is not a free-for-all but rather should be a place with a more clearly defined legal architecture.

A useful first step towards establishing this legal architecture would be a move away from the simplified binary divide of the intellectual public domain and the intellectual private domain of intellectual property law – or, at least, away from the notion that the intellectual public domain is some undifferentiated concept equating to the 'commons' in Roman law. After this first step, a blueprint for developing such an architecture might include: first, an appreciation of the difference between what is publicly or communally owned in intellectual space and what is in the commons – that is, unowned – in intellectual space and thus ripe for appropriation; secondly, an associated recognition that some things can never be owned, at least privately, because of their cultural significance; and, thirdly, the development of the concept of group and communal rights, belonging to less than the public as a whole, bounded by property on the outside, but inside promoting freedom and space for creativity, innovation, invention and cultural conservation.[73] Failure to develop the same

who divides festivals of urbanized societies into 'carnivalesque and folklorized' with only the first growing out of a community and being really a rupture, but concludes, based on empirical work, most such festivals contain elements of both.

72 See, e.g., Lawrence, 'Rules of Misrule', p. 134.

73 On each of these points, see further F. Macmillan, 'Altering the Contours of the Public Domain', in C. Waelde and H. MacQueen (eds), *Intellectual Property: The Many Faces of the Public Domain* (Cheltenham: Edward Elgar, 2007). See also the emerging concept of 'i beni comuni' (community goods) in, e.g., A. Ciervo, *I Beni Comuni* (Rome: Ediesse, 2013).

complex architecture in intellectual or intangible space as that which we have developed in tangible space for the preservation of heritage and cultural property only invites constant encroachment by the type of private propertization in intellectual space that undermines and destroys claims to cultural property and heritage in that space. A clear understanding of the reality of the relationship between intellectual property and cultural heritage and property is an urgent political and legal project. This point might perhaps be reinforced by recalling Slaughter's salutary observation about the way in which the current state of the relationship between intellectual property and cultural property can be mapped onto geopolitical relations:[74] the idea that the global north lacks intangible cultural property is socially and culturally impoverishing; the suggestion that all culture in the global south is open to appropriation is simply unjust and outrageous.[75]

[74] Slaughter, 'Form and Informality'. And see text accompanying nn. 48–52, above.
[75] See further Macmillan, 'The Protection of Cultural Heritage'.

10 Franchising carnival
Issues of rights and cultural identity

Sharon Le Gall

1 Introduction

In March 2011, it was reported that South Africa would be hosting a Trinidad-style carnival later that year. The South African government had already set up a unit to manage the festival and was receiving 'technical support' from Trinidad and Tobago.[1] The interest in Trinidad Carnival was because of the 'social cohesion that Carnival produces'.[2] The same report stated that Uganda was also planning to have a Trinidad-style carnival in Kampala.[3] This chapter will reflect on franchise-like activity in relation to carnival in Trinidad and Tobago over the past fifty years, and the possible reasons for the replication of this festival in approximately sixty cities in North America and Europe.

Section 2 covers a brief history of the Trinidad and Tobago Carnival, of which calypso/soca (music), mas (masquerade) and pan (the steel pan musical instrument) are taken to be the defining 'authentic' elements. The rationales for the global proliferation of the festival will be explored in section 3. As festivals are catalysts for creativity, intellectual property is generated at those times and governed by existing intellectual property laws where applicable. Carnival also embodies properties in traditional knowledge and intangible cultural heritage. However, there is an uneasy accommodation of those diverse properties in carnival within intellectual property and emerging traditional knowledge laws that will be discussed in section 4. The difficulties involved in 'formally' franchising the carnival 'product' will be explored in section 5.

The development of this unique trade is facilitated by intellectual property laws and the state, but largely led by entrepreneurs who facilitate new commercial opportunities through commercialization of cultural expertise or 'know-how'. However, franchising carnival is not wholly due to

[1] See D. Joseph, 'The Future of T&T Carnival', *Trinidad & Tobago News* (online), 27 March 2011, at http://trinidadandtobagonews.com/selfnews/viewnews.cgi?newsid 1301281408,84750,.shtml.
[2] *Ibid.* [3] *Ibid.*

an economic logic of commodification, nor simply an outcome of private ambitions to establish a new global cultural trade. Carnival also encompasses a serious negotiation of identity occurring within and across communities, nation states and internationally. The attraction to carnival is due to a genuine interest in exploring and renewing cultural expression of identity, and it is this dimension that is also an important driver of the franchise activity.

2 Trinidad Carnival

2.1 Introduction – festivals: definitions and meanings

Defining festivals and their typology with any precision is difficult, 'and to an extent will always fall short of corresponding realities', probably because it necessitates 'having to define a limited time and space frame in which a multitude of social interactions, aesthetic signs and narrative discourses can be observed'.[4]

Festivals, of which carnivals are a part, have been defined simply as 'themed public celebrations',[5] or more elaborately as 'periodically recurrent, social occasion[s] in which, through . . . a series of co-ordinated events . . . members of a whole community [participate directly or indirectly] united by ethnic, linguistic, religious, historical bonds, and sharing a worldview.'[6]

Sociologists and anthropologists have offered diverse reasons for the place and meaning of festivals in societies. Some rationales include the need for people to set aside times and places for celebration, the opportunity to provide a socially sanctioned forum for unleashing social tensions (that would otherwise prove destructive) and the means through which people express identities, connect with their place and communicate with the outside world.[7]

Festivals are a part of Caribbean culture. There is the Jonkonnu of Jamaica, with variations of this festival celebrated in Belize, St Kitts and Nevis and Guyana; Hoosay of Guyana and Trinidad; and carnival

[4] D. Picard and M. Robinson, 'Remaking Worlds: Festivals, Tourism and Change', in D. Picard and M. Robinson (eds), *Festivals, Tourism and Social Change: Remaking Worlds* (Clevedon: Channel Vision Publications, 2006), p. 4 (footnote omitted).

[5] D. Getz, *Event Studies: Theory, Research and Policy for Planned Events* (Oxford: Butterworth-Heinemann, 2007), p. 31.

[6] A. Falassi, 'Festival: Definition and Morphology', in A. Falassi (ed.), *Time Out of Time: Essays on the Festival* (Albuquerque, NM: University of New Mexico Press, 1987), p. 2.

[7] See Getz, *Event Studies*, p. 32.

celebrations in Barbados, Grenada, Dominica, and St Vincent and the Grenadines, amongst others.[8]

2.2 *Carnival in Trinidad and Tobago*

Carnival in Trinidad and Tobago is the largest pre-Lenten festival in the Caribbean and has influenced the content and observance of the celebrations in the region. From a historical perspective, during the period of British rule prior to emancipation (from 1797 to 1834), Carnival in Trinidad was an important festival for whites and free persons of colour, particularly in urban Trinidad. Enslaved Africans were virtually excluded from participation.

The most significant event affecting the population structure was the abolition of slavery in 1834, and the termination of the subsequent compulsory apprenticeship period. Following emancipation, Asian immigrants were brought in as indentured labourers.

Carnival of 1834, the year of emancipation, already exhibited signs of a takeover by working-class people who had previously been restricted from joining the celebrations. During that period, Africans developed the Canboulay as 'a kind of commemoration' of their emancipation.[9] This was a re-enactment of what took place on the plantation during slavery when there was a cane fire, and the first indigenous aspect of post-emancipation carnival in Trinidad seems to have been derived from the Canboulay performed by the former enslaved Africans. A torchlight procession and a re-enactment of scenes associated with slavery took place to the accompaniment of African drums on the night of every 1 August, the anniversary of emancipation day. Africans organized themselves into bands with kings, queens and other royal figures in a manner similar to that of the pre-emancipation regiments.[10] Sometime during the 1840s, Canboulay was shifted from August to the beginning of the pre-Lenten Carnival, with processions beginning in the early hours of the morning of Carnival Monday re-interpreted as J'Ouvert or Jouvay ('break of day') celebrations.

During the decades that followed emancipation, there were unsuccessful attempts to suppress carnival through police action and legislation.[11]

[8] For an overview of festivals in the Caribbean, see J. W. Nunley and J. Bettelheim (eds), *Caribbean Festival Arts: Each and Every Bit of Difference* (Seattle, WA: University of Washington Press, 1988).

[9] See E. Hill, *The Trinidad Carnival: Mandate for a National Theatre* (Austin, TX: University of Texas Press, 1997), p. 23.

[10] See S. Stuempfle, *The Steelband Movement: The Forging of a National Art in Trinidad and Tobago* (Philadelphia, PA: University of Pennsylvania Press, 1995), pp. 17–19.

[11] In 1881, the Chief of Police led 150 policemen in an attempt to contain the bands. The bands retaliated and several persons, including police officers, were injured. The

Restrictions on drumming encouraged the development of new forms of instruments for carnival, which included chac-chacs, old boxes and bits of metal. By the beginning of the twentieth century, the tamboo bamboo[12] became the primary form of carnival percussion. Varied lengths of bamboo were either thumped on the ground or hit with sticks to produce varied sounds. The tamboo bamboo was the replacement for the African drum, the use of which was prohibited by the Ordinance for the Better Preservation of the Peace.

Early versions of the steel pan entered the post-emancipation carnival celebrations in the 1930s. It developed in a diffuse, cumulative and collective manner resulting in some uncertainty over who actually invented it.[13] Common to the numerous accounts of the origin of the steel pan was the Alexander's Ragtime Band and it is suggested that this band was the first to have made the complete transition from bamboo instruments to steel pan instruments in their nascent stages. By 1946, a new set of steel pan instruments had, in large part, replaced the paint tins and dust bins used previously, and by 1948 a number of steel bands were able to play calypsos and sambas, as well as their own compositions.

Initial legislative attempts to restrict the playing of the steel pan and the debates that ensued in the Legislative Council have been characterized as having little to do with 'playing noisy instruments' (as described in the amendment to the Summary Offences Ordinance, 1945) and more to do with issues of class, power and culture: part of the agenda of colonization practised in Trinidad and Tobago at that time.[14] However, the period between 1947 and 1951 (and following years) arguably marked the beginning of the acceptance of the steel pan as a national art form. Steel bands toured the Caribbean and Europe, the steel pan was included as a category in the national music festival and a music festival was created exclusively for the instrument. In 1973, Pan Trinbago (still extant) became the official organization with the primary responsibility for the management of the steel bands.

From a historical perspective, carnival has successively belonged to the social and cultural domain of different groups or classes in society that accordingly placed different accents on the expression of dominant

following year, the carnival was peaceful, but, by 1883, there was a resurgence of violence, which led to the passing of the Ordinance for the Better Preservation of the Peace, 1884.

12 The word 'tamboo' is derived from the French word 'tambour' for drum.

13 Some of the names commonly associated with the nascent stages of this instrument are Winston 'Spree' Simon, Elliott 'Ellie' Mannette, 'Fisheye' Ollivierre, Bertram 'Bertie' Lloyd Marshall, 'Mando' Wilson and Anthony Williams: see S. Gonzalez, *Steelband Saga: The Story of the Steelband – The First 25 Years* (Trinidad and Tobago: Ministry of Education and Culture, 1978), pp. 1–2.

14 See Stuempfle, *The Steelband Movement*, p. 8.

values and subordinated counter-values.[15] Originally, the French elite used carnival as a way of defining and celebrating their community and cultural heritage. Following emancipation, the formerly enslaved Africans, no longer relegated to the margins of the public festivity, appropriated the event and recreated it in terms of the Canboulay. In the decades that followed emancipation, Africans increasingly used carnival as an occasion to assert their identity. Attempts to sanitize carnival through legislation and brute force had partial success as the event was redefined as a 'traditional Trinidadian celebration suitable for the enjoyment of the general public'.[16] This redefinition of carnival paved the way for the commercialization of the festival, though the Canboulay tradition in J'Ouvert or Jouvay continued to be asserted in resistance to the '"improvement" programme'.[17] This commercialization has continued from 1945 to the present, or what Richard Burton calls the period of 'modern carnival'.[18]

Many have decried the commodification of the current carnival celebrations that 'is exemplified by the assembly-line production of indistinguishable costumes bought and sold in a market transaction'.[19] What Trinidad and Tobago Carnival represents today, and its core values, have not been the subject of national discourse,[20] but it is arguably a source of varying degrees of economic benefit for some, an opportunity to engage in political leveraging for others and a means to display and celebrate identity and national pride for most.

3 The replication of Trinidad-style carnivals

3.1 Caribbean diaspora

Trinidad-style carnivals can be found in other Caribbean islands. They have been transplanted to more than sixty cities in North America and Europe.[21] Three specific art forms associated with the festival – calypso/soca (music), mas (masquerade) and pan (the steel pan musical

[15] See P. van Koningsbruggen, *Trinidad Carnival: A Quest for National Identity* (London: Caribbean, 1997), p. 253.

[16] Stuempfle, *The Steelband Movement*, p. 31. [17] *Ibid.*

[18] See R. D. E. Burton, *Afro-Creole Power, Opposition and Play in the Caribbean* (Ithaca, NY: Cornell University Press, 1997), p. 199.

[19] See G. L. Green and P. W. Scher, 'Introduction: Trinidad Carnival in Global Context', in G. L. Green and P. W. Scher (eds), *Trinidad Carnival: The Cultural Politics of a Transnational Festival* (Bloomington, IN: Indiana University Press, 2007), p. 22.

[20] See S. Burke, *Policing the Transnational: Cultural Policy Development in the Anglophone Caribbean (1962–2008)* (Saarbrücken: Lambert Academic Publishing, 2010), p. 152.

[21] See C. G. T. Ho and K. Nurse, 'Introduction', in C. G. T. Ho and K. Nurse (eds), *Globalization, Diaspora and Caribbean Popular Culture* (Kingston, Jamaica: Ian Randle Publishers, 2005), p. vii.

instrument) – have been the source of inspiration for other carnivals that attract large numbers of visitors and generate significant revenues for their external host cities. The economic impact study commissioned by the London Development Agency, for example, found that in 2002:

> the Notting Hill Carnival generated approximately £93 million and supported the equivalent of 3,000 full-time jobs – clear evidence that what takes place every August Bank Holiday weekend on the streets of Notting Hill is a multi-million pound income-generating event.[22]

While some of the Trinidad-style carnivals such as Labour Day in New York, Notting Hill Gate in London and Caribana in Toronto are decades old, more recently, versions of that festival have been or are proposed to be hosted in Nigeria, Uganda and South Africa.

Different reasons have been offered for the replication of Trinidad Carnival in the Caribbean diaspora. The migration of Trinidad and Tobago and other Caribbean nationals to North America and the United Kingdom has resulted in the 'diffusion of the festival arts weaned in the Caribbean' as the re-enactment of the festival acts as a means of 'cultural expression, survival, and social demarginalization'.[23]

Trinidad and Tobago Carnival, according to Nettleford, 'fully demonstrates the interlinking of migration, transmission and maintenance of the intangible of a people' that is assured through cross-fertilization, adjustments and adaptations over time with the resulting products taking on indigenous characteristics but retaining the influences of the migrants' place of origin.[24] Also, there is an openness about Trinidad Carnival at its core that allowed its transmission by migrants, even though some aspects of the festival are somewhat closed and have not been transferred to the host cities.[25]

Another rationale for the proliferation of Trinidad-style carnival is linked to the festival as a means of asserting identity in national and diasporic spaces. Trinidad and Tobago Carnival, as a cultural identifier, is evidenced not only in its place of origin, but is a significant aspect of

[22] See Greater London Authority, *Notting Hill Carnival: A Strategic Review* (London: Greater London Authority, 2004), p. 9, at http://legacy.london.gov.uk/mayor/carnival/docs/review_final_rpt.pdf.

[23] See R. Nettleford, 'Implications for Caribbean Development', in Nunley and Bettelheim, *Caribbean Festival Arts*, p. 196.

[24] See R. Nettleford, 'Migration, Transmission and Maintenance of the Intangible Heritage' (2004) 56 *Museum International* 78, 80–1.

[25] Interview with R. Gibbons, Former Director/Head of the Centre for the Creative and Festival Arts, Faculty of Humanities and Education, University of the West Indies Tunapuna, Trinidad and Tobago (30 June 2011) (referring to the traditional mas characters, the portrayal of which are more involved in terms of costume, dance and speech styles, and are more difficult to reproduce and may require some level of tutelage from more experienced exponents of the particular traditional mas characters).

the cultural life of Trinidad and Tobago nationals in the Caribbean diaspora. For growing diasporic communities, 'festivals, carnivals . . . provide important moments of visibility and occasions of concentrated celebrations of identity beyond the confines of their "host" communities'.[26] Some scholars suggest that overseas carnivals are:

> primarily about identity formation because they are inevitably linked to the diverse forces that give race, ethnicity, gender and sexuality in the host countries 'new' meanings. They claim that the overseas carnivals are not so much about reiterating a Trinidadian or Caribbean identity for that matter, but more about rejoicing in the opportunity to become somebody new, in a new place (space).[27]

Carnival also presents opportunities, albeit short-lived, for the marginalized populations in the diaspora to exert political agency.[28] Generally, carnivals in the diaspora have become symbols of

> alterity and present their participants with opportunities to make powerful statements about themselves, and their existence in a different place. The carnival is also a sphere for social and political discourse that is not merely a reflection of politics but a site for political activisim.[29]

3.2 African continent

Whereas issues of identity formation and social and political activism inform the discourse on the proliferation of Trinidad-style carnivals, the recent hosting of the festival on the African continent introduces other rationales. Calabar Carnival in Cross River State, Nigeria, which is modelled after Trinidad and Tobago Carnival, is billed as 'the biggest street party in Africa'.[30] However, Calabar Carnival can be distinguished from the other Trinidad-style carnivals in North America and the United Kingdom in that 'it is a Trinidadian-style carnival held in an African city without pre-existing Caribbean influence'.[31] It is not a diasporic carnival 'driven by nostalgia for home and a need to reaffirm community unity abroad'.[32]

[26] Picard and Robinson, 'Remaking Worlds', p. 2.
[27] Burke, *Policing the Transnational*, p. 170.
[28] In Brooklyn's Labour Day Carnival one can find signs with commentary about US and Caribbean politics: see P. Kasinitz, '"New York Equalize You?" Change and Continuity in Brooklyn's Labour Day Carnival', in M. C. Riggio (ed.), *Carnival: Culture in Action – The Trinidad Experience* (New York: Routledge, 2004), p. 271.
[29] Burke, *Policing the Transnational*, p. 172.
[30] A. B. Carlson, 'Calabar Carnival: A Trinidadian Tradition Returns to Africa' (2010) 43(4) *African Arts* 42.
[31] *Ibid.* [32] *Ibid.*, p. 44.

Calabar Carnival emulates Trinidad and Tobago's twenty-first-century carnival with its commercial tendencies, characterized by large mas bands, mass-produced costumes (often imported) and based on fantasy themes. The potential for economic returns was attractive to the Nigerian delegation that visited Trinidad; Nigeria is considered a developing democracy with unstable oil revenues. Calabar Carnival is seen as creating an image for Calabar, 'like a brand that will attract tourists to fuel other profit-making ventures', and therefore be beneficial in ways beyond the direct revenues from the event itself.[33] It is suggested that the inspiration for Calabar Carnival was the need to attract a critical mass of tourists to Calabar for an even grander project – Tinapa – which was 'billed as "Africa's Premier Business Resort"' and which will include a sound stage for Nollywood productions.[34]

Economic rationales aside, political narratives are present in Calabar Carnival. Carnival is both competition and politics. Bands are identified with a unique colour for easy visual identification, like political parties, and associating with a particular band is 'a process of social and political positioning' that can facilitate being connected to the 'right people' and potentially lead to social or economic advancement.[35]

4 Identifying properties in carnival

4.1 Intellectual property protection for carnival

Festivals have been characterized as sites of 'vernacular creativity'.[36] In Trinidad and Tobago, where the carnival festival dominates the cultural landscape, it is not surprising that much of the creative output of the country is linked to carnival. Whether that creative output meets the standards required for intellectual property protection is another matter.

4.1.1 Protection for the 'overall theme and programme' or 'format' of carnival

'Carnival in a box' is a proposal put forward by a local initiative, Project Foresight, which comprises a 'complete Carnival package in containers that can be delivered along with performers and event management

[33] *Ibid.*, p. 48. [34] *Ibid.*, p. 58. [35] *Ibid.*, p. 49.

[36] See D. Noyes, 'Toward a Network Model of Invention: From Homeric Epic to Open-Source Software', draft paper presented at 'Con/texts of Invention: A Working Conference', Case Western Reserve University, Cleveland, OH, 20–23 April 2006, p. 20 (copy on file with author).

to any venue in the world'.[37] It includes all aspects associated with a major carnival event such as the overall theme and programme; the costume design and manufacture involved in a mas band; the musicians and accompanying bands – in particular, steel bands and Caribbean-style artists; carnival managers and event organizers; and pre- and post-event promotional goods and services.[38]

The 'Carnival in a box' proposal refers to the 'overall theme and programme' associated with the festival as an element thereof which can be 'delivered in a container'. However, that 'theme' or 'programme' is not articulated but is evidenced in practice each year. At the state level, Trinidad Carnival assumes a particular format managed through various agencies, including the National Carnival Commission (NCC), Pan Trinbago, the Trinbago Unified Calypsonians Organization (TUCO) and the National Carnival Bands Association (NCBA). The festival is 'launched' by the state approximately two to three months prior to the days of the street parade. That launch may include a rehearsal of the 'Canboulay', but usually includes a procession of 'traditional' mas costumes, and steel band, calypso and soca performances throughout the country.[39]

There are a series of activities and competitions surrounding the principal constituent artistic forms of Trinidad Carnival that give the festival its unique sequence and shape within what is referred to as the 'carnival season'. With respect to mas, there are a large number of band launches where designers display their offerings for the upcoming festival (usually in a party environment) and prospective participants are encouraged to register to 'play mas'[40] with that particular mas band. Interestingly, these 'band launches' usually precede the official launch of carnival by the state.

[37] See K. Nurse *et al.*, 'Sector Foresight Project: Creative: Trinidad and Tobago "Best Bet" Investment Cases', *The Trinidad and Tobago Foresight Project* (Trinidad: National Institute of Higher Education, Research, Science and Technology, 2007), p. 21, at www.niherst.gov.tt/s-and-t/projects/foresighting/creative-sector-chpt4.pdf.

[38] *Ibid.*

[39] The launch of Carnival 2011 featured a parade of traditional carnival characters by various regional carnival committees which showcased 'real' carnival costumes such as the Pierrot Grenade, Indians, Fancy Sailors and the Dame Lorraine: see G. Cardinez, 'Carnival Launch Described as the Best Ever', *Trinidad Express Newspapers*, 8 December 2010, at http://trinidadexpress.com/featured-news/Carnival-launch-described-as–the-best-ever-111504954.html.

[40] The act of 'playing mas' refers to adorning a costume, based on a particular theme which is decided by the bandleader, and joining others (referred to as masqueraders) in the same 'mas band' who are similarly dressed, on Carnival Monday and Tuesday. A 'mas band' may vary in size from a few dozen or less to several thousand: see C. Martin, 'Trinidad Carnival Glossary', in Riggio, *Carnival: Culture in Action – The Trinidad Experience*, p. 292.

Steel bands begin to practise their arrangements of a calypso or soca (song) for the annual Panorama steel pan competition organized by Pan Trinbago approximately two to three months before the start of the competition, where winners are chosen in the single pan, small, medium and large band categories. There are three rounds of competition culminating with the winning steel band being announced on the Saturday preceding Carnival Monday and Tuesday (the days of the street parade). Similarly, calypso, soca and chutney soca competitions are held during the months leading up to the days of the street parade. The Soca Monarch is 'crowned' on the Friday preceding the days of the street parade on what is referred to as 'Fantastic Friday', and the Calypso Monarch is traditionally 'crowned' on the Sunday before the days of the street parade on what is referred to as 'Dimanche Gras'. The Soca Monarch competition is organized by a private enterprise that receives significant state and corporate support, and the Calypso Monarch competition is organized by TUCO. The king and queen of carnival, which are the costumes that symbolically 'lead' their respective mas bands, are also 'crowned' on Dimanche Gras night. The NCBA is responsible for managing this competition.

Following the Dimanche Gras competitions, J'Ouvert or Jouvay is the precursor to the street parade of the masquerade bands later on that day and Carnival Tuesday. During Jouvay, 'ole mas characters' parody public figures (local and international) or provide witty commentary on social or political issues (local and international). Jouvay mas bands usually portray a general theme but, notably, costumes are simple and participants are usually covered with paint, mud or machine oil.

On Carnival Monday afternoon (sometimes earlier) and Carnival Tuesday, the more elaborate costumes, or what are referred to as 'pretty mas', are presented. There are competitions for the best mas band in several categories according to size and type of portrayal (for example, historical or creative themes).[41]

The preceding paragraphs provide the general (though incomplete) 'theme and programme' or 'format' of Trinidad Carnival. The form of intellectual property protection that may be best suited to protecting that overall format for carnival will be copyright. The category of works protected by the local copyright legislation includes protection for dramatic works, stage productions of dramatic works, musical works and works of mas.[42] There is no provision, however, for the kind of 'work' that incorporates, as does Trinidad Carnival, the aforementioned 'works' and more.

[41] See National Carnival Bands Association (NCBA), *CBA Rules and Regulations (Senior Bands)* (2013), at http://ncbatt.com/index.php/carnival/carnival-regulations.

[42] See Copyright Act 1997 (Trinidad and Tobago), s. 5(1) (Copyright Act).

Further, given copyright law's difficulty in recognizing rights in television show formats,[43] by comparison, it is unlikely that protection for the overall 'theme and programme' for carnival will succeed. However, the 'Carnival in a box' concept refers to the 'accumulated knowledge and expertise' associated with producing a carnival,[44] and such know-how can arguably be the subject of licensing agreements. When requests are made to the NCC for 'technical assistance' in producing Trinidad-style carnivals, such assistance may be governed by contractual arrangements for which a fee may be stipulated. The challenge is that not all requests for 'assistance' are made through formal channels, as the organizers of the diasporic carnivals generally make their arrangements for technical and other partnerships directly with the relevant 'cultural entrepreneurs' from Trinidad through the informal and unstructured networks that have developed between 'home and host' festivals over the years.[45]

This underscores that the know-how associated with the production of a carnival resides within formal and informal, as well as public/collective and private/individual, domains. However, with respect to the more recent versions of Trinidad-style carnivals on the African continent, more formal arrangements have been pursued. For example, the Nigerian delegation, mentioned above, that in 2005 travelled to Port of Spain, Trinidad, to attend carnival and learn how the event was produced, comprised twenty-five people, including the Cross River State Carnival Commission, the state governor and other government officials. The delegation studied the organizational structure of the carnival. They met with organizers in order to learn the logistics of band organization, costume design and event planning. And, later the same year, they brought several Trinidadians to Calabar, including officials from the NCC and the NCBA, and a university professor who researches Trinidad and Tobago Carnival.[46]

Although the 'overall theme and programme' may not attract copyright protection, trade mark protection may be available for names associated with Trinidad Carnival events – for example, 'Jouvay', 'Dimanche Gras', 'Panorama', 'Soca Monarch' and 'Chutney Soca Monarch'. Where these events are organized by the state through its specialized agencies, issues of ownership and rights to the relevant event 'names' should be relatively straightforward. However, where events are largely privately run, with

[43] See K. Bowrey and M. Handler, 'Instituting copyright: reconciling copyright law and industry practice in the Australian film and television sector', in this collection.

[44] See Nurse *et al.*, 'Foresight Project', p. 24.

[45] See Burke, *Policing the Transnational*, p. 175.

[46] See Carlson, 'Calabar Carnival', 48.

assistance from the state, the picture is less clear, especially in the absence of national discussions on the 'ownership' of carnival.

The consequences of an absence of national debate were evident in 2010 when a privately owned local television station was prevented from filming and broadcasting scenes from Trinidad Carnival in the environs of Port of Spain, where the principal events occur, on the ground that another local television station (state-owned) had 'purchased' the rights to broadcast the festival, presumably from the NCBA.[47] However, those 'licensed' broadcasts were taking place at the main competition venues while the privately owned station was transmitting interviews with masqueraders after they had crossed the various stages at the competition points, and with persons who had gathered at parks and other open spaces to enjoy the celebrations.

There remains a lack of clarity about who owns the rights to carnival, and the parameters of those rights, since there is a confluence of private and public interests in the production and hosting of the festival that are yet to be defined and articulated.

4.1.2 *Protection for the constituent artistic forms of carnival – calypso/soca (music), mas (masquerade) and pan (instrument)*

Calypso/soca (music) Intellectual property protection can be considered in relation to specific aspects of a carnival. The music created for, and associated with, the festival is generally held in private hands, with attendant rights being managed by the local or other copyright-collecting agencies. Each year, new music is created for the carnival season that, in large part, supersedes the music of the previous year. That music can be classified under an all-embracing category – calypso – that can be further subdivided into categories that include vintage calypso, soca, chutney soca, groovy soca and rapso. Also, complex musical arrangements of calypsos and soca are created for the annual steel pan competitions. Any issues surrounding the use of new music created for the carnival season will be negotiated with the owners of the works themselves, with or without the involvement of the copyright-collecting agency.

Arguments for the protection of the genre 'calypso' and its progeny, divorced from their expression, are more difficult (if not impossible) to

[47] See C. Moe, 'CNMG Moves against Gayelle over Carnival Rights', *Trinidad Guardian*, 17 February 2010, at http://guardian.co.tt/archives/news/general/2010/02/17/cnmg-moves-against-gayelle-over-carnival-rights.

support in copyright law, though similar issues have been discussed in relation to the protection of traditional knowledge.

Mas The Trinidad and Tobago Copyright Act offers protection for a 'work of mas', which is defined in s. 3 as:

> an original production intended to be performed by a person or a group of persons in which an artistic work in the form of an adornment or image presented by the person or persons is the primary element of the production, and in which such adornment or image may be accompanied by words, music, choreography or other works, regardless of whether the production is intended to be performed on a stage, platform, street or other venue.

A 'work of mas' attracts protection as a derivative work since such a work may comprise or rely on other protected works.

The inclusion of a category of protection for 'mas', at first glance, appears to be superfluous, since elements of it are already captured by existing copyright categories. For instance, the drawings for the particular costume worn by the individual may qualify as an artistic work; the 'performers' of 'mas' are protected (at least in theory) from the unauthorized fixation and reproduction of their performances (which with thousands of potential 'performers' in 'mas bands' seems almost impossible to enforce); the 'choreography' used as part of the performance of the 'mas' may qualify for copyright protection if it is original; and the words and or music accompanying the performance of the 'mas' may qualify as literary or musical works, respectively, under copyright law. However, what the inclusion of this category of works does is to expand the range of possible owners of copyright works to include what may be referred to as mas 'bandleaders', that is, the individuals who make the necessary arrangements to 'put the band on the road', so to speak.[48]

The bandleader or 'producer' of the 'work of mas', as the owner of the work, presumably has the right to reproduce the work, broadcast the work or communicate the work to the public. These rights have been identified as most applicable to the ways in which a 'work of mas' may be used as the legislation does not identify the specific rights which may be afforded to this category of work, separate from other copyright works.[49]

48 Copyright Act, ss. 3 and 26(5), read together, provide that a 'producer' of a work of mas is the natural person or legal entity by whom the arrangements necessary for the making of the work are undertaken, and such producer shall be the original copyright owner.

49 See Copyright Act, s. 8(1).

These rights are 'assigned' to the NCBA as a condition of participating in its carnival competitions.[50]

While a 'work of mas' is protected within national copyright law (as opposed to elements thereof which may be subject to separate copyright protection), its reach does not extend beyond Trinidad and Tobago where Trinidad-style carnivals are hosted or proposed to be hosted. Such protection internationally may be achieved by negotiation with the festival organizers in each host city. Alternatively, reliance could be placed on protecting the copyrightable elements of the 'work of mas'.

Pan The potential for the development of 'franchise [steel pan] factories in offshore markets' was referred to in the 'Pan Tree' investment proposal, which is another investment idea promoted by the Foresight Project.[51] That initiative is complementary to the hosting of Trinidad-style carnivals and will entail securing intellectual property rights to the manufacture of the steel pan and the know-how associated with the tuning of the instrument. The know-how related to establishing and managing a steel band orchestra was also identified as a valuable asset by the project.

Protecting the steel pan, which was declared the national instrument in 1992, has been a part of the national discourse for decades, prompted by non-nationals claiming that the steel pan originates from them or their institutions, the existence of manufacturers of the instrument in Asia, Europe and North America, or the acquisition of intellectual property rights for various aspects of the instrument. In the year that the steel pan was declared the national instrument, for instance, an article in one of the daily newspapers referred to a 'stunning declaration' that the University of West Virginia in the USA wanted to be the world centre for the steel pan.[52]

More recently, the issue of the protection of the steel pan resurfaced in response to reports of the grant in 2002 of US Patent No. 6,212,772 B1 to two US citizens, George Whitmyre, of Elkton, Maryland and Harvey J. Price, of Wilmington, Delaware, for the 'Production of a Caribbean Steel Pan' using a hydroforming press. What has emerged from the national discourse in response to the Whitmyre/Price patent and other developments are the claims that there should be some form of recognition of the geographic origin of the steel pan, and some means of

[50] See National Carnival Bands Association of Trinidad and Tobago (Incorporation) Act 2007 (Trinidad and Tobago), s. 4(b) and (c) and the NCBA Rules and Regulations (Senior Bands), r. 18.

[51] See Nurse *et al.*, 'Foresight Project', p. 78.

[52] See T. Joseph, 'America Declares its Hand', *Trinidad Express Newspapers*, 19 June 1992.

controlling and licensing the use of the technology involved in the manufacture of the instrument. Ultimately, the Government of Trinidad and Tobago was unsuccessful in its attempt to have the Whitmyre/Price patent revoked.[53]

The process of manufacturing the steel pan lends itself to patent protection. Although that process has not changed fundamentally over the years and traditional or original methods of manufacture are still being used locally and internationally,[54] the range of the steel pans, the materials used in their production (for instance, the chroming of instruments) and some of the tools used in the manufacture of the instrument have changed.[55]

In Trinidad and Tobago, several patents have been granted to individuals in relation to the steel pan and its accessories. In 2009, a patent for improvements on the traditional process of making the steel pan was granted to a local university professor in relation to what is referred to as the 'G Pan'. The patent was assigned to the Government of Trinidad and Tobago.

With respect to the traditional or original process of making the steel pan, patent law requires the fulfilment of certain criteria that cannot be met in relation to it given the circumstances of the invention and development of the instrument. Those criteria include the identification of an inventor or inventors, and novelty. Also, patent law does not accommodate the cultural importance of the instrument to Trinidad and Tobago, whose system is predominantly characterized as a tool to promote new industries and is not normally used to further or promote non-economic ends such as the protection of artefacts that embody cultural identity.

Hyo Kang has stated that patent law reproduces novelty in relation to a history of 'previously accumulated novelties' called prior art, which is a legal construct divorced from an invention's past.[56] Her observations underscore the inability of patent law to accommodate cultural and other factors that are relevant when intellectual objects, which are also objects of cultural significance to a group or a country, are considered

[53] The claims in that patent were able to delineate 'different pressures and clamping methods', which preserved its novelty over the process used by the Steelband Research Project at the Caribbean Industrial Research Institute, University of the West Indies, in the mid-1970s: telephone interview with R. Aching, Senior Examiner (Technical), Intellectual Property Office, Ministry of Legal Affairs (26 August 2008).

[54] See interview with Professor Clemént Imbert, Deputy Dean, Electrical and Computer Engineering, Faculty of Engineering, University of the West Indies, Trinidad and Tobago (28 October 2006).

[55] *Ibid.*

[56] See H. Y. Kang, 'Invention and Agency in Patent Law', paper presented at 'Con/texts of Invention: A Working Conference', p. 4 (copy on file with author).

for intellectual property protection. Although the concept of invention implicitly relates the object to a history of technoscientific practices, 'the legal production of the invention eliminates or rather "eclipses" . . . all previous social relations . . . at the moment of its transformation into an invention'.[57] Kang states further that at the point of transformation of an artefact into the subject of patent law it undergoes a negation of its social past to become a part of the legal history of prior art.[58] It is this negation of its social and cultural past that occurs when attempts are made to reinterpret the steel pan as patentable subject matter. As a result, much, if not all, of the steel pan's importance as a signifier of cultural identity is lost.

4.2 *Other properties in carnival*

4.2.1 *Property in traditional knowledge*

Carnival today still embodies some aspects of its earlier practices in what can be referred to as 'traditional knowledge' in its constituent artistic forms, particularly 'mas'. Any attempt at franchising carnival must be cognizant of not only the intellectual property it embodies but its other 'properties' in traditional knowledge, even though national and international regulation is still under review. Interestingly, this 'traditional' aspect of carnival has not been transmitted to the Caribbean diaspora. One possible explanation for this is the decline in the portrayal of traditional mas in contemporary carnival celebrations in Trinidad. Another is the suggestion that this aspect of carnival is 'closed' as opposed to the other aspects of carnival, which are 'open' and relatively easier to replicate.[59]

What we now refer to as traditional mas characters were popular in carnival celebrations from the late nineteenth century onwards. The mas characters that have 'survived' and have been 'revived'[60] in twenty-first-century carnival include the Midnight Robber[61] and the Pierrot Grenade.[62] Traditional mas utilizes essentially the same type of costumes each year though they are remade annually, sometimes with different colours and some design modifications. As Errol Hill has argued:

57 *Ibid.*, pp. 4–5. 58 *Ibid.*, p. 5.

59 See interview with Gibbons (30 June 2011).

60 The NCC and other interested parties have attempted to preserve traditional mas characters.

61 For a description of the Midnight Robber character in terms of dress, dance and overall portrayal, see Hill, *The Trinidad Carnival*, pp. 90–1.

62 For a description of the Pierrot Grenade character in terms of dress, dance and overall portrayal, see *ibid.*, p. 92.

> It is not unusual to find an individual playing one of these characters for upward of twenty years . . . In one instance a traditional mask was played by the same family over three generations, so that the accumulated traditions of masking, dancing, singing, speech, and band organization associated with this particular masquerade were handed down intact from father to son to grandson.[63]

Although traditional mas characters are not a central part of Trinidad Carnival, some would argue that they give the festival its distinctive character and there have been attempts to revive that custom.

The protection of traditional knowledge (used here as a general term) has been the subject of international discussion for decades. The WIPO Intergovernmental Committee on Intellectual Property and Genetic Resources, Traditional Knowledge and Folklore (IGC) has produced two draft international instruments – one dealing with traditional cultural expressions (the Draft TCEs Articles) and the other with traditional knowledge (the Draft TK Articles) – which are under review. Recently, it was proposed for consideration that the Draft TCEs Articles include 'works of mas' as protectable subject matter.[64] That proposal has been attributed to the delegations of Mexico and Trinidad and Tobago. It should be noted that, thus far, there is no proposal to include 'festivals' as protectable subject matter.

Based on the criteria for protection of traditional cultural expressions set out in a recent version of the Draft TCEs Articles, a 'work of mas' should be 'distinctive of', 'the unique product of' or 'associated with' the cultural and social identity of the beneficiaries defined therein, which include indigenous peoples or local communities.[65] A 'work of mas' should also be the result of creative intellectual activity[66] and be held, maintained, used or developed as part of the cultural or social identity or heritage of the indigenous peoples or local communities.[67] The terms 'distinctive', 'unique' and 'associated with' are criteria that replaced the apparently more problematic term 'characteristic', which appeared in earlier versions of the Draft TCEs Articles, and was intended to convey

63 *Ibid.*, p. 87.

64 See Intergovernmental Committee on Intellectual Property and Genetic Resources, Traditional Knowledge and Folklore, 'The Protection of Traditional Cultural Expressions: Draft Articles', *World Intellectual Property Organization* (Twenty-Fifth Session, Geneva, 15–24 July, 2013), WIPO/GRTKF/IC/25/7, art. 1 (option 1), Annex, p. 4 ('Draft TCEs Articles').

65 *Ibid.*, art. 1(2)(b) (option 1), Annex, p. 4. These are criteria for which there is no consensus by the IGC.

66 *Ibid.*, art. 1(2)(a) (option 1), Annex, p. 4.

67 *Ibid.*, art. 1(2)(c) (option 1), Annex, p. 4.

'notions of "authenticity"'.[68] Authenticity is contested in the context of Trinidad Carnival since the constituent artistic forms of the festival, including mas, have all been transformed over the past 200 years and continue to be transformed today. Thus, there is no 'authentic' expression of the constituent artistic elements of carnival which best represents the cultural identity of Trinidadians and Tobagonians.

Notwithstanding the absence of the requirement that traditional cultural expressions be 'characteristic' of the cultural community and thus apparently avoiding issues of 'authenticity', other restrictive terms are introduced requiring traditional cultural expressions to be 'distinctive' or 'unique' products of the respective local communities. Such criteria may be difficult to satisfy given the intercultural nature of Trinidad Carnival and its constituent art forms, with its European and West African influences, as it is envisaged by the draft articles that only those traditional cultural expressions that can be 'localized or identified uniquely with a particular people or community could be protected'.[69]

Further, the requirement that the traditional cultural expressions be products of 'creative intellectual activity' including 'communal creativity' introduced criteria that were more onerous than that required under copyright law and raises difficult questions about the standard of creativity that needs to be established.[70] Proposing such onerous criteria for the Draft TCEs Articles defeats the purpose of creating an alternative protective framework to accommodate subject matter excluded from copyright protection specifically and intellectual property protection generally.

5 Challenges to franchising carnival

The technical expertise for the hosting of Trinidad Carnival resides within formal and informal spheres, and thus it is difficult to control its distribution, which is necessary to franchise it. Related to this is the fact that there are collective and individual interests (and arguably rights) in carnival. The steel pan, for example, is said to have developed in a

[68] See Intergovernmental Committee on Intellectual Property and Genetic Resources, Traditional Knowledge and Folklore, 'The Protection of Traditional Cultural Expressions/Expressions of Folklore: Revised Objectives and Principles', *World Intellectual Property Organization* (Ninth Session, Geneva, 24–28 April 2006), GRTKF/IC/9/4, Annex, p. 13.

[69] Intergovernmental Committee on Intellectual Property and Genetic Resources, Traditional Knowledge and Folklore, 'Record of Deliberations at the First Intersessional Working Group', *World Intellectual Property Organization* (First Intersessional Working Group, Geneva, 19–23 July 2010), GRTKF/1WG/1/4, p. 14.

[70] *Ibid.*, p. 16.

diffuse, cumulative and collective manner resulting in some uncertainty over who actually 'invented' it. There are individuals who have made significant developments to the shape and sound of the contemporary steel pan, some of whom have secured patents and other forms of intellectual property rights, while others have not. Any attempt to articulate and franchise rights to the steel pan must be cognizant of collective/national and individual/private interests. Balancing those interests will be challenging and would require carefully implemented national legislation.

In addition, the singling out of the steel pan for further national attention (with international implications) may rouse old and ongoing political and ethnic strains. The debate about the steel pan's designation as the national instrument in the 1990s raised concerns about the equality of cultural representation in a multicultural state where the steel pan may be considered by some as a symbol of 'Afro-Trinidadian' rather than 'national' cultural identity.

The established overseas carnivals (in London, New York and Toronto), while rooted in Trinidad Carnival, are also products of their host environments,[71] and the idea of franchising any aspect of Trinidad Carnival in relation to those festivals seems unlikely to succeed. Also, the exponents of those carnivals are less likely to respond positively to formal state initiatives (through the agencies of the NCC, Pan Trinbago or TUCO, for example) to 'regulate' what they have been able to do 'unregulated' for decades facilitated by informal networks with the informal/private creative sector in Trinidad. However, there are new opportunities for franchising the festival in relation to the interest shown by countries on the African continent in which state/formal relationships are engaged and provided that the challenges at the national level, including the balancing of collective and individual interests as well as the 'corralling' of the various 'properties' in carnival, are overcome.

Franchising some traditional aspects of carnival may be possible simply because the technical expertise involved in producing and performing traditional mas characters resides within a smaller domain and is therefore easier to 'capture' and 'control'. However, the legal framework for the protection of traditional knowledge is non-existent at the national level and under review at the IGC.

[71] Even one of the more recent versions of Trinidad Carnival – Carnival Calabar in Nigeria – has been described as a 'foreign carnival tradition on which indigenous art forms and festivals have been sprinkled' presumably to make the festival more acceptable for local consumption: see A. H. Esekong, 'Promoting Culture and Tourism in Nigeria through Calabar Festival and Carnival Calabar' (2012) 3 *Mediterranean Journal of Social Sciences* 287, 291.

6 Conclusion

Trinidad Carnival has been exhibiting franchise-like behaviour for decades, long before carnival was considered as something to be commodified, long before Trinidad and Tobago intellectual property laws were shaped around aspects of the carnival, and long before the legal/business construct of the 'franchise' was envisaged. It grew in an organic way without a policy or legal framework,[72] facilitated by Caribbean migrants who, as Nettleford put it '[yearned] for a psychic, if not physical, return [home]'.[73] This may provide one rationale for the emergence of the more-established overseas carnivals, but there is no singular or dominant explanation for the franchise-like behaviour. Opportunities to assert cultural identity and even exert political agency have been said to be provided to communities in the Caribbean diaspora where carnival is re-enacted that are not the usual or immediate consequences of the franchising process.

The hosting of Trinidad-style carnival in a growing number of cities in the African continent is a recent development in the 'export' of the festival. The cultural and historical ties that Trinidad and Tobago has with the African continent may influence the kinds of relationships that may eventually develop between Trinidad Carnival and the festivals held in Nigeria, Uganda and South Africa. Those relationships may very well resemble a franchise in form, but may actually be cultural exchanges in substance. As Carlson noted in relation to the large-scale import and adaptation of Trinidad Carnival in Nigeria, Nigerians are tracing the path of their ancestors to the Caribbean, celebrating the interactions and influences their ancestors had in that region and manifesting that history in a new performance style. 'As carnival "returns" to Africa, it is difficult to determine exactly what is returning: it is the idea of a return that matters'.[74]

[72] See interview with Gibbons (30 June 2011).
[73] See Nettleford, 'Implications for Caribbean Development', p. 197.
[74] See Carlson, 'Calabar Carnival', 45.

Index

Cambridge Intellectual Property and Information Law

Titles in the series (formerly known as *Cambridge Studies in Intellectual Property Rights)*

Brad Sherman and Lionel Bently
The Making of Modern Intellectual Property Law
978 0 521 56363 5

Irini A. Stamatoudi
Copyright and Multimedia Products: A Comparative Analysis
978 0 521 80819 4

Pascal Kamina
Film Copyright in the European Union
978 0 521 77053 8

Huw Beverly-Smith
The Commercial Appropriation of Personality
978 0 521 80014 3

Mark J. Davison
The Legal Protection of Databases
978 0 521 80257 4

Robert Burrell and Allison Coleman
Copyright Exceptions: The Digital Impact
978 0 521 84726 1

Huw Beverly-Smith, Ansgar Ohly and Agnès Lucas-Schloetter
Privacy, Property and Personality: Civil Law Perspectives on Commercial Appropriation
978 0 521 82080 6

Philip Leith
Software and Patents in Europe
978 0 521 86839 6

Lionel Bently, Jennifer Davis and Jane C. Ginsburg
Trade Marks and Brands: An Interdisciplinary Critique
978 0 521 88965 0

Geertrui Van Overwalle
Gene Patents and Clearing Models
978 0 521 89673 3

Jonathan Curci
The Protection of Biodiversity and Traditional Knowledge in International Law of Intellectual Property
978 0 521 19944 5

Lionel Bently, Jennifer Davis and Jane C. Ginsburg
Copyright and Piracy: An Interdisciplinary Critique
978 0 521 19343 6

Megan Richardson and Julian Thomas
Framing Intellectual Property: Legal Constructions of Creativity and Appropriation 1840–1940
978 0 521 76756 9

Dev Gangjee
Relocating the Law of Geographical Indications
978 0 521 19202 6

Andrew Kenyon, Megan Richardson and Ng-Loy Wee-Loon
The Law of Reputation and Brands in the Asia Pacific Region
978 1 107 01772 6

Annabelle Lever
New Frontiers in the Philosophy of Intellectual Property
978 1 107 00931 8

Sigrid Sterckx and Julian Cockbain
Exclusions from Patentability: How the European Patent Office is Eroding Boundaries
978 1 107 00694 2

Sebastian Haunss
Conflicts in the Knowledge Society: The Contentious Politics of Intellectual Property
978 1 107 03642 0

Helena R. Howe and Jonathan Griffiths
Concepts of Property in Intellectual Property Law
978 1 107 04182 0

Rochelle Cooper Dreyfuss and Jane C. Ginsburg
Intellectual Property at the Edge: The Contested Contours of IP
978 1 107 03400 6

Normann Witzleb, David Lindsay, Moira Paterson and Sharon Rodrick
Emerging Challenges in Privacy Law: Comparative Perspectives
978 1 107 04167 7

Paul Bernal
Internet Privacy Rights: Rights to Protect Autonomy
978 1 107 04273 5

Peter Drahos
Intellectual Property, Indigenous People and their Knowledge
978 1 107 05533 9

Susy Frankel and Daniel Gervais

The Evolution and Equilibrium of Copyright in the Digital Age

978 1 107 06256 6

Edited by Kathy Bowrey and Michael Handler

Law and Creativity in the Age of the Entertainment Franchise

978 1 107 03989 6